SAITO-HA SHITO-RYU KARATE-DO
For the Modern Warrior

Strengthening the Mind, Body and Spirit

by
Del Saito

STRIVING
FOR
PERSONAL
PERFECTION

Expressions

The book is truly an expression of the remarkable personality and professionalism of Master Soke Del Saito. Basically, it is the result of hard work that demonstrates a vast experience and shows the way to be followed by all those who believe that **KARATE is a way of life!**

In Budo Spirit!
Ionel Bara, President
World Traditional Okinawa Karate Federation

My sincere congratulations to my friend and associate for 50 years, Del Saito, for his excellent publication, **SAITO-HA Shito-ryu Karate-do for the Modern Warrior**. Both well-written and researched, the book is presented in a clear and organized layout. I met Del when he arrived in San Bernardino, California as a young member/instructor of the International Karate Federation with a new dojo and a serious attitude for development of Shito-ryu. From his beginnings until today, I observed Del's development from a junior level instructor to a master of his style of karate. This maturity is reflected through his research, study, and development of the dynamics, mechanics, values, and spirituality of Shito-ryu. I am proud to endorse and add my pen to this fine publication representing Del's insight and written mastery of SAITO-HA Shito-Ryu Karate-do.

Ray L Dalke
University of California, Riverside
Instructor, emeritus
Founder, American JKA
JKA Instructor, certified 1972

"A masterpiece about the different aspects of traditional karate-do and its intrinsic teachings. Sensei Del Saito deftly distills the key qualities of effective training while treating the reader to a feast of technical and philosophical insight. This is one of the most detailed books on the art of Shito-Ryu Karate ever published. An essential read for any practitioner of martial arts – regardless their style - looking to amplify their knowledge and performance."

Jose M. Fraguas, 7th Dan karate-do
Best-selling author of "Karate Masters" Series
Editor-in-Chief of "Masters" and
"USA Karate" Magazines.

My family has been training in Saito-ha Shito-Ryu Karate-Do for 5 years under the guidance of Del Saito Soke. Reading this book has provided a greater understanding of the art, history, as well as an in-depth look into the effects on the mind, body and spirit of karate. This book will be a cornerstone of reference for our family as we continue our journey and growth in karate. We are incredibly lucky that Del Saito Soke chose to settle in Grants Pass, Oregon in 1980 (a fact I learned reading the appendix of this book!!!!). Through his guidance our son has overcome severe separation anxiety and is no longer an "introvert". Our son now leads classes and is able to talk openly in front of groups. We appreciate everything Saito Soke has taught us through Saito-Ha Shito-Ryu Karate-Do and look forward to the understandings our children will obtain by their reading of this book.

Jerred & Shaye Shoemaker Family

Congratulations on a job well done. The book is very well written and informative. It really does enforce the real meaning of what karate stands for. I really feel that it is a honor and a great privilege to have been a former student with a continuing friendship.

Dr. Dick Thompson, PhD
35 year veteran and instructor of aviation

Saito Soke's new book captures the very essence of the principles taught by him to his students over many decades which focus on the development of good character, a healthy mind and body, and the higher calling for serving others. Since the late 1960s, Saito Soke has lived by example with his healthy attitude and wholesome philosophy that nourishes one's mind, body and spirit. Our family is most blessed to still have Del Saito and John Isabelo as sensei and mentors (myself, since childhood days of training at the small Pupukea dojo in Sunset Beach, Hawaii). I highly recommend this book especially to parents who want to instill good moral character, inspire confidence, discipline and leadership skills in their children.

God Bless,
Joel and Venus Lovingfoss & Ohana

This book is truly a great insight into the world of karate do from one of the last remaining true masters of karate. Saito Soke's reflections and teachings share the true meaning of karate and why it is so important in today's world. From technical, historical, and philosophical approaches, Saito Soke conjures a vivid vision of the path that he has walked and continues to walk everyday. It is a must read for anyone involved in the wonderful world of karate.

Tony Mendonca
Director TKFI USA
Mechanical Engineer

As a representative of the Traditional Karate-Do Federation International Saito-Ha Shito-ryu in Brazil, I can say that around the world, there are few masters with the technical, cultural and intellectual capacity of Soke Del Saito. As your disciple, I assume a great responsibility to preserve and promote the teachings of Saito-Ha Shito-ryu International, in the most authentic way, for my Sensei Kai and the 4500 students in my country. I am absolutely sure that this book will serve as an important and unique reference for karatekas and people interested in knowing the essence of Traditional Karate-Do and the Budo Spirit. I am deeply grateful for the opportunity to give my simple contribution to this great literary work.

In Budo Spirit,
Ubiratan de Souza Lima, Kyoshi 7th Dan

As a student and the mother of a student at the Traditional Karate-Do Federation International, I remain astonished at Del Saito Soke's consistent passion and dedication to teaching the young and the inexperienced from the first day they visit the dojo. I have yet to see another world expert willing to give themselves with this kind of humility. And as an author, I am impressed, but not surprised, by the monumental task he undertook of assembling this book. Any readers that would choose to learn from him in this format can be confident he is a man and a teacher who walks out the philisophies and integrity he teaches every day--on and off the mat.

Aimee L. Salter
Author of Amazon #1 Book for Teens, Every Ugly Word.

Del Saito has done it again! Since the year I met him, I have never ceased to be amazed at the vast knowledge that this great man treasures. I was lucky enough to enjoy the Italian founding party of Saito-ha Shito-ryu, where I had my first serious approach to becoming part of this impressive family and it was official in August 2009. This book is a must-read (and not just once) for karate practitioners, of any style, and those who are considering getting started in their practice, as well as their families. Del Saito Soke leaves nothing out, he touches on social, historical, family, technical issues and opens the doors of our Shito-ryu branch, making it clear that the main goal is to preserve the knowledge that has been developed over many years. It is an honor for me to be able to follow the path of Budo guided by a great teacher, father and friend.

Osu!
Joan Gombau, TKFI Director of Catalonia & Andorra

This book is an amazing representation of the depth of Saito Soke's knowledge in his martial art studies , his teachings and his personal wisdom about life and it's values. The art of teaching is to simplify that knowledge for your students until it becomes theirs through years of training, guidance and personal maturing. I read this book and I feel like I am back in the dojo again. An impressive study guide. Thank you for your teachings! Thank you for your friendship!

Chad Hamrin, International Yoga Teacher

I was delighted to read this book from cover to cover. The memories of the teachings of a master who has spent over 6 decades crafting his art are truly inspiring. As the wife of a karate sensei, and a practitioner of karate myself, it brings a clarity and focus of the approach my husband brings to his dojo through this book. I can see the profound influences Saito Soke has had on our dojo and the countless lives he touches every day. A truly delightful read and recommended to all.

Dr. Brandi Mendonca
MD, MPH

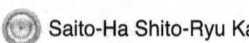 Saito-Ha Shito-Ryu Karate-Do

Congratulations, Del Saito Soke on your wonderfully well written book. It reflects your great ability in expressing the true way of teaching the history as well as the modern way of karate. You have inspired hundreds if not thousands of karatekas as well as the non-practitioners. Students and parents look up to you with great admiration and guidance. Our relationship during the Sunset Dojo days at Pupukea, Haleiwa, Hawaii goes back in the early days of 1964 under the teaching of Sensei Alfred Kahalekulu and has grown beyond "Friends". You are truly a man with open mind allowed me to train in Shihan Walter Nishioka's school during your absence from Hawaii and then permitted me to continue Shito Ryu Saito-ha. Carmen and I as well as the rest of the family congratulates you on your book and your success.

Aloha,
John Isabelo, TKFI Representative of Hawaii
Retired Homicide Dedective, HPD

Fifty years ago, at the tender age of 12, my mother took me to a store-front dojo on Baseline Avenue in San Bernardino, CA. sensei taught me respect, confidence, self-control, kumite, kata, how to teach, how to lead, how to run a business, and a whole lot of life lessons. Congratulations on a wonderful book that is full of truth, guidance, and wisdom. For many it will be a deep well of many new things and a road map; for others it will be a keen reminder of what we have learned and more besides. From either direction, we have a great opportunity through this book to learn and grow deeply in spirit and love for karate – and for Del Saito who handed the tradition on to us in the best way!

Rollin A. Ramsaran, PhD
Academic Dean of the Seminary
Professor of New Testament and Christian Origins

Soke Saito has brilliantly put over five decades of experience in karate-do into words. The wisdom Soke Saito imparts to the reader should be mandatory reading for martial artists of all styles and ages. I had the privilege to study karate-do under Soke Saito and know that this book takes his countless teachings and wraps them up in a perfect package.

Kevin Quinn
Retired DEA Special Agent

I have known Soke Del Saito for many years. He invited me to the launching of Saito-Ha Shito-ryu in Hawaii along with the heads of other karate organizations. One of his top students, John Isabelo and his granddaughter Casey Isabelo trained with us for several years when Soke Saito moved to the mainland. They both were shining examples of what karate-ka students should be like so I knew that Saito was a good sensei. I enjoyed his book which mentions local Hawaiian foods & culture and his remembrance of growing up on the North Shore. Unusual in a karate book. I congratulate him for the book which carries on the legacy of traditional/classic karate.

Walter K. Nishioka
Shihan & Founder of International Karate League

I am reminded of the time I was sitting in the San Bernardino dojo at 2:00 am, bo resting on my shoulder with instructions to not let it fall and repeating "concentration at the task at hand" 500 times. For a 15 year old that and many other experiences help mold my attitude and character for a lifetime. Del Saito's attention to detail and the basics were core principles in our training and more importantly were the attitudes of respect and hard work. These ideas as well as a concise history of karate and many other gems are contained in this excellent book. I would highly recommend this book for those interested in martial arts.

Eesha Bhattacharyya, M.D.
Board-Certified OBGYN, Kailua and Honolulu, Hawaii

I began training with Saito Soke in 2007 and I've been hooked ever since! His teachings have transformed my life. In this book you'll find a lifetime of karate knowledge and expertise at your fingertips.

Robert Burstein Sensei
President, Southern Oregon Crane

SAITO-HA Shito-ryu Karate-do for the Modern Warrior is indeed a voluminous documentation representing Del Saito Soke's 60 years of diligent study, incessant practice and unwavering spirit. From the inception to the completion, this work is a testament to the vast experience and extraordinary insight exemplary of Soke. a true Master of the art of karate-do and founder of Saito-ha Shito-ryu Karate-do. As a native of Hawaii with a Japanese heritage brought up in an environment of active martial arts culture in the islands, Soke was exposed to and experienced martial arts from multiple styles, masters and perspectives, while maintaining focus on the principles of dedicated training, self-control and moral standards. These early influences are the foundations of his veritable understanding of traditional Karate-do, a way of life that he embraces. These valuable life experiences are now shared by Soke in this production with all those who wish to learn. Modern karate practitioners are indeed fortunate to have this as a reference for their own training and self-development along their martial path

The book begins with a historical timeline of Karate and the influential masters. This is followed by the philosophy of karate-do in which Soke Saito emphasizes the standpoint of a true Sensei, who inspires and encourages students to learn while setting an example of living life with honor, integrity, humility and compassion. The concept of "Shu – Ha – Ri" is introduced as an essential quality of a karate sensei. As a karate student, the benefits of karate training should be well understood, that is, karate facilitates the development of body, mind and spirit, while builds character and morality. The student learns that "practice of karate-do leads, not to violence, but to harmony." Soke Saito devotes a chapter to these important concepts. The practical aspects of Shito-ryu karate: from proper attitudes, dojo etiquettes, gi folding, promotions, to fundamentals, basic techniques, kata and bunkai/oyo, kumite, self-defense, and kobudo, are all presented systematically and succinctly with descriptive and pictorial demonstration of techniques and movements. The last section of the book focuses on wellness and health, including proper nutrition, conditioning, and sensei-student-parent relationship which is key to success for a karate student. The Appendix is a rich resource of martial arts information and a reference for karate students. Not only is this a textbook for karate students, it is a guide for karate sensei's.

By viewing "through the looking glass", this book by Master Del Saito Soke would be a valued manual for practitioners of Saito-ha Shito-ryu Karate-do. In addition to imparting the knowledge for the way of life of a martial artist, it reveals the way of how to live life to the fullest.

Ceci Cheung, PhD
UCSD and OHSU Professor Emeritus
TKFI Shihan

I walked into the Grants Pass dojo in 2000 looking for a place where my young daughter and I could train in a sport/activity that we could do together. As a boy I trained for a short time in a traditional Kung Fu dojo and recalled the discipline and exercise presented in each class. I wanted to attend a similar place that focused on character, morals, ethics and teaching young kids (and adults like me who needed it) the life skills to assist in growth, and be a productive member of society.

From the time I first walked into the dojo, I felt it was a place where I could grow. My daughter would hear the same values I was trying to instill in her at a young age. Saito Soke was patient, skilled, and caring for all of the students on the mat regardless of age or abilities. Even a 30-something adult like me could see there was something to be learned. His understanding of the "Art" and delivery impressed me from day one.

We joined the dojo family after one class and I have never looked back in regret. Although my daughter no longer trains, I plan on having my grandkids join me on the mat one day. Through local, state, national and international karate tournaments we were exposed to so many different cultures and experiences. This helped my daughter to understand how blessed she is to live in a free country and to respect and value her freedom and opportunities. For me, seeing other students from around the world has given me a whole new perspective on karate-do and the true "art" in karate. I am thankful every day for what karate has done for me, physically and mentally, and what I have learned from my time with Saito Soke.

This book provides a glimpse into the true "Do" (Way) of karate and will help you glean knowledge about traditional karate-do. The concepts and techniques are broken down and clearly explained. If you are looking to grow mentally and physically in your journey and follow a life-long path for growth and understanding in true karate-do, this book is your road map.

Be wary of self-appointed "Masters" who, like snake-oil salesmen of the past, sell you a bill of goods without foundation. Study this book as you research the background and experience of your selected dojo and sensei. Many dojos, in my opinion, are "belt factories," (as long as the check clears, you will gain rank). Use this book to help you understand how to find the right dojo and ensure you are learning the "art" and are not just gaining belt rank to signify your place. Take your time, enjoy the journey and you will be part of the "Do" for many years to come.

Domo Arrigato Saito Soke for providing this book!
Jim Hamilton, Deputy Police Chief
Grants Pass Dept. of Public Safety
TKFI Shihan

SAITO-HA Shito-ryu Karate-do for the Modern Warrior

First Edition

Copyright © 2020 Del S. Saito

All rights reserved. Except for brief passages quoted from other authors, no part of this book may be reproduced in any form or by any means, electronic or mechanical, including photocopying and recording, or by any information storage and retrieval system, without permission in writing from the author or publisher.

ISBN: Paperback Book - 978-0-9900041-5-8
       E-Book - 978-0-9900041-4-1

Budo Heritage Publishing

Printed in the U.S.A.

Cover photo by Heath Thompson
Cover design by Zak Graham

DEDICATION

To my mom and dad, Clara and Toshio Saito, my brother Burt, my karate-do sensei Kenzo Mabuni Soke, and to my Iaido teacher Masayuki Shimabukuro Sensei, who all demonstrated the true example of dedication, sacrifice, love and service; all of whom were called home and now are spiritual beings for eternity. With each breath I take, they still awaken my senses, and I continue to keep their legacy alive.

 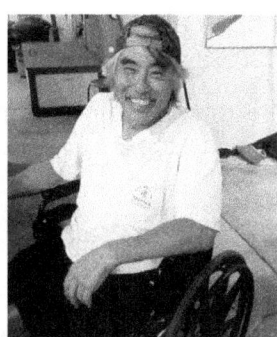  

ACKNOWLEDGMENTS

This work has been a synergistic outcome coordinated with many of my students, karate masters, friends, and supporters. It began in the 1980s when I decided to collect all of my notes, thoughts, and experiences together and present them in an organized book. My hope is to assist others in making their journey in karate both rewarding and enjoyable. The information set forth in this book will share with you, the student of karate, information I have attained in my lifelong passion with devotion to this martial art.

I express my heart-filled humble gratitude to the friends, instructors, students, and colleagues who have supported my journey, and who have made this work possible.

Kenzo Mabuni Soke	For being my sensei, friend, and mentor, and for his trust and support which provided me the inspiration to write this book.
Masayuki Shimabukuro	My Iaido sensei who taught me the martial way by his humble example.
Tony Mendonca	Director of our TKFI Shihan Kai, a son to me since his early years of training, for his excellent suggestions that has improved the quality of this book.
Laura Quinn	For her assistance in preparing this text in its infancy several years ago.
Ceci Cheung	For her valuable feedback and encouragement.
Janie Burstein	For her friendship, passion, fortitude and many hours spent editing this book.
Aimee Salter	For her professional and caring advice for this book.
Kevin Quinn	For his painstaking editing on this project.
Charles Goodin	For sharing his compilation of Hawaii's martial arts history.
David Lowry	For his wisdom and helpful thoughts on karate.
Joel Lovingfoss	For his professional assistance in the production of this book.
Bob and Jan Loeser	For their assistance in my computer issues.
Leone Bara	President of the World Traditional Okinawa Karate-do Federation for his support and friendship.

To my present Shihan Kai members who have dedicated their lives to our organization and commitment to service.

Tony Mendonca	Ubiratan de Souza Lima	Joan Gombau	Dwight Grover
Ceci Cheung	Gowtham Ragunathan	Jim Hamilton	Amir Mahdavi

To the instructors and students who shared and supported the promotion of this book with their commitment, support, inspiration, shared experiences and modeling for the numerous photos.

Jim Hamilton	Robert Burstein	Chuck Aoto	Ken Frownfelter	Kelsey Kitts
Sebastian Gattey	Matthias Gattey	Hendry Santoso	Michele Barnes	Lisa Pickart
Elise Gattey	Logan Mendonca	Abby Jones	Benji Thai	Crystal Hang
Dwight Brown	Steve Schiffman	Jade Elardi	Braxton Shoemaker	Tracey Raggi
Jerred Shoemaker	Kaitlyn Hausman	Vallori Abbey	Vanessa Abbey	Kailey Kitts

Alexandria Elesky	Sherry Archambault	Misty Hamilton
John and Carmen Isabelo	Joel and Venus Lovingfoss	Jessie Nelson
Glen and Leslie Parks	Rumi Kosugi Matsuyama	Brandi Mendonca
Pirouz Pirnia	Kevin and Peggy Quinn	Dwight Brown and family
Takashi and Sachie Katada	Fausto and Annamaria Arabi	Sabine and Mark Gattey
Francesco and Alessandra Arabi	Jennifer and Jake Thibodeau	Sam Manuel

And to my wife Ida for her faithful encouragement, and for putting up with me during this undertaking.

There are so many others who have contributed to this book in various ways that it would be impossible to thank them all here. I am equally indebted to all, and appreciate your encouragement and support.

Photo by Geri Takahashi & Heath Thompson

FOREWORD

*"Those who are thinking of the future of karate should have an
open mind and strive to study the complete art."*
- Kenwa Mabuni

*"To win one hundred victories in one hundred battles is not the highest skill.
To subdue the enemy without fighting is the highest skill."*
- Gichin Funakoshi

I once witnessed a "karate Grandmaster" who struck his student in the chest and described it as the "death touch." Supposedly, this death touch could either bring quick paralysis or slowly destroy his student's ki which will cause heart failure in the time chosen by the "Grandmaster." Since this was only a demonstration, the "Grandmaster" chose to inflict temporary paralysis, which was quickly remedied by a touch to the students neck. Fortunately for me, being a teenager, I was already involved in a reputable karate dojo and was not even slightly impressed.

Unfortunately, much of what passes for karate instruction today has strayed far from the teachings and beliefs of such masters as Mabuni and Funakoshi (considered to be the first Okinawan instructors to migrate to Japan), who shared their knowledge of karate-do with the Japanese people. All too often karate is taught "buffet style", especially to the beginner student: "Ah yes, I'll teach you a little of this, lots of that, but none of the other stuff." They are merely giving these students a grab bag of tricks, not the concrete fundamentals so important to establishing a firm foundation. Continuing such a "diet" produces weakness, not strength. Unfortunately, many of these students will just accept what they have been taught, not realizing that their fundamentals lack the ingredients to build upon. I certainly don't fault the students for learning what their instructors are teaching them. I can only forewarn prospective students and parents to be very aware before committing to a karate program. Be aware of these "McDojos."

True karate, or karate-do, is a system with deep traditional roots. This tradition extends well beyond merely teaching how to punch, strike, block, and kick. Historically, it's devoted to cultivating mental, spiritual, and physical balance. Karate-do provides a holistic approach to building a strong mind, body, and spirit.

In my karate journey, being of Japanese ancestry I had to learn to deal with a bit of prejudice while serving in the Air Force, and when I began teaching in California. If I had learned the "death touch" technique, with all the other hocus-pocus taught by some outrageous methods of martial arts, I would probably have attempted to take an approach that would have landed me on my behind side with a couple of black eyes. Although my first instinct was to retaliate and fight back, I was able to remain calm, smile and wave at those who tried to get a rise out of me. My sensei's teachings kept reminding me that it was always better to avoid a fight and walk away at the first sign of trouble. Fortunately, those seeds were deeply planted in my head and I was able to resist stooping down to the level of my adversaries.

Don't misunderstand, in Saito-ha Shito-ryu, you will learn an excellent system of self-defense. But more, you'll discover that each sensei in the TKFI (Traditional Karate-do International) dojos revere words like honor, respect, morality, humility, and tradition. In TKFI dojos the words of men like Mabuni and Funakoshi aren't dismissed as hollow echos from the past - they are embraced. These same dojos contain students from all walks of life - men and women, young and old, the weak and strong - all training side-by-side, sharing, giving, and growing together.

Like other martial arts, karate is based on experience and observation. Many of the components or aspects can only be fully understood through constant practice and trust in your sensei.

Karate training teaches one to fight to avoid fighting. This paradox – the idea that participating in an aggressive martial art can make one less aggressive, is at times difficult to grasp. Yet this fundamental belief that forms the nucleus of karate has been proven by many masters and their students as a way to learn to achieve self-control.

I attribute much of my growth as a positive human being to my sensei, as he echoed the same teachings taught by my parents. Learning that my instructor had many of their same views made me pay closer attention when my mom and dad took the time to instruct me on being a positive influence and contributing member of society. Through the many years of both learning and teaching karate, I was able to acquire patience which is a vital pulse in steering students technically while helping them polish their character. Through the wisdom, knowledge and care of my sensei and parents, I was able to tame my aggressiveness, exercise self-control and continue to enjoy the privilege of sharing karate with those seeking my instruction.

The TKF International logo is in part from the author's Kamon (family crest/emblem). What is seen in the Saito Kamon is the katabami (wood sorrel) plant, which is very strong and can survive in extreme circumstances. TKF International never displays the sword needlessly, but always keeps it sharp and ready be it necessary to defend against those that try to bring harm to its cause. The feathers on an arrow keeps the arrow's flight straight, and so must our warrior path be true and our target in focus. It also represents the Five Way Spirit of Shito-Ryu Karate-Do as written by Master Kenwa Mabuni,

INTRODUCTION

I was one of the fortunate students that was personally invited by my first sensei to study karate. Those who sought instruction were tested when they first entered the dojo, and only after the third or fourth visit did our sensei acknowledge their presence and invite them to train. We all underwent vigorous physical challenges to prove that we had the desire and spirit before being allowed to move further with instruction—not only testing our dedication, but also measuring how prepared we were for the physical difficulties we would face.

Training was extremely rigorous. Our gi (uniform) was drenched in sweat after each workout. There was no need for the sensei to remind us about bending our knees, keeping our posture correct or staying focused. A quick strike with a shinai (bamboo sword) was all that was needed. This type of training, though frowned upon in our modern culture, developed true "warriors" who could be relied on, not only in battle, but in life. This is the intention behind the original art form.

The karate-do epic for the modern warrior, greatly influenced by the Chinese, Okinawans and Japanese over 400 years ago, was one of the greatest human discoveries of the martial arts. It could not have merely happened by chance, and exists today as a result of the culminated efforts from people of different cultures and races.

Okinawa, divided into three kingdoms, experiencing subjugation and political upheavals, did not merely survive but maintained its dignity, healthy life-style and budo spirit. The influx of foreigners filled the islands with new and curious ideas; new customs, food, and household items, and the sharing of their martial arts. Okinawans were able to preserve their own customs and styles while integrating the more applicable concepts, and were able to create the living cells of karate. This art was nurtured and seriously practiced, wasn't developed in a day, nor was it easy. Through their dedicated masters and artistic techniques, they were able to transmit their knowledge to those willing to learn, and eventually reached people all over the globe.

It is interesting to note that although others from foreign lands had a great deal of influence in the formation of karate, most of the credit is given to those that eventually embraced a worthy educational process that could be both understood and documented.

Many instructors have come and gone, and what and how they have taught their students is now being revealed by their teachings. True masters of karate are those that have demonstrated great character while sharing their understanding of the art. I have been blessed to have both instructors that I revere, and those that only boast their titles to take unfair advantage of their students and associates. I have also learned from those that have demonstrated betrayal and unworthiness, which made me become stronger in my pursuit for a more wholesome approach to this treasured art. Instead of laboring or elaborating on the negative, I have chosen to create my own variations (with the blessing of my sensei, Kenzo Mabuni) in the expression of karate's common principles, with the ultimate hope of illuminating the art of karate-do. Although I have named my style Saito-ha Shito-ryu, I continue to learn from all other styles as Kenwa Mabuni, the founder of Shito-ryu, advocated.

I have written this book to provide a guide for students, instructors, parents and all those interested in the art of karate. The techniques and its components take years of study to fully understand, as well as the attributes it offers. Be it in the practice of fundamentals, kata, kumite, kobudo and self-defense, the ultimate goal is to be a better person physically, mentally and morally. My intention is to

Saito-Ha Shito-Ryu Karate-Do — For The Modern Warrior

"There are no styles of Karate-do, just varying interpretations of its principles."

Mabuni Kenwa

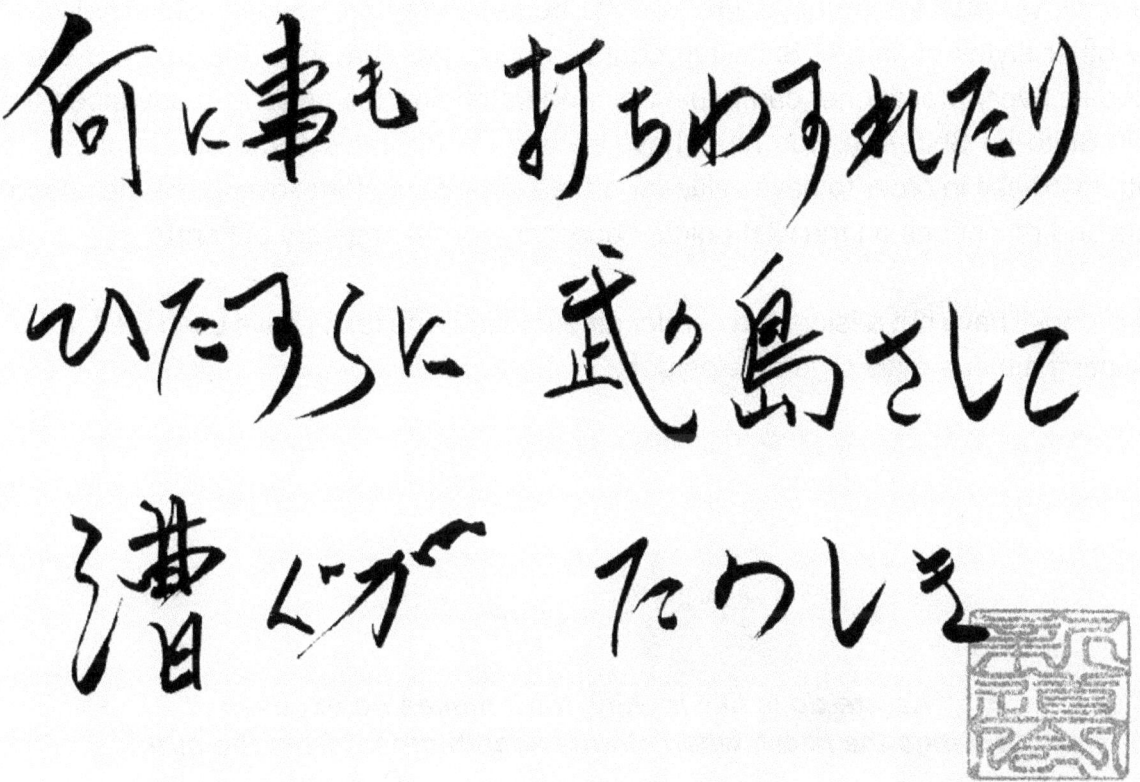

**Clearing my mind of everything
with devotion and joyful anticipation
I row my boat toward the island of Bu.**

Mabuni Kenwa

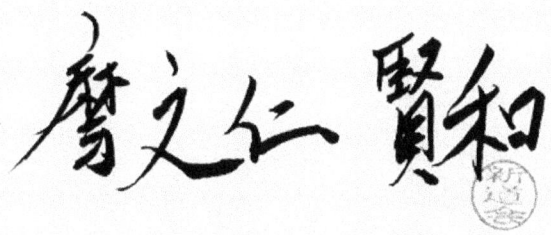

guide you through the study of karate, which I have learned through 59 years of experience. Whether you're a beginner or an advanced student, it is my wish that this book not only helps polish your techniques but helps you to define your character as well. I am also hopeful that you will discover and consider the moral education imparted in this book - that is the training of the heart and mind for righteousness. It calls for discipline, etiquette, structure and positive habits. A true understanding and practice of karate-do leads not to violence and conflict, but instead to harmony and strong principled character.

This book will also assist those who wish to become very proficient in Shito-ryu karate-do as well as any other styles of karate. Shito-ryu contains principles that form the basis of every system practiced today. Every practitioner can benefit by understanding the basic and advanced techniques embodied in Saito-ha Shito-ryu. You must have an open mind, release the bonds of your ego, and learn to better yourself in order to have value for others. Thank you for allowing me the space to share my thoughts and reflections on the vital points necessary for the mastery of karate.

NOTE: In this book I have not designated gender differences in the text. I have used the form of "neutral he," representing either a male or female person.

> *"Karate-do is like loyalty, for it makes no excuses*
> *but stings the heart, when clouds keep hiding it from the sun."*
> *D. Saito*

CONTENTS

Expressions
Dedication
Acknowledgments
Foreword
Introduction

Chapter 1	A Historical Timeline	19
	Okinawa-te 20	
	China Hand to Empty Hand 25	
	Introduction of Karate in the United States 25	
	Karate in Hawaii 26	
Chapter 2	The Philosophy of Karate-do: View of a Sensei	28
Chapter 3	The Benefit of Karate in a Modern Society	33
	Karate for the Mind 34	
	Karate for the Body 37	
	Karate for the Spirit. 38	
Chapter 4	Introduction to the Dojo	42
	Honbu Dojo 43	
	Sensei 43	
	Sensei-Deshi Relationship 44	
	Dojo Etiquette 44	
	Other Formalities, Rules and Principles 46	
	Folding the Gi 49	
	The Purpose of Uniforms and Colored Belts 52	
	Tying the Belt 53	
	Method 1 53	
	Method 2 53	
	Competition method 54	
Chapter 5	Promotions	56
	Ranking System 56	
	What the Color of Belts Represents 57	
Chapter 6	Training with Proper Attitudes and Habits	59
	Realistic Expectations 59	
Chapter 7	Fundamentals as Foundations of Karate	60

> Standard Components   60
>> Form (katachi)   60
>> Posture (shisei)   60
>> Balance and the Center of Gravity (antei and itten)   61
>> Power and Speed (chikara no kyojaku and waza no kankyu)   61
>> Hip Coordination (koshi or shiri)   61
>> Focus (kime)   61
>> Rhythm (Rizumu)   61
>> Timing and Distance (hyoshi and maai)   62
>> Spirit (gei and shiki)   62
>> Stances (dachi)   62
>> Blocks or Reception (uke)   65
>> Thrusts (tsuki)   69
>> Proper way to form a fist   69
>> Strikes (uchi)   72
>> Kicks (keri)   75
>> Footwork (futtowaku)   79
>> Fundamental Training Concepts of Shito-ryu Karate   81
>> Supplementary Training   82
>> Stretching   87

Chapter 8   The Language of Karate: Kata and Bunkai/Oyo   90
> Ingredients of Kata
>> Enbusen   92
>> Kishin no yoi   92
>> Bunkai   93
>> Oyo   93
>> Kokyu and Tai no Shinshuku   93
>> Kiai and Kime   93
>> Chakugan and Metsuke   94
>> Waza no Kankyu   94
>> Chikara no Kyojaku   94
>> Keitai no Hoji and Shisei   94
>> Jushin no Antei   94
>> Zanshin   95
>> Summary   95
> Kihon Kata   95
> Kihon Kata Nijugo   96
> Kihon Kata Zenkutsu Dachi Dai Ichi   100
> Kihon Kata Tsuki   103
> Pinan Katas   104
>> Pinan Shodan and Oyo   105
>> Pinan Nidan and Oyo   111

    Pinan Sandan and Oyo 116
    Pinan Yodan and Oyo 121
    Pinan Godan and Oyo 129
  Seienchin and Oyo 135

Chapter 9 Kobudo 149
    The Roku Shaku Bo 150
    The Nunchaku 151
    The Sai 153
    The Eiku or Kai 154
    The Kama 155
    The Tonfa 156

Chapter 10 Reflexes Applied to Karate 158
    Transmission of the Reflex Signal 158
    Spinal Level Reflexes 158
    Rebound Reflex 159
    Low Brain Level Reflexes 159
    High Brain or Cortical Reflexes 159
    Muscle spasm 159

Chapter 11 Kumite 160
    Basic Sparring (kihon kumite) 161
    Semi-free Sparring 161
    Free-Sparring (jiyu kumite) 162
    Dojo Kumite and Tournament Kumite 162

Chapter 12 Kyo 164
    Sources of knowledge 164

Chapter 13 Self-Defense 166

Chapter 14 Competition 172
    The Olympic Dream 176
    Cage and Ultimate Fighting Competition 177
    Competition in Life 177

Chapter 15 Considerations for Parents 180

Chapter 16 You the Student 185

Chapter 17 Examining the Sensei 187

Chapter 18   Nutrition   192

Chapter 19   Living Life to Its Fullest Potential   194

APPENDIX 1
    Founding and first launching of Saito-Ha Shito-ryu Karate-do   197

APPENDIX 2
    Keizu (Genealogical Table)   198

APPENDIX 3
    Combinations   199

APPENDIX 4
    Fun Drills   200

APPENDIX 5
    Catalogue of Kata   201
        Kihon Kata   201
        Shito-ryu Hongata (Itosu-Ke)   201
        Shito-ryu Hongata (Higaonna-Ke)   202
        Kenwa Mabuni Shito-Ryu Kata   202
        Supplemental Kata   203
        Supplemental Kata (Ruei-Ryu Influence)   203
        Saito-Ke Kata   203

APPENDIX 6
    Terminology   204

APPENDIX 7
    Author's Journey   224

APPENDIX 8
    Memorable Photos Past & Present   234
    Contributors to Martial Arts   238
    Permanently Etched   242
    Fun with Talented Friends   250
    Honbu Dojo - Our Home   253
    Collage of Treasured Moments   255

APPENDIX 9
    Through the Looking Glass   260

Chapter 1
A HISTORICAL TIMELINE

Many of those reading this text may not realize the importance of the historical understanding of karate and be tempted to skip this chapter. The earlier masters of karate had to devise clever methods to pass on their knowledge to others. Finding a dedicated student in itself was a difficult task. What comes to mind is Daniel-san in the Karate Kid movie. Sensei Miyagi had him perform menial tasks for him before teaching him the techniques of karate. Similarly, without realizing that my sensei was always training me, he had me help him with his chores, sit patiently while he and his friends played Hawaiian music for hours, and had me tend to his string of fish during his evening spear fishing expeditions at Shark's Cove. Out of respect, I only questioned his motives to myself, and only after receiving my Black Belt did Kahalekulu sensei share the importance of consistency of teaching and learning. I was taught that a dojo was not just in a building, but extends to anywhere you are. Earlier masters realized the importance of this philosophy to train their students to become the best they could be, and my sensei passed on that realization to me.

Another point of interest is that in earlier times karate was practiced in secrecy. I was also taught that our techniques were not to be shared to anyone else. The element of surprise was of utmost importance to prepare for genuine challenges and threats. We are able to learn from history in order to preserve the value of our treasured art, and to also learn not replicate those actions that are not advantageous for continued study and practice.

A true written history of karate does not exist, although several authors such as Patrick McCarthy, Takao Nakaya, and John Sells have compiled historical data to formulate a chronological record of information that sheds light on this unique martial art. Though it can be traced back hundreds of years, its origins are shrouded in mystery, as much of its development and practice required great secrecy due to sociological constraints of the time. The earlier masters were unable to transfer their knowledge to an educational system, largely due to geographic boundaries and their own needs for safety and protection.

India's influence on the original martial arts training techniques is certain. According to popular legend, sometime early in the sixth century, an Indian monk of noble birth traveled to China to visit Emperor Wu, in the city that is now known as Nanking. This monk was Bodhidharma (Daruma Taishi - Ta Mo in Japanese) and his father was King Sugandha of the Kshatriya or "warrior" caste of southern India. His journey to China began as a result of his unhappiness in having to assume the role of his father's position. Thus he went to seek enlightenment and form his philosophy and practice of deep contemplation. This Chinese Chan was later recognized by the Japanese as Zen. It was said that in one kingdom, Bodhidharma "meditated in front of a wall for nine years."

Bodhidharma eventually settled at the Shaolin-szu (in Japanese called the Shorinji), a temple in the Honan province of China. Upon arrival, he commenced teaching the monks his meditative philosophy, but soon discovered they were too mentally weak to perform these rigorous meditations. Therefore he developed a series of physical exercises, including his "eighteen movements," to strengthen their minds. This system included combat techniques which were based on many of the ingredients of India's yoga and kshatriya training, and also the basis for Lo Han boxing. It is also said to have included a form of weaponless fighting called "vajramushti," or "one whose fist was impenetrable." It is interesting to note that these techniques were developed in an era of peace; this important fact is evident in the psychological, physiological and social factors in martial arts. Shorinji kempo eventually emerged as the name given for these techniques.

The history is uncertain whether Bodhidharma actually introduced kempo, or if it already existed in China. Nonetheless, it is clear his influence sparked the interest of these combative exercises within the Shaolin temple walls.

Okinawa-te

Around the sixteenth century, a cultural exchange began between the people of the Fukien province in southern China and those of the Ryukyu Islands, an archipelago in the Pacific between Kyushu, Japan and Taiwan, China. The largest of these islands was Okinawa, which was valuable for its location and its accessibility to trade. This accessibility, however, made the Okinawans vulnerable. Twice their weapons had been banned under martial law, so it was natural that the people of the island devised their own self-defense systems to protect their families and their land. The White Crane style "Gung Fu" was instrumental in some of the formation of "ti" (technique), "tode" (China Hand), and "unante" (empty hand), the earlier names for karate. According to some historians, the Fujian White Crane was developed by a female martial artist who imitated the movements of the white crane, observing its movements, methods of attack and spirit. Some of these techniques have been passed down to the Okinawan Goju-ryu, Uechi-ryu and Chito-ryu styles.

Although I have stated that there are no true written texts on the history of karate, some of the self-defense techniques, mental training, and other fighting information was obtained from the Wubei Zhi or in the Japanese Bubishi (Record of Martial Preparation). This ancient comprehensive manual of combat originated from Fuzhou in China's Fujian province. Often referred to as the "Bible of Karate," it was compiled in 1621 by Mao Yuanyi, an officer in the Ming Dynasty. This manual includes military theories, including those of Sun Tzu, a Chinese general, military strategist, writer and philosopher and the author of The Art of War. It also includes some theories dating back to the last years of Eastern Zhou Dynasty, more than 1,800 years before Mao. This book contains chapters on different battles and what strategies were used to defeat the enemy, methods of training the troops, martial arts techniques (including the use of weapons), the attacking and defending of cities, and marine navigation. The Bubishi also covered history, etiquette, anatomy, healing and medicine. Some masters of karate consider the Bubishi the earliest manual of Okinawan Karate.

Nevertheless, the Okinawans considered China to be a highly civilized and advanced culture and eagerly received the arrival of their art known as Shorinji kempo. Shorinji kempo had both differences and similarities to the systems they had already developed, and they quickly assimilated the most effective styles into their practice. Veiling themselves with the innocent names of "ti," "tode," or "China-hand" (or simply "te" or "hand"), the Okinawans polished their art in utmost secrecy. Due to the weapon bans of the time, they cleverly incorporated farm implements and other useful tools into their art. Some of the more popular weapons were the bo (a wooden staff or stick), the sai (a forked metal device), nunchaku (wooden flails or horse bridle), the tonfa (a mill grinding handle or a crutch) and the kama, (a sickle with a handle that is a sharpened right-angled metal blade). (See Kobudo in Chapter 9)

It is said that their styles varied in accordance with their origins. In the north or mountainous regions, where horses were the main means of transportation, the use of kicks was widespread. In the south, where rowboats were utilized due to the abundance of rivers, the use of hand techniques was created. I also believe that their culture, stature, attire, and maybe even hairstyles had a great influence on how their karate styles were developed. Keep in mind that the Okinawans were peace-loving people, and although they at first developed their techniques for self-defense, they ultimately continued to practice their treasured art to preserve it and used it to ensure better health and peaceful existence. Another important consideration of style development should also be placed on linguistics, of which I elaborate in Chapter 8.

The three regions of Okinawa, which could be classified as styles, were developed at Shuri (the ancient capital of the Ryukyu Kingdom), Naha (the current capital) and Tomari (the seaport and fishing district). Shuri-te, having the Northern Shaolin influence, uses rapid moving stances and higher kicks and is characterized by fast, offensive motions generating power instantly. Naha-te, having the Southern Shaolin influence, is characterized by sanchin dachi (three point stance) and circular steps, and emphasizes breathing control, powerful open hand techniques and low kicks. Tomari-te is a combination of the two, incorporating both the Northern Shaolin and Southern Shaolin techniques. All three traditions share the common components of the external and the internal planes. The external plane exists in the physical realm, which is the body, incorporating strength, flexibility and endurance and which requires repetition and rigorous training. The internal elements are managing pain, sensing the body and its surroundings, and also includes the spiritual plane, which consists of education, discipline and ethics.

In the early 1900s the weapon bans were lifted, and at last the Okinawans could practice their art without the fear of punishment. With the inclusion of ethics in this practice, favorable approval began in this society, so administrators incorporated karate into the curriculum of their schools to make it available for everyone to practice, not just the upper class. As good and peace-loving people, the Okinawans understood their external ability was in direct proportion to their internal balance. Hence, they strove to hone the sharpness of their martial art skills from within.

Some of the more notable individuals who laid the foundation for karate are presented below. Their method of training was to teach students how to deal with conflict by keeping mentally and physically fit. They had strict guidelines and expectations in dealing with morality and ethics. They were not side-tracked, as many karate clubs of today are, by focusing on competition and tournaments.

NOTE: Several of the dates in this section are not certain due to the unavailability of records.

Kanga "Tode" Sakugawa (1786-1867)

Born in Shuri in 1786, Tode Sakugawa, aka Kanga Sakugawa, began his martial arts training under an Okinawan monk named Peichin Takahara at the age of seventeen. At age 23, Sakugawa was advised by Takahara to train under Kusanku, a Chinese master in Kung Fu. For the next six years, Sakugawa learned all that he could and became a great master. Tode Sakugawa was an important factor in the development of "te" (hand) on the Ryukyu Islands.

Sokon Matsumura (1809-1899)

A student of Kanga Sakugawa, he taught Itosu, Azato and others. Being tall and thin, he developed great kicking and jumping techniques which added to his fame. The originator of Shurite, Matsumura served as chief bodyguard to the last three successive kings of Okinawa. A story is told that Sho Ko, one of the kings, ordered Matsumura to fight a fierce bull in an upcoming festival. Understanding the importance of fighting strategy, he snuck in to where the bull was penned for several nights before the contest. Matsumura wore the same unwashed clothes, covered his face, and agitated the bull by poking him with a stick. When the bull was in a state of complete agitation, Matsumura revealed himself and totally confused the fierce bull. The bull couldn't escape, was unable to hurt his adversary, didn't like the pain and showed signs of fear when he saw Matsumura's face. The day of the contest finally arrived and the bull was released to meet his tormentor. He charged at Matsumura, but as soon as the bull smelled the scent of the clothes and saw Matsumura's face, he stopped dead in his tracks, turned and retreated. The king was so impressed to witness such a display of bravery, that he gave Matsumura the title of "Bushi" (warrior).

"Ankoh" Itosu Yasutsune (1830-1916)

Born in Shuri, Okinawa, Itosu trained under karate bushi Matsumura and Tomari-te's Kosaku Matsumora. He was famous for his superior strength and strong hands. It was said that Itosu defeated Azato in arm wrestling and could break a thick stalk of bamboo with the mere grip of his hand. He was given the nickname "Anko" or "iron horse" because of his strong rooted stances as he performed his techniques. Itosu taught that conflict should be avoided at all costs. He said "As you practice karate, look brightly with your eyes and keep your shoulders down, stiffen your body as if you are on the alert. Always concentrate attention on what is around you. A man with character will avoid quarrels and love peace. The more he practices karate he should teach others."

In 1901, Itosu introduced Okinawan karate into the Shuri elementary school system as part of the physical education training program. Since the traditional katas were too difficult for the younger students to learn, Itosu developed the five Pinan katas still taught today in several styles of karate. Karate quickly gained popularity and by 1905, Master Itosu was teaching at the Dai Ichi College. In 1908, he wrote a letter to the Prefecture Educational Department recommending the introduction of karate to all Okinawan schools, including those on the Japanese mainland.

His letter was written as follows:

"Karate practice should be used as a means of self-defense, and in order to protect one's parents and loved ones. It should be used to improve your health and should not be used for your own selfish interests or to deliberately hurt someone. The purpose of karate is to train the human body to become as hard as rock and as strong as iron (steel). To effectively develop the hands and feet to be used as spears or arrows, and to develop a strong spirit and brave heart through continuous practice. If karate were introduced at the elementary school level, the children would be well prepared for the military in the future."

It is notable here that both the First Duke of Wellington and Napoleon also discussed the concept that "tomorrow's victory can come from today's playgrounds."

Kanryo Higashionna (1853-1915)

Kanryo Higashionna was born March 3, 1853, in Nishimura, Naha City. He was born when Okinawa was under rule of the Satsuma Clan of Japan and was tenth generation of Higashionna in Haru lineage. It is interesting to note that his name was pronounced "Higashionna," which is a derivative of Chinese and Japanese characters. Japanese was not the standardized language of Okinawa until 1872.

One of Higashionna's first teachers was Arakaki Seisho, one of the King's Bushi (warriors). He is responsible for many significant modern katas, including "Seisan." Arakaki spoke Chinese exceptionally well, and so it was recommended he travel to China for further training.

While Higashionna was a teenager, a new government under Emperor Meiji was being established on Okinawa, bringing Japan into the modern world. This new government, referred to as the Meiji Restoration, did not come to power easily. There was much instability as samurai rose up against this change, as the warrior class was disinherited.

Higashionna traveled to Foochow, China during this time and studied a Southern Shaolin style under Master Ryu Ryuko, and he also became a prominent pro-China activist. During his stay in China, Higashionna became interested in the making and selling of bamboo wares, which he did during the day in order that he might train at night.

Higashionna imported several Chinese forms from the Fukien Province of China and, upon returning to Okinawa after thirteen years, systemized the art of Naha-te with these contemporary Chinese arts.

He and his famous disciple Chojun Miyagi, (who later founded Goju-ryu) devoted their lives to the improvement and advancement of the art of Naha-te.

Gichin Funakoshi (1868-1957)

Gichin Funakoshi is recognized as the man most responsible for maintaining the systems that have nurtured the fundamentals of modern-day karate. Funakoshi was born prematurely in Shuri, Okinawa. By his own admission he was "rather a sickly baby" who was not expected to live long. Because of his frail condition, he notes that he was coddled and pampered by his grandparents. When he was eleven, it was Funakoshi's good fortune to meet Yasutsune Azato. Master Azato was one of Okinawa's foremost karate experts and Funakoshi began his karate training. After several years of discipline and hard work learning the martial arts, Funakoshi's health reversed. He became strong and robust and lived until he was almost ninety. Funakoshi notes that he was never sick again or in need of a doctor.

Funakoshi also trained under "Ankoh" Itosu Yasutsune, who was considered an equal to Azato in karate skill. After becoming an expert in his own right, Funakoshi took an active role in introducing karate to the Okinawan public.

In 1917, Master Funakoshi demonstrated karate at Butokuden in Kyoto, Japan, the official Martial Arts center at that time. In 1921, the emperor of Japan visited Okinawa, and Master Funakoshi was again selected to demonstrate karate at the famous Shuri Castle. In 1922 he was invited by the Japanese Ministry of Education to introduce karate to the Japanese people at a physical education exposition. The Japanese became greatly interested in the art and encouraged Funakoshi to travel all over Japan to personally teach the art of karate. The major university in Japan invited him to create a karate curriculum, and soon hundreds of students were being trained under his guidance. He is the father of the martial art style known as Shotokan.

Kenwa Mabuni (1889-1952)

Like Funakoshi, Kenwa Mabuni was a member of an old samurai family, who studied with Master Itosu beginning at the age of thirteen. While attending the Shorin-ryu School, where Itosu taught, he learned the Pinan, Passai (Bassai Dai), Chinto, Wanshu, Gojushiho and Kushanku (Kosokun Dai) katas, as well as several others. Mabuni also studied Naha-te under Kanryo Higashionna. These men were the highest authorities of karate at that time and were the founders of the two schools of Okinawan karate. Both instructors passed away when Mabuni was in his twenties.

Of all the modern Okinawan karate pioneers, Mabuni is considered one of the most well learned in the Okinawan arts of tode and kobujutsu, the ancient Okinawan weapon arts.

It was most likely Mabuni who taught the Pinan and other katas to Funakoshi and Hironori Otsuka, the founder of Wado-ryu.

Mabuni began to develop a method of karate that blended the two schools, which he first called the "hanko" or half-hard style. Later, he changed the name to "Shito," deriving the name from the alternate reading of the ideograms found in the names of his former teachers. "Shi" was for the "ito" of Itosu, and "to" for the "Higashi" of Higashionna. Thus was the birth of the martial art style still known today as Shito-ryu.

Shito-ryu is a blend of the two major fountainheads of modern karate; Naha-te, represented by Higashionna's Shorei, or Goju-ryu style, and Shuri-te, represented by Itosu's Shorin-ryu. It is the oldest official blend in a recognized style of karate and was established between 1930 and 1935 when Mabuni moved permanently from Okinawa to Osaka, Japan. Schools at that time had to declare a name for the styles they practiced under the order of Butokuden. Today, several styles exist that were developed from the two main schools of karate, but Mabuni's Shito-ryu was one of the first.

Kenzo Mabuni (1927-2005)

Kenzo Mabuni is the son of Kenwa Mabuni. He was born on May 30, 1927 in Shuri City, Okinawa. In 1929, when he was 2 years old, his family moved to Osaka, Japan where he resided until his passing on June 26, 2005. Kenzo Mabuni began his karate training at the age of 13 and had continued his training for 60 years. On August 1, 1943 he earned the rank of Judan (10th degree Black belt) from his father Kenwa.

His organization, Nihon Karatedo Kai, was founded by his father in 1939. After his father's death in 1952, Kenzo accepted his mother Kame's request that he take over the Nihon Karate-do Kai organization that his father founded. He inherited the responsibility and became the 2nd Governor of Shito-ryu, and successor to this organization. Kenzo Mabuni followed his father's syllabus the way it was written and named his style, "Seito Shito-ryu" or pure Shito-ryu.

Kenzo Mabuni devoted his life to the preservation of Shito-ryu Karate. In 1993 he was invited to come to America by the late Shotokan Master, Osamu Ozawa. This was the first exposure of the Seito Shito-ryu System outside of Japan. In 1994 he was again invited to the United States and a following of his style began. Mabuni's organization, Shito-ryu International Karate Do Kai, now has branches in North and South America, Europe, Asia and the Oceania regions where he served as the

Kaicho, (President), and Soke (Grandmaster) for this organization.

Tsukasa Mabuni Soke, Kenzo and Hiroko Mabuni's eldest daughter, presently presides over the Seito Shito-ryu Karate-do Kai Organization based in Japan.

In this historical ladder created by earlier masters, I will be able to keep their legacy secured while adding a few more rungs to keep up with the changing times. As students throughout the world continue to seek my instruction, and being a direct "descendant' from the master of Shito-ryu, I am taking this opportunity to make a favorable impact throughout the world through Saito-ha Shito-ryu Karate-do.

China Hand to Empty Hand

On October 25,1936, a council of distinguished karate teachers agreed to change the name "karate', which translated as "China-hand", to its modern characters meaning "empty-hand."

Master Funakoshi described "empty" in these words, "As a mirror's polished surface reflects whatever stands before it, and as a great valley carries even small sounds, so must the student of karate render his mind empty of selfishness and wickedness in an effort to react appropriately toward anything he might encounter. " Thus, "empty" means' to rid the mind of negative thoughts and feelings and to create space for useful actions more worthy of cultivation. "To this character of "kara" the ideograms for "hands" or "te" and "the way" or "do" were added. It was at this time that karate became more worthy of being accepted as an art form than one of brutal tendencies.

Introduction of Karate-do to the United States

Karate was first introduced to American Servicemen stationed in Okinawa after World War II. Upon returning to the United States, some of them began teaching their newfound art to their family and friends.

In 1948, Masatoshi Nakayama was named the chief instructor of the Dai Nippon Karate Kyokai (Japan Karate Association), and remained so until his death in 1987. Nakayama was instrumental in preparing JKA's young college graduate instructors to propagate the JKA Shotokan system throughout the world.

It was Tsutomu Ohshima whom they initially sent to America. He arrived in Los Angeles in 1956, at the age of twenty-six and began teaching at the Konko Temple. In 1957, Ohshima began the first university karate club in the United States at the California Institute of Technology in Pasadena, California. Soon after a strong base of American students was built, and other JKA instructors followed Ohshima such as Hidetaka Nishiyama, Takayuki Mikami, Shojiro Sugiyama, and Teruyuki Okazaki.

Although Ohshima is given credit for being the first to teach the recognized style of karate in the United States, it was Robert Trias (1923-1989) who first started teaching "Shuri- ryu," a more eclectic style, in America. He started his first commercial school in Arizona in 1946 after serving in the United States Navy during World War II. While in the service, he had learned a combination of Chinese art, Shuri-te, and later Goju-ryu. Known to some as "the father of karate in America," he also founded the United States Karate Association.

With these first generation pioneers of karate in the United States and its territories, the road was paved for other notables to emerge onto the karate scene. This has impacted martial arts as we know it today.

Some of the instructors worth mentioning (several who are no longer with us), are Gosei and

Gosen Yamaguchi, co-founders of Goju Kai Karate Do USA; Richard 'Biggie' Kim, who established the Zen Bei Butoku-Kai International; Peter Urban, founder of American Goju-ryu Karate Do (USA GoJu Karate); Osamu Ozawa, organizer of the Annual Traditional Karate Tournament International in Las Vegas; William Dometrich, founder of United States Chito-ryu Karate Federation; Don Buck, one of the first non-oriental instructors of Kyokushinkai style of Karate who opened Oyama's Karate in the USA; Dan Ivan, martial arts pioneer and who was instrumental in bringing Fumio Demura to the America; Chuck Merriman, founder of Karate International; Fumio Demura, director of Shito-ryu Karate-do Genbu-kai; Tak Kubota, founder of the Gosoku-ryu style of Karate; Ray Dalke, the highest ranking American ever in the Martial Art of Shotokan Karate; Tomohiro Arashiro, who established Okinawa Ryuei-ryu Karate Kobudo Ryuhoukai in the USA; Doug Perry, Representative for the Shorin-ryu Shorinkan Kyokai in North America; and Kunio Miyake, who established Shuko-kai International in the United States.

Karate in Hawaii

It is also interesting to mention that some 2,500 miles southwest of California, in a cluster of islands known as Hawaii (a U.S. territory at that time), Okinawan immigrants were arriving to work on the sugar and pineapple plantations. The immigration to Hawaii began in 1900 and would continue until the mid-1920s. Choki Motobu, Chotoku Kyan, Chojun Miyagi (who taught Goju-ryu for one year) as well as others, shared their karate and kobudo with their families and friends, as well as with the citizens of Hawaii. This was even before karate was introduced to the Okinawan school system and before Kenwa Mabuni and Gichin Funakoshi went to mainland Japan.

James Mitose (1916-1981), an influential Hawaiian who left Hawaii when he was four years old, received a formal education and extensive martial arts training in Japan. Mitose is responsible for developing and preserving Kosho Shorei-Ryū Kenpo. He returned to Hawaii and accepted all students, something that was not done in the Okinawan communities before this time. Mitose taught many Hawaiians Kempo, especially after the attack on Pearl Harbor. This was to prepare the residents in the event of a Japanese invasion. Mitose trained such notables as Bobby Lowe, who in the mid-1950s became Mas Oyama's Kyokushin representative in Hawaii; William Chow who taught Ed Parker, the Father of American Kempo; Kenneth Funakoshi, founder of the Funakoshi Shotokan Karate Association; and Adriano Emperado, promoter of Kosho Shorei-ryu Kempo and Escrima.

Other prominent instructors in Hawaii include Thomas Shigeru Miyashiro, first nisei karate sensei; Walter Nishioka, founder of the International Karate League; Tommy Morita, representative for Dr. Chitose and later Shoshin Nagamine sensei's Matsubayashi-ryu; James Miyaji, Hawaii Zen Bei Butoku Kai; David Krieger, co-founder of the International Karate Federation and President of the Nuclear Age Peace Foundation; Chuzo Kotaka, President of the International Karate Federation; and Lee Donohue, President of the American Karate Kai.

Since then, hundreds of karate schools have sprung up throughout the United States, with ties to Okinawan, Japanese, Chinese, Korean, Indonesian and Polynesian martial art forms.

Some of these schools are promoting the true philosophy of karate, while others emphasize the fighting aspects of martial arts. The purpose of studying karate should always be to promote a better existence for mankind, both physically and spiritually. Anyone can train the physical body to fight, but the one thing that differentiates the truly strong from the rest is the training of the mind and the spirit.

Hawaii instructors from several martial arts disciplines training together.

Students from the North Shore of Oahu taking a serious photograph under the direction of Al Kahalekulu sensei (6th from left).

Chapter 2
THE PHILOSOPHY OF KARATE-DO: VIEW OF A SENSEI

All people have the spirit - it is just a matter of careful guidance. It is just like jade in the matrix - if you throw it away, it's just a rock, but if you cut and polish it, it is a gem.
- *Gaoan*

Being a true sensei, or "one who has blazed life's path," may be compared to being a point man in combat. The sensei assumes the most exposed position in leading his student through uncharted territory. He assumes responsibility for his men and is willing to pay the ultimate sacrifice for those in his care. My philosophy is that in order to be a good sensei, student, or both, you must first conquer the enemy within yourself. Each new day provides new opportunities to claim victories over oneself, by making responsible and positive choices. One must learn to "identify the enemy" in order to properly prepare to act wisely. In the study of karate, one must also know when your enemy is being your friend, and your friend is being your enemy.

As in other disciplines, a teacher is one who guides and imparts knowledge to the student in the hopes of shaping their character, preparing them for a productive future, and teaching them to be a contributing member of society. But in karate the role of the teacher extends beyond that of the conventional teacher in that not only does the teacher pass on his knowledge, he also leads by example with his character and by the way he lives his life. Because of the strong influence the karate teacher has on the future of their students, it is very important for the teacher to act and live life with integrity and honor. In Japanese, the word "sensei" (meaning "teacher") denotes "the one who comes before." This has significant implications in that in order to be a teacher, he has had to both walk and experience the path previously and thus be able to steer the student in the proper and most constructive direction. (More on the meaning of "sensei" in Chapter 4).

In my karate journey as well as my own life's walk, I have been blessed to learn from some of the most talented instructors. Those that I have admired have taken the time to share their knowledge with me, and always imparted much more than just the technical aspect in their instruction. In my infancy of learning martial arts, I was primarily drawn to learn the combative techniques that could mold my skinny body into a Charles Atlas body and give me the ability to give those that messed with me a "dirty likin." As I matured in my karate practice, I realized that the sensei's role was comparable to the role of parents. Senseis not only teach students how to perform a task correctly, but also take the time to teach methods that will improve one's character. I take this to heart and continue to include "life lessons" in my classes that both students and parents appreciate.

Karate transmits a fundamental nature of reality; it is a process of learning and mastery. The Japanese terms for this thought process are "Shu•Ha•Ri," and these are the stages used to outline the overall student's karate progression and continued relationship with their instructor. These stages are essential for learning and mastery.

Shu (mamoru) means "to obey" and "to protect." This is the learning stage where students absorb all the teacher's lessons while the teacher disciplines, nurtures and encourages the student's progress. The student learns by observation and carefully listening to the many instructions. They are to emulate the sensei without question.

Ha (yabureru) means "to break" or "to frustrate." This is the stage where the student has acquired many of the fundamental technical and philosophical concepts of karate and formulates their own interpretation to fit into their existence. The teacher allows the student to explore their inquisitiveness and begin to draw on their own individuality. In this stage teachers become frustrated with student's countless questions. Nevertheless, the student is given wider range to explore their views while still respecting their teacher as the master of the art.

Ri (hanareru) means "to separate" or "set free." This is when the student has reached a higher black belt rank and embodies many of the instructor's core teachings of the physical, mental and spiritual stages, and also separates from the teacher. This separation does not mean that the teacher and student are no longer associated. Actually, a stronger bond is created by the many years of their treasured relationship both inside and outside the dojo.

Tony Mendonca, one of my longest and faithful students, shares his story on Shu-Ha-Ri.

Obey, break, separate....Shu Ha Ri...Obey, break, separate.
Believe it or not... as long as I have been training, I often repeat this phrase. It has impacted every aspect of my training, and my life. From how I train, teach, act with my children and wife... everything. It is such a powerful and simple tool to help you filter and reflect on what actions you need to take to better yourself and others in this world.

Shu - Obey
For me this was the easiest part and in the beginning, and the most attractive. I came from a very unstable home with a single mother that was always at odds with local law enforcement. She also suffered from mental illness, was often protesting and often in jail. I longed for stability, structure, and a definitive place where it would be simple to understand the rules. I had begged my mother to allow me to take karate for years. And it was she, surprisingly, that enrolled me in class.

I still remember the first time I met Saito Sensei. My mother took me to the dojo and we entered his office. He looked me straight in the eyes and said "I don't allow any horseplay in my dojo." I just looked at him, nodded, and prayed that I would escape alive. His stare was so penetrating, I was terrified. I had changed my mind; this guy and karate were way too frightening and I was already planning a way out. He was scarier than any of the karate guys in the movies I had seen, whether they were the hero or villain. I was sure if I stayed in his presence and made a mistake, he would melt my brain with his mystical karate powers. I could not wait to get out of the dojo and make my escape. It was a Friday at 3:30pm, so I figured if I left now I had the weekend to figure out how to change my name, migrate to Canada, and hide out in the Yukon so this crazy, insane karate guy would not murder me during training. But then he smiled and said "Great. Class starts at 4pm. And look, you already came dressed to practice for your first time!"

I was frozen. Somehow, he had read my mind and knew of my partially formed plan. He was so adept at trapping his prey and now I had no escape. Fifteen minutes later, my mother left (it was the 80's and parents trusted their children's instructors, so they did not often stay to watch). I was shown by a senpai how to bow onto the mat and then was introduced to the other students in class. I stood in line and prepared for my death. As we closed our eyes, I rationalized that it had been a good 6 years. I had a lot of bike rides, a dog that loved me, and had eaten my share of Dairy Queen soft ice cream.

All in all, it had been the best I could have expected. And so I was prepared to perish at the hands of a karate master.

But something completely different happened. Sensei started to teach us. He was strict, sharp, and did not repeat himself. He would crack a shinai on you if you made a mistake. But he was also fair and consistent. Don't get me wrong, he did not go from villain to fluffy rabbit. I was still terrified. But I knew this guy wanted to bring the best out of me. And if I just did what he asked, he would make me stronger. For the first time in my very confused and unprepared life, I knew the importance of making positive choices. All I had to do was obey this guy and I would be a better person. I would bring value to my life and I could be a great role model for others. I was soon hooked and I was hungry. This simple idea of submitting one's self to a good teacher changed who I was and who I would be forever. It no longer mattered that my home life was uncertain, that my mother was unstable, or that I did not know if we would have a home from day to day. In this place called the dojo, within these four walls, with this man, I was safe, I was valued, and I was taken care of. For the first time, I experienced structure, true discipline, and felt my intrinsic value.

The act of obeying in the presence of a master is the first step in a karate journey. This is also true in everyday life. Humility is the backbone of having the ability to progress. And in martial arts this starts with "shu."

Ha - Break

I was 18 and was participating in the finals of the men's open kumité for our state championships. The match had started and I had scored on the first exchange with a reverse punch. My opponent accepted the decision but with a bit of cockiness. We continued the match and we attempted to bait each other. As we fluidly moved around the ring, he faked, shifted, caught me flat footed, and landed a beautiful "jodan mawashi geri," (a roundhouse kick to my face). The referee stopped the match, but no flags from the judges had been raised. The referee was visibly astonished and so was I. It was clear that I had been scored upon and my opponent should have been rewarded with an ippon (1 point). My opponent was outraged. Hand in the air, shaking his head in disgust, and looking at me as if I was the cheater.

This was this first time I experienced what I had thought "Ha" was. In that moment, the way I was taught was to continue the match no matter what the official's decision was. But the whole situation was not right with me. It appeared that the judges were biased. If that was so, that meant that my sensei was also biased. So, I had to do something to make this right.

With the crowd echoing their sentiment about the decision, I was pondering on what to do. Since competitors are not allowed to talk in any way to the opponent, officials, or coaches, asking for reconsideration or review was not possible. Officials' ruling were final and could not be protested on judgment calls. So, I did the only thing I could think of to make it right. As the referee started the match I walked toward my opponent, leaned in, and motioned with my hand for my opponent to kick me again in the face. The look on his face was priceless. He was so confused and astonished. But then he shrugged his shoulders and executed the kick and was awarded an ippon. I was hoping that I made the right decision to preserve the integrity of the sport. I was wrong. Instead, I made the judges look foolish. Of course that was not my intent, but my understanding of break, or "ha" still lacked the maturity of its meaning.

Back on the line, I looked over my shoulder and sensei was shooting eye-daggers at me. I had to complete my plan to make it right. The referee awarded the ippon and now I was behind in the match with about 60 seconds left. The referee started the match and I sprinted off the line and landed the same kick on my opponent as he had landed on me... called a "take back." The referee started the match again and I immediately scored again with the same kick. Now I had him.... the referee restarted for the fifth and final time... I shifted, faked, shifted and scored a third time with the same technique, winning the match.

As I was awarded the victory, my opponent congratulated me and I knew I had his respect. The crowd was cheering and my fellow peers nodded in approval of my actions. I had taken an unfair situation, turned it on its head and broke the established rules of protocol. But I did not do it for glory or ego. I did it because the situation was unjust and I felt it was making my sensei look the same.

Was my sensei happy? Nope.... I got called over to the head table and received a "grade A tongue-lashing" for disrespecting the officials. He was right, and he had no choice but to reprimand me. But that is life sometimes. To break, to irritate, to stray from the rules and do what you think is right is a natural and healthy part of karate and life's journey.

Author's comment: Yes I was upset at his actions yet proud for what he was trying to convey to all concerned. Tony had arrived to a state of mind that many students do not achieve.

Ri - Separate

I do not think I had a conversation longer than "Hi" and "Bye" with my sensei until I was about 24. Even though I had been teaching classes for years, ran several dojos for him, and was his second in command, I never really understood how to get beyond the "shu"(obey), and the occasional "ha" (break). I was a sponge, listening and learning all I could from sensei's teachings. It was not yet my time.

One day sensei Saito called me into the dojo and wanted me to do some extra kumite practice. He had a Japanese exchange student living with him who was a really strong competitor in Japan. And I had just returned from a long weekend of Nationals team training. He wanted to see how I was coming along and he wanted to test me. It was only the three of us in the dojo that night and he pushed us to the brink. We started with light timing matches and then increased the pace. He pushed harder and harder but to see if he could break me or find a weakness. But I was up to the challenge. We did two hours of matches and it was either a draw, or I won, but I never lost a match. I received a small nod after the training, which for normal folks would have been a hug followed by "great job" and with 12 high fives. The nod was golden to me.

It was shortly after that day that Sensei Saito, (Hanshi), asked my opinion on something. I cannot recall what it was and I don't believe that is what really matters. It was the fact that he thought that my input had value. After that my sensei started to become my friend as well as my teacher. He would guide and instruct me and would allow free dialogue and exploration between us. This gave me the confidence to explore my own karate journey and to seek out how I could grow and transcend some of the initial barriers. That initial push of encouragement allowed me to go back to school and become an engineer, experience life outside of the dojo, teach and give seminars, travel the world, and finally come to open my own dojo.

One cannot hope to combine something new or improve upon something without experience. And that is what my sensei encouraged me to do. Experience life but use that experience to better the lives of those you touch. Every day that I teach, I think of three things: Am I teaching the proper foundations to my students; am I continuing to learn and grow so that I can become more independent; and am I taking the knowledge received from all of my experience in training, in competition and in life to add something to what he has created?

I am still my Sensei's student, and I always will be. But I am now also his friend and companion on our journey.

Shu•Ha•Ri is circular in concept; that is all the stages flow within the other. Following this method of progression and learning, dedicated students are provided with a compass to surpass their master, both in knowledge and skill. This result will continue to advance the art so that it can be enjoyed by future generations.

Karate cannot be learned over a brief period of time. To understand karate fully, one should practice continuously and seriously (every day) for many years with these basics kept in mind:

The hands and feet should often be trained on the "Makiwara" (striking post), striking it one to two hundred times. This technique is properly achieved by dropping or relaxing the shoulders, opening your lungs (inhaling deeply) without raising the shoulders, taking hold of your strength (holding your breath briefly), gripping the ground with your feet and sinking your intrinsic energy (ki, chi, Internal Life Force) to your lower abdomen (tanden) as you do this practice.

Karate should be practiced with the proper stances, executed by keeping the back straight, lowering the shoulders, allowing the strength to develop in the legs, positioning the feet firmly on the ground and delivering the ki through the tanden, while keeping the upper and lower body parts connected throughout the movement.

Karate techniques should be practiced repeatedly, over and over, a great number of times.

The correct analysis (bunkai) of the techniques should be learned and then properly applied (oyo) to the given circumstances.

Karate practitioners should decide whether the emphasis is purely on physical fitness training or only on the practical use of the body.

Karate should be practiced with great intensity with the concept of always being prepared to defend yourself, as if on the field of battle.

Karate should be practiced correctly to develop the proper strength of technique. Historically, those who have learned to master karate as children have lived to an old age. Karate helps in the development of muscles and bones, aids in the digestive process and keeps minds clear and focused. As previously stated, in past times karate had been practiced in physical education classes from the elementary school level onwards. The benefits of this early training and continuing training leads to rigorous health and well-being.

In my nearly sixty years of travel along the karate path, I have experienced many highlights in my career and have learned valuable life lessons. In the following chapters, YOU will see the history and techniques applied to everyday life in our modern times. By reading everything I have included in this book, I am hopeful that you will better understand karate and the range of benefits it has to offer, including the benefits of healthy mind, body and spirit.

Chapter 3
THE BENEFIT OF KARATE IN MODERN SOCIETY

Karate originated in Okinawa as a form of self-defense used by the natives against the sword-wielding Samurai on horseback from mainland Japan. Because the Okinawans had no weapons that could withstand the ferocious sword, they trained their bodies to be weapons, and, with the aid of farm tools, were able to fend off the Samurai. This required discipline and incessant training, for these were battles of life or death.

Although it was the farmers that utilized the self-defense aspects of karate, it was the Yukatchu, or aristocrats, of the Ryukyu Kingdom that were put in charge of military defense. They were all part of a complex caste system that was responsible for the development and training of what we now know as karate. Also incorporated with these scholar's responsibilities was the advancement of education, culture, and history. So we must certainly embrace and acknowledge all the contributions of karate, not simply the fighting aspects.

The world today is filled with advanced technology, and such things that were once considered luxuries, like indoor plumbing, are now considered commonplace. Life is fast-paced and filled with every activity imaginable. Modern medicine has accomplished remarkable feats, including face transplants! Plastic surgery has become an acceptable form of weight loss and self-improvement. Kids have their own cars, cell phones, video games, computers and all the benefits of the grown-up world, without the experiences that are gained from becoming a well-rounded adult. Cars, lawnmowers, shopping carts and even living room sofas now have cup holders. The windshield wipers on some automobiles now go on automatically with the fall of a raindrop. And now, we wonder, how did we survive before the existence of the universal remote control?

The United States population is roughly ten percent of the world, but consumes ninety percent of its goods. Yet with all of our luxury items, commodities and technological advances people are less healthy than ever. Nearly two-thirds of America's population is overweight. The incidence of Juvenile Diabetes is growing in children at a staggering rate. The average American family eats fast food at least two times a week, and this loss of a healthy diet has been detrimental to the health of so many Americans. The number of children diagnosed with Autism each year is astounding. Attention Deficit Disorder has become rampant in schools in huge numbers, and these children are routinely treated with strong anti-depressants, amphetamines, and even opioids. The world is more cynical and politically divided than ever. People today have become so much more self-absorbed, all trying desperately to keep their boundaries while the world closes in around them. It is not surprising that, considering all of these factors, life has become increasingly and overwhelmingly complex. There is an inherent lack of balance in today's society.

This trend is vastly different from what life was like in Okinawa years ago. It was not as complicated back then, when boundaries were clearly established and maintained. Karate was developed by the Okinawans as a means of protecting their families and developing strength of character, honor and respect. They also realized that with these basic qualities, people could be successful in all walks of life.

Karate trains the mind, body and spirit. Without the ability to be strong in one's mind, it is easy to become discouraged. The physical body suffers as well. It is no wonder to me that the Okinawans, even today, live longer and age incredibly well.

The art of karate transcends time. Its values and teachings have not changed, and its principles have been proven to be effective throughout the centuries. In our increasingly complex society, what better way to achieve self-confidence, respect, physical strength, flexibility, stamina and overall better health than through the practice of karate? Karate provides a level of consistency desperately needed in a constantly changing world. It is a practice where discipline and training are nurtured, along with focus and respect. It fosters a healthy balance in life.

Karate also transcends age barriers. Anyone can begin training at any time in their life, no matter what age (although it is best for a young child to wait until he has the ability to pay attention and learn). Karate provides families with the opportunity to participate in something positive together. It is rare these days to be able to spend time with family members on a regular basis doing something everyone can benefit from and enjoy. Women, especially, greatly benefit from the self-defense and the confidence-building techniques provided through practicing karate.

Correct posture is another benefit of karate. A strengthened core and improved flexibility are directly related to good posture. Posture reflects a person's level of self-confidence, and determines how are people perceived by others. It is natural that observations are made regarding a person before words are spoken. Good, strong posture plays a role in positive first impressions. Poor posture adversely affects the internal organs, especially the lungs. It compresses the thorax, which intensifies respiration activity. Karate, taught properly, increases body awareness and aids in the bio-mechanical relationships of the muscles to improve posture.

There is a philosophical benefit of karate as well. The repetition and practice of the physical movements promote the balance of the mind and body. In turn, a well-balanced mind provides us with thoughts that are filled with spirit, confidence and motivation. With the practice of karate these positive thoughts become stronger and more prevalent, thus replacing emotional blocks such as anger, fear and frustration.

Lao Tzu, a Taoist sage, beautifully explains this premise. He wrote:

*"Thirty spokes share the wheel's hub; it is the center which makes it useful.
Shape clay into a vessel; it is the space within which makes it useful. Cut doors
and windows for a room; it is the holes which make them useful. Therefore,
profit comes from what is there, usefulness from what is not."*

The benefits of karate are so valuable in this modern age, and they are just as vital to maintaining balance and strength now as they were five hundred years ago. The foes that exist today have different faces. One, for example, complacency, is perhaps the most pervasive. Obesity, poor physical health, addiction, the dissolution of the family, low self-esteem, difficulties in personal relationships and countless others add to the list. These foes have become both external and internal enemies. Karate training is not only great physical exercise; it is a life-long, fulfilling discipline that strengthens the mind, body and spirit.

KARATE FOR THE MIND

Throughout his life, James Allen (1864-1912) sought tranquility amidst the violent tides of change brought about by the Industrial Revolution in late nineteenth-century England. He wrote a small book on his personal philosophy and the premise of positive thinking, and simply called it <u>As a Man Thinketh</u>. He wrote:

"They themselves are makers of themselves. Only the wise man, whose thoughts are controlled and purified, makes the winds and storms of the soul obey him."

In a chapter titled "The Effect of Thought on Circumstance" he wrote:

"A man's mind may be likened to a garden, which may be intelligently cultivated or allowed to run wild; but whether cultivated or neglected, it must, and will bring forth. If no useful seeds are put into it, then an abundance of useless weed seeds will fall therein, and will continue to produce their kind."

Just as a gardener cultivates his plot, keeping it free from weeds, growing flowers and the fruits which he requires, so may a man tend the garden of his mind, weeding out all the wrong, useless and impure thoughts, and cultivating toward perfection the flowers and fruits of right, useful and pure thought. By pursuing this process, a man sooner or later discovers that he is the master gardener of his soul, the director of his life. He also reveals, within himself, the laws of thought, and understands, with ever increasing accuracy, how thought forces operate in the shaping of his character, circumstances, and destiny. Thought and character are one, and can only manifest and discover itself through environment and circumstance. The outer manifestation of a person's life would always be a reflection of his inner state.

Man is buffeted by circumstance so long as he believes himself to be a creature of outside conditions, but when he realizes that he is a creative power, and that he may command the hidden soil and seeds of his being out of which circumstances grow, he then becomes the rightful master of himself."

The power of the mind is well known. There are many books on the power of positive thinking. The training and development of a strong mind is more than a matter of just controlling thoughts. It is a simple concept, but is far from easy. If it were easy there would be no need for contemplation or reflection on the reasons for mistakes. It would be a matter of "Oh, well...there's always tomorrow." The need to try harder, accomplish more, perform better or become stronger would not exist. Discouragement would not be an issue.

When addressing mental training in the martial arts, there are distinctions in cultural awareness. This can be seen, for example, in an international athletic competition where it is obvious that one opponent somehow gained a psychological advantage over another. Despite the importance and power of vital psychological components, people in the West still tend to overemphasize the mere physical aspects of training, focusing on the development of technique, power, speed, and strength. Training in the West is far more externally oriented. An example of this is the common use of chemicals such as creatine and steroids being incorporated into training, and the thought process of "he who buys the most expensive protein shake" will ultimately win. In short, the mental aspects of competition are not the focus.

In the Far East, the internal aspects of martial arts have always taken precedence. On the battlefield a "whirlwind of death and fear swirled around combatants" and the quality of discipline, spirit, physical commitment, mental focus, and calm were more important than training, skill and technique. During times of war, young samurai were trained from birth to be completely committed to action with no thought of self or their own life. Their lives were solely dedicated to absolute, unwavering discipline and relentless repetitive practice, mixed with psychological-religious training to prepare the mind.

> *"Bless those who curse you, pray for those who mistreat you".*
> *Luke 6:28*

It should be noted that, for the samurai, the highest level a warrior could hope to achieve in an encounter would be a peaceful resolution without ever drawing the sword. All the training a samurai warrior received was to ensure cultivation of strong character, simplicity, self-restraint, equanimity, concentration, firmness, and the ability to remain emotionally neutral.

Traditional karate today continues to emphasize training of the mind and the building of internal discipline. The practice of etiquette forces the individual or ego to become humble in the school and when training. The fighting spirit is developed in doing that extra push up, keeping your stance when it's painful, or overcoming challenges in learning difficult techniques. In kumite, or sparring, students face natural fears and negative thoughts and must learn to instead become instinctively calm, contemplative and able to study the opponent with objectivity. Frustration leads to ineffective reactions, and that may lead to failure. Performing a kata in front of the class teaches a student how to deal with situations that are uncomfortable. The dojo becomes more than just a gym of physical activity, but rather a place for students to intimately relate to matters of the spirit. Endless practice and basic repetitions force the mind to let go and allow the body to take over as the techniques are internalized.

Focus is also a mental component which works in perfect harmony with the physical body. Focus creates awareness from within and allows the body to perform without hindrance. Focus also refers to understanding the limitations of a person's body - knowing not to hyperextend the arms or legs, not to kick higher than the body allows, and not to overpower each movement. By learning to relax the muscles, one gains the ability to react quickly and concentrate the power of a movement, without having to first release tension.

Meditation is one of the most essential and beneficial elements of karate training. Society, as mentioned, is increasingly busy and distractions are constant in daily life. Schedules are hectic. Tensions runs high. Cell phones are a constant source of distraction. Anyone can be reached anytime, anywhere. Teens communicate more with Siri than their parents!

Meditation opens the door to a more peaceful coexistence with the universe. It quiets the mind and calms the storm. It creates a refreshed mind in which to cultivate positive and productive thought. Meditation can be done many ways. At the dojo, it is taught in the kneeling position, with a focus on taking some deep breaths and releasing all idle thoughts and worries with slow, deliberate inhalations and exhalations. This quiet and still time also provides each student with an opportunity to practice their breathing by expanding and contracting their belly, then expanding laterally to their rib cage, followed by directing their breathing to their chest and finally to their back between the scapulas. Meditation helps to bring the mind to the present, preparing the student for the ensuing training session.

Meditation can also be done in the form of prayer several times each day, allowing time for introspection and balance, and a healthy pause from the daily hustle and bustle. It allows us a time to free ourselves momentarily from the never-ending noise pollution and overstimulation of every day life, and refreshes our brain cells. A person can also pause several times a day and just sit in silence. There is great solace to be found in a quiet mind.

> *"Let us draw near with a true heart in full assurance of faith, having our hearts sprinkled from an evil conscience, and our bodies washed with pure water".*
> **Hebrews 10:22**

Recent research also supports the idea that physical exercise encourages the brain to function at optimum levels. Exercise prompts nerve cells to multiply, strengthening their connections with neurons and protecting them from degeneration. A 1999 study involving mice at the Salk Institute further explored this premise. The study set out to discover how healthy brain cells affected the neurons in the brain. The goal was to find out if healthy brain cells translate into those behavioral benefits which enable one to learn more efficiently and quickly. The two groups of healthy mice were housed separately in cages that were identical except for one detail: One group of mice had running wheels installed in the cage.

"The mice just love the wheel! They run on it as soon as you put it in their cages," said Van Praag, one of the researchers. "If you let them run as much as they want, they run all night long."

For several weeks researchers tracked data as the runners voluntarily racked up two to three miles on their wheels every night. The scientists then tested the groups to see whether the groups differed in their ability to solve a popular learning test called the "Morris Water Maze." Although both groups of mice swam at about the same speed, it was quickly ascertained that the running group learned the location of a platform hidden under the maze's opaque water significantly faster than their less fit counterparts.

This study ultimately concluded that there was definitive evidence proving that physical exercise promotes healthy brain function. There have been many documented cases where professional (and even amateur) athletes have accomplished amazing feats. Recently a blind man reached the summit of Mt. Everest for the first time. The most heart-warming and inspirational moments in life happen when seemingly staggering odds are stacked in the way of one who overcomes them.

The body can be made strong with a healthy diet and daily exercise. Almost anyone can achieve a high level of strength and condition through hard, physical work. But in the end, the one with the strongest mind will achieve their highest aspiration.

KARATE FOR THE BODY

> *"Men are born soft and supple; Dead, they are stiff and hard.*
> *Plants are born tender and pliant; Dead, they are brittle and dry.*
> *Thus whoever is stiff and inflexible is a disciple of death.*
> *Whoever is soft and yielding Is a disciple of life.*
> *The hard and stiff will be broken.*
> *The soft and supple will prevail."*
>
> *- Lao Tzu*

The benefits of physical exercise have been clearly established. Modern technology provides many tools with which to measure physical fitness. Heart rate monitors are a basic tool used by most professional runners, cyclists and many other athletes. Exercise equipment like treadmills and elliptical machines have onboard computers that will not only measure data about the effectiveness of a specific workout in reaching the target heart rate, but will also save this data to monitor the progression of fitness.

Physical fitness is tangible in that as it is being achieved, the outcome is visible. People notice other people who are in shape and fit. Many strive to look like cover girls and underwear models.

Hectic schedules and time restraints sometimes challenge the ability to take the time for a good workout. Others obsessively dedicate their lives to this activity, yet neglect their spirits and minds.

When it comes to fitness, America is a "fast food" nation with a burning desire to look "perfect" without doing the hard work. Plastic surgery seems an easier way to achieve a certain look or appearance, but the internal component of exercise that involves edifying the mind is crippled by using this process. The ease of availability for body image surgeries has created a spoiled and complacent sector in our society. Plastic surgery was so expensive ten years ago it was only available to the elite. Now surgeries are auctioned off on eBay! Fad diets, erratic work out schedules and other "quick-fixes" only add up to disappointment. These temporary solutions don't provide long term solutions for physical health and well-being. It seems that our society has its measurement for success skewed. Material possessions and flawless appearances are the prizes most sought after, but these in the end are the things that are least rewarding.

It cannot be disputed that physical activity is tantamount to good health. Karate is an excellent way to become physically fit. It does not age-discriminate because training is done at the level of the individual's pace or ability. It can be as difficult or as easy as it is practiced. It meets the student at their level.

Karate is one of just a few athletic activities that combines the use of soft and fluid movements that require relaxed muscles with no tension, and also movements that require quick, hard contractions of large muscle groups. This works muscles in the necessary way to build strength and flexibility. Karate also uses both fast and slow movements during training, building muscle strength as certain skills are developed. This dynamic method creates a flexible musculature system that is firm and defined, allowing supple movement and rhythmic fluidity. Contrarily, exercise programs that build bulging muscles actually restrict fluidity in movement.

Warming up muscle groups to avoid strains or injury is particularly important to any athletic activity and is always done at the beginning and end of each class. Breathing techniques, core balance and body awareness are incorporated into all facets of training.

People who take the time to exercise generally take time and interest in eating properly. Diet is an important contribution to a healthy fitness program and life. Nutrition should never be neglected. A poor diet counteracts the benefits of exercise, causing fatigue. Tired muscles are more likely to break down and blood sugar levels rise and fall creating mood swings, which leads to discouragement and frustration.

Adequate rest is another factor in physical health. More than half of the American population suffers from insomnia at least two nights during the week. Rigorous physical activity is an excellent way to ensure a good night's sleep.

Stamina, cardiovascular health, core strength, muscle strength, flexibility, good posture, longevity and good reflexes are just a few of the physical benefits of karate training.

In summation, karate is a well-rounded physical exercise that imparts the added bonus of building mental and spiritual strength.

KARATE FOR THE SPIRIT

Spirit is defined as: "The vital principle or animating force within living beings; the soul." It is further defined as "vivacity" or "courage" and "the real sense or significance of something." Of the three elements of mind, body and spirit, the spirit is the most intangible. It is represented in the character of an individual. Spirit is the life force that tells your mind not to quit when things are difficult and to go that extra mile. A person's spirit can be seen in the results of their daily lives and accomplishments. A person who lacks spirit lacks depth.

Spirituality is not contained simply in religious belief systems. Karate and Eastern culture at its birth was strongly influenced by Buddhism, as that was their religion at the time. Buddhism is a religion that promotes selflessness and striving to become a person of high quality with strong moral values, while discouraging the focus on the outer world and material things. In fact, most cultures look to a higher source to find spiritual strength. This higher source is extremely important and enables one to achieve spiritual awareness. Spirituality requires the letting go of the "self" or "the ego."

Japan also has long been influenced by Shintoism and Bushido, or "The Way of the Warrior." The way of the samurai has held a particular fascination for those in Western culture. The samurai was trained to become selfless, putting family, honor and respect above all things, and to sacrifice his own life if necessary, without question.

The values in Western culture were very similar, especially in their original context. Modern society has become less humanistic and more self-serving, and in recent years the results have not been favorable. Seemingly, these days it is only in times of great tragedy that the founding fathers' spirit that created America rises up and embraces its people, unifying them again. These difficult times, and the heroic acts of individuals that reach out to others, are the essence of what exemplifies spiritual strength. If life was always easy there would be no need to seek a higher power or to develop spiritual strength. But life is not easy.

Karate is an art and practice which advances inner growth. By applying a foundation of self-discipline, unity is created in the mind, body and spirit. This unity creates a better understanding of life on both the physical and spiritual planes.

Master Kenwa Mabuni wrote of the "Five Way Spirit" (Go Do Shin) of Shito-Ryu:
- One • Determination: Never forget the spirit of first beginning.
- One • Morality: Never neglect courtesy and etiquette.
- One • Development: Never neglect effort.
- One • Common sense: Never lose common sense.
- One • Peace: Never disturb harmony.

Master Mabuni believed each statement was of the highest priority (hence the delineation and use above of the word "One" in the ranking for each).

Underlining the Importance of Go Do Shin

These 5 precepts are important to understand and practice. It's easy to memorize them and say them after each class, but careful attention should be focused on the meanings of each one and applied each day:

Never Forget the Spirit of First Beginning (Will)

Whether it be the first day of school, the first trip to Disneyland, or the first date, that excitement that stirred the spirit at that time must also be similarly applied each day to karate practice. Daily routines often leave us in a less glamorous mood, and the passion once had is often somehow lost. So it is good to greet each day, each karate class, and each good thing within your grasp with an expectant spirit. Seize every opportunity to better yourself while helping others, stay focused, and accomplish great things. Remember not to take things for granted, and appreciate God's favor and protection throughout each day.

Never Neglect Courtesy and Etiquette (Morality)

To possess the traits of character we admire, moral education is essential; we must train the heart and mind to soar above evil. By modeling positive behaviors and with the proper training, good habits of courtesy and etiquette are formed. Adults must take the issue of morality seriously, especially in the presence of children, and must understand that their morals are constantly being taught to those around them, often without even realizing. Their example is vital in shaping a child's character, and virtues such as honesty, compassion, courage, and perseverance can be grasped and demonstrated by children when proper examples are modeled.

Today we are witnessing a seemingly never-ending political nightmare where political parties are refusing to accept anyone's opposing views. Good people can be either conservative or liberal, so let's not form negative judgement on either side, as this clouds our moral obligation as human beings and ambassadors of optimistic growth. The personal conflicts between opposing conservative and liberal viewpoints can obscure our obligation to offer positive instructions to all students. Remain courteous and respectful.

Never Neglect Effort (Growth and Determination)

Karate students should always strive to give their best effort while training. They emerge successful in life if they are determined to grow with a strong and positive fighting spirit. They push aside their weaknesses of laziness and hopelessness and replace them with confidence and perseverance. They should not dwell on temporary set-backs but rather fight on to a victorious finish.

Never Lose Common Sense (Common Sense)

Karate teachers cannot teach a person to reach an intelligent conclusion or make a sound judgement on practical matters. They may, however, educate students to be more aware and allow time to think and make wise decisions on their own. The Latin word for education is "educare," which means "to draw out." The sensei, through their teaching style and appeal, helps to draw out the best in each student in order for them to apply common sense.

Never Disturb Harmony (Peace)

Unity, tranquility, and balance are essential in keeping harmony and peace in each student's environment - at home, in school, in their community, in their country, and even the world they live in. This is not to say that one should put themselves in "neutral" and not get involved in the struggle of good against evil. In karate practice students learn about timing, distancing, and space. They come to understand how to reflect harmony without having emotions dictate their actions. Civic decency, brotherhood, human rights, and the peace these actions accord, will be attained only when people can practice and attain peace in their own lives.

Master Mabuni also listed these spiritual weaknesses as noteworthy:
- Doubt or Skepticism
- Negligence
- Egotism

A spirit that is cultivated and nurtured provides a foundation of success because it radiates calmness and an ability to endure all things. There are efforts and there are results. The strength of the effort is measured by its result. Things do not happen by chance. Strength, power and spirituality are the fruits of effort - they manifest as thoughts completed, objectives accomplished, and visions realized.

Winston Churchill, a hearty man of solid inspiration, single-handedly saved England during the Blitzkrieg during World War II. England endured endless nights as the Third Reich flew planes over London, unloading thousands of bombs on the land and causing mass destruction. Hitler, along with the rest of the world, felt that the fall of England would be imminent and easy. But they did not know the bulldog-like tenacity of Winston Churchill. He went on the air, time and time again, calling his nation to hang on. He encouraged them to keep believing and to never lose hope. England survived by this tenacity.

Years later one of his alma maters, an exclusive prep school, asked him to speak at graduation. Churchill accepted the invitation. The headmaster at the school was elated. For weeks the student body was told "Winston Churchill is coming, the most powerful orator in history. Bring your pencils and paper, and take note of every word he says."

Finally the greatly anticipated day arrived. The graduation service began. The students sat at the edges of their seats with pencils in hand and papers poised. The guests and parents settled in for a long, inspirational speech. After many glowing and flowery introductions, Winston Churchill arose from his chair, approached the podium and turned to address the eager crowd.

"Gentleman," he said, "Never give up. Never give up. Never, never, never, never, never, never, never!" Then he turned around, returned to his seat and sat down. The students were stunned. The audience was amazed. And none of them ever, ever, ever forgot it.

When the body is tired and the mind is weak, be strong in spirit, and simple and powerful in speech.

> *"Karate is a treasured gift from God. It enables us to generate courage while filling ourselves and emptying ourselves at the same time."*
> *- Del Saito*

Chapter 4
INTRODUCTION TO THE DOJO

Finding the right school in which to learn and practice karate is of the utmost importance. The dojo, literally translated, means "place of the way" or "formal training hall." It is an integral part of the Koryu (old tradition) arts and Budo ("warrior way") training. The dojo mirrors a church, meaning that it is not merely a building, but a place for fellowship in training of the mind, body and spirit. A Japanese proverb we always should reflect upon is "Jikishin dojo kore nari," or "a pure heart is a dojo."

Traditionally, the shomen, or front wall, was well defined as this was where the shrine was placed. This was also the place of the sensei. To the right was the joseki, or "upper place," for the senior students and to the left is the shimoseki, or "lower place," for the junior students. Historically, one of the reasons for this arrangement was to afford the sensei maximum protection from an intruder.

The dojo is the place where everything comes together. In the beginning it will feel like entering a different world, as ritual and formality are practiced. The dojo should be clean, simple, well lit, and have proper ventilation. The dojo should be fully supported and cared for by the students, not the instructors.

Before signing up at a karate school it is best to visit a dojo a few times to watch the instructor and the students' attitudes during training. Their respect for their sensei should be obvious. Ask questions about the instructor's training background. Check on class schedules to ensure the practicality of attending classes at their designated times, and see that there are enough classes during a week to ensure the discipline and skill are addressed. Another important question to ask is whether karate is taught as sport, or as an art, at their organization. The answer is usually as both, but you may find some schools only emphasize the sporting aspects. There should be a profound emphasis on building and perfecting character. The sensei, or instructor, should be able to demonstrate skills that are clear, well-practiced and polished. Ask about the teaching of kata and bunkai. Question the instructor about their promotion system. Be wary of schools that hand out belts without having an established and defined promotion curriculum. Ask who will be teaching the classes. A qualified instructor conducting the classes is more effective than a beginner or novice student in this position. Inquire about all the fees and tuition. Tuition may seem very reasonable, at some dojos, but by the time you include the other costs that are attached, you may be paying more than you bargained for.

Jesse Enkamp, best-selling author, and founder of Seishin, lists some warning signs of the "McDojo," a studio that is more interested in focusing on the "bottom line" and bolstering student's egos than providing them quality instruction of substance and clarity.

Warning signs might be:
- Students having a proliferation of badges/patches on their gi
- Students being awarded their black belt in 1-2 years
- The instructor has studied marketing longer than Karate
- The instructor demands respect, he doesn't earn it
- A red gi for the grandmaster, black gi for instructors and white gi for regular students
- New students aren't allowed to watch a class
- Advancement to the next rank is very expensive
- Bunkai/oyo (applications) are not taught to the karate moves

- Low kicks are never practiced
- Prospective students are required to become a member before even trying a lesson
- The sensei is a "grandmaster" with 7th dan or above, yet is 30 years or younger
- Students are taught to be subservient and not to ask questions

Another red flag revealing these compromising studios is that the teacher will offer all the best techniques learned from many different martial arts.

Unfortunately, despite all the warnings, hundreds if not thousands of students will still enroll in these "McDojos." And sadly, even after finding out that their level of instruction lacks quality, they do not leave and seek a different dojo with a better instructor. These cultish environments can be brainwashing to students who do not know better. This is NOT karate in its purest sense, so the outcome will not be positive.

Honbu (or Hombu) Dojo

A honbu dojo is the administrative and stylistic headquarters of an organization or group. It is also referred to as the "home dojo" where students and instructors from all the branches congregate to train, share teaching techniques, learn business and marketing strategies, take examinations, and share time with the headmaster. Students who train at the honbu dojo are expected to excel in all areas of karate-do and set the highest standard for other affiliated dojo members to follow.

Sensei

"Sensei" is comprised of two written Chinese characters (kanji). "Sen" means literally "before" or "preceding." "Sei" is the character that means "life" or "to be born."

Dave Lowry, one of the most knowledgeable martial arts authors of our times explains, "The "sensei" is "the life that came before." "This is a poetic way to denote someone who has walked along "the way" before you and who may now show you the path as well."

The sensei is the very essence of the dojo. His character must flow through his students at many levels and touch every aspect of their lives. The sensei is an exceptional teacher in that he has extensive knowledge and is able to convey this knowledge in the best possible way. He is an impartial judge who can see his students progress without showing favor. A sensei may become harder on students as their skills advance. The sensei knows to correct technique in a time-appropriate fashion, and is kind but firm with beginners.

Some students may classify the sensei as a teacher or friend, but he is not just one of these but both, and more. The sensei always has his students' best interests at heart. He may take opposing views with them to test their reactions, or put forth untruths to see if they are readily accepted. Silence may be the best form of praise a student receives from their sensei. He will observe the student in and out of the dojo, watch how they interact with family members and friends, at home or at work, and watch their interactions with fellow students.

The sensei always keeps his true course, even though he may adapt to different situations. His inward ideals and principles are constant and unflappable. He persists when there is no apparent reason, gives while others take, and asks nothing in return. It is important to understand these dynamics of the sensei to the dojo and its members, as it should always be a mutually beneficial relationship that results in effective training and application.

James Allen gives an apt description of the qualities of a sensei:

"The strong, calm man is always respected and revered. He is like a shade-giving tree in a thirsty land or a sheltering rock in a storm. Who does not love or desire a tranquil heart, a sweet-tempered, balanced life? It does not matter whether it rains or shines for they are always serene and calm, possessing the poise of character which we call serenity. It is precious wisdom."

Other Important Attributes of a Sensei

To reiterate the importance of a worthy sensei, I will discuss some areas for you to be aware of in order to maintain a positive and healthy training journey. I have mentioned the characteristics of an ideal sensei, however I must also share my observations of some karate instructors in recent years. There are instructors that cleverly veil themselves with fancy titles and degrees that have little, if any, use for the actual teachings of karate-do. They take unfair advantage of their students just to assert their physical superiority. They confuse loyalty with control. A sensei is one who continues to train regularly and is able to teach and guide his students by example, not the one with a high rank and a pot belly to boot. It is too easy for the modern sensei to equate the success of his dojo with the quantity of students, profits, and tournament achievements. The essence and substance of a sensei's teachings should be focused on personal growth for students, and students should be emulating his living example. Just as vibrant roots continue to absorb water and nutrients in order to keep branches healthy and strong, sensei too need to continue to nourish themselves regularly with discipline, instruction, and personal training (tandoku renshu) in order to maintain soundness for all who depend on him. If not, they are mere instructors and should not be called "sensei."

Sensei-Deshi Relationship

The relationship between the sensei (teacher) and the "deshi" (student) is a critical element in the teaching of karate. Traditionally, karate is passed on from the sensei to the deshi by direct transmission of information and knowledge. The sensei sets the example and the student imitates and follows. The success of the sensei's teaching and the ability of the student to learn is based on two things; the trust of students for the sensei, and the compassion and understanding the sensei bestows on the student. It is a mutual relationship characterized by reciprocal trust, respect, effective communication and commitment.

Dojo Etiquette

Once a sensei and a dojo have been chosen, it is important to quickly learn the appropriate etiquette for the dojo. Tradition forms the backbone and nucleus of karate-do. It is important that students are aware of the dojo's rules and etiquette in order to preserve this tradition.

There are profound differences in the far Eastern and Western cultures. These differences become clear when training begins at a dojo. Respect, bowing, order, and discipline are natural to Far Eastern students and are learned at an early age. Due to cultural differences, the challenges Westerners face when learning to be a member of the dojo community might include:

Bowing - Westerners are accustomed to greeting one another with a handshake, wave or "high five."

Cleaning - Westerners believe chores should be done by a janitor and that students should not be asked to do chores, especially since they are paying tuition for classes.

Senpai /Kohai - The practice of having a "big brother" or senior student working closely with a young student. There is a belief that only the sensei or paid school personnel should be working one-on-one with a student as these others are not seen as "qualified" to work closely in a teaching position.

Staying in Tempo with Others - Most Westerners like to walk to the beat of their own drum and have trouble following dojo protocol and etiquette.

Taking Shoes Off Before Walking on the Mat - Most Westerners are accustomed to wearing shoes in the house.

Appearance/Uniforms - Most Westerners are unaccustomed to the use of uniforms in school. In the West, individuality is emphasized. Extreme ways of drawing attention to one's appearance are commonplace, "My blue hair/facial piercings are just a way I express myself."

These cultural differences, once understood, are easily addressed. Students come to understand the importance of the dojo formalities, dress, attitude and service while they practice. They learn that one can excel without having to look or act differently.

The actual formalities of dojo etiquette vary throughout the world, however many share similar procedures. The more students perform the formalities of karate, the more intensely they will understand and eventually appreciate humble expressions of respect.

When entering or leaving the dojo, students should pause momentarily at the entrance and bow. This bow demonstrates respect for the place where people from all walks of life gather together to train and grow while creating stronger values for themselves. The bow is also a reminder that karate is to train the mind, body and spirit. In addition, when black belts are in the dojo and class has not yet begun, students should walk over and greet them with a bow. By doing so, students acknowledge their appreciation for the hard work and knowledge those with high ranks have acquired.

At times parents refuse to enroll their children in karate classes due to the misunderstanding of the bow. They say, "We do not allow our children to bow to anyone but God." I agree that bowing the head should display a sense of prayer, reverence, or worship. However, the bow practiced in the dojo is simply a gesture of respect. The bow is performed by bending at the waist, demonstrating humility, awareness, and sincerity.

When class is about to begin, the command, "Seiretsu!" or "line up!" is announced, and then dojo members align themselves in order of seniority from joseki (upper seat) to shimoseki (lower seat). Traditionally, the seniors would line up farthest away from the entrance while the juniors would line up closest to the entrance. I have reversed that arrangement and have placed greater responsibility on the senior students to protect the less proficient by placing them nearest the entrance.

Once students have lined up in rank, meditation will follow. This is done in the "seiza" (kneeling or seating position). At the command "Mokuso" ("Quiet oneself in order to reflect one's heart and state of mind") all students will maintain an erect posture, with the shoulders and arms relaxed and pause briefly to rid their minds of negative thoughts, bring their minds to the present, and to achieve a state of readiness for the ensuing lesson.

The dojo kun (oath or code) is then recited by all with enthusiasm and vigor. For example, many of the Shito-ryu organizations recite their founder's oath as follows:

"Seek perfection of character.
Be faithful.
Endeavor to excel.
Respect others.
Refrain from violent behavior."

The highest ranking student on the right will make the command "Shomen ni, rei!" ("To the front, bow!") and while still kneeling, the students will place their hands on the floor (forming a triangle) in front of them, and bow until their foreheads are about an inch above the floor. After pausing for a moment to show respect to the place of training, students will rise back to the kneeling position slowly and in order, one at a time, from highest-ranking to lowest. The senior student will then give the command, "Sensei ni, rei!" (to the teacher, bow!) The students will bow facing the instructor while saying, "Onegai shimasu" ("I'm requesting that you train us hard.") Again, they assume the kneeling position and remain calm and attentive until the next command is given.

At the end of each training session students will again line up for meditation. After meditating, the Go Do Shin is recited followed by the command, "otagai ni, rei" ("To each other, bow!"), and students will then pair up and bow to show respect and gratitude to their fellow students. After this bow is completed, students return to the original kneeling position facing the front of the dojo. This next bow could include the senpai (senior student), and shidoin (assistant teacher). The sensei will then choose to make some remarks about the training and closing comments, and the command "sensei ni, rei" ("To the teacher, bow!") will be given. The students will bow simultaneously saying "Arigato gozaimasu." The final command of "shomen ni, rei" ("To the front, bow!") will be given. Prior to leaving the dojo, it is respectful for students to bow to all senior students and the black belt students.

Sherry Archambault and Janis Howard demonstrating proper way to bow while standing.

Other Formalities, Rules and Principles:

Whenever the instructor calls upon a student to demonstrate a technique, they must bow before and after the demonstration. When a student is paired with another student during practice, they must bow to each other before and after the practice.

If friends or children are invited to observe a class, they should be advised beforehand of proper dojo etiquette.

After each class, all students should participate in clean-up activities, such as wiping down the mats and equipment, and putting away all equipment used during training.

Gis (uniforms) should be fresh and clean at all times.

Instructors should be addressed as "sensei" at all times in the dojo, and students should be encouraged to do so even outside of the dojo. Students should bow and greet their sensei at all dojo ac-

Students demonstrating the proper way to bow as a group.

tivities and tournaments.

Karate-do Precepts for Character Development:
"Henceforth, I shall faithfully train to strengthen my mind and body.
I am willing to endure rigorous training to achieve my goal.
As my strength increases, I shall seek to cultivate a gentle heart.
I shall not use my skill outside the dojo except in the most extreme circumstances.
At all times I will try to avoid inflicting injury upon another person.
I will not brag about my skill nor use it maliciously.
I shall train with the spirit of humility."

Rules of Conduct:
1. Vulgar language is never allowed, whether inside or outside the dojo. You represent the TKF International and your example should never discredit karate or the organization.

2. Smoking is prohibited in the dojo at all times. (If you have this habit and wish to break it, we can make some accommodations to help you).

3. Alcoholic beverages are never allowed in the dojo. Never come to practice intoxicated or with the smell of alcohol on your breath. Confidence and strength come through hard training and are not found in a bottle.

4. Non-prescribed or mind-altering drugs are strictly prohibited at all times. Your best high is through proper training of the mind, body and spirit.

5. A dignified appearance is always proper and will reflect on the attitude towards the organization of non-participants.

6. Do not speak ill of other instructors or their students. "The mountain does not laugh at the river because it is low, nor does the river speak ill of the mountain because it cannot move."

7. Improper behavior or any violation of TKF International Rules of Conduct may result in termination of membership.

8. It is the responsibility of the instructor to ensure that the students follow dojo etiquette during karate class.

9. Your students' karate gi should be kept clean and in good repair at all times. Unauthorized patches are not allowed on the gi.

10. Students are asked to keep their fingernails and toenails clean and clipped. Jewelry should not be worn during training.

11. Once the practice session begins, no student is to break rank unless given permission to do so.

12. Students should be ready to start training at the designated starting time. Any student arriving late is to bow onto the mat (when acknowledged by eye contact with the instructor), enter to the side of the class, meditate, and warm up briefly before joining the ranks, with the least amount of disturbance to the class.

13. No street shoes are allowed on the main dojo floor.

14. No food or chewing gum is allowed during training sessions.

15. Injuries or illness must be reported immediately to the instructor.

Karate By-Laws:
1. Never use hands and feet without a just cause.
2. Never accept, nor challenge anyone to a duel.
3. Never speak ill of the absent.
4. Respect the rights of others at all times.
5. Develop tolerance through the knowledge of these arts.
6. Avoid all arguments.
7. Curb impetuousness and think before acting.
8. Be extremely hesitant in using any dangerous counter-techniques, even in one's own defense.
9. Participate in all class projects.
10. Practice the arts patiently, diligently and in the proper state of mind.
11. Be honest, humble, courteous, and sincere at all times.
12. Never carry a chip on your shoulder.

13. Always strive for spiritual, mental and physical strength.
14. Avoid all pettiness.
15. Forgive the ignorant and practice self-control at all times.
16. Never boast or use profane language.
17. Treasure these arts and never display them needlessly.

Karate Resolutions:

1. Never invite trouble by an uncalled for look, remark or action.
2. Make every effort to smile or talk, and not fight, my way out of trivial situations.
3. Never become involved in the domestic quarrels of neighbors.
4. Ignore the ranting of a rowdy, belligerent person, drunk or otherwise.
5. Never start a fight with a weaker person just to assert physical superiority.
6. Steer clear of all trouble-prone areas, or walk away from such places, at the first sign of trouble.

Folding the Gi:

Place the jacket, back down, on the floor and stretch it out smoothly. Fold the right front jacket flap over to one side. Next fold the left side flap over the right jacket. Fold the sleeves in over the front of the jacket. Fold the jacket in half and then in half, again. Place the neatly doubled pants on top of the folded jacket, folding the pant legs to just below the bottom of the jacket. Fold or tightly roll the jacket and pants from the bottom up. Place it on the doubled- folded belt, and bring the loose ends through the looped end and pull it tightly.

In these modern times, students often take their gi to a professional cleaner and will bring their uniform to the dojo on a hanger. This is acceptable and the gi need not be folded. However, for students who do not use a hanger, folding the gi is required. It is unsightly to see students carry their wrinkled gi as if it just came out of the washer.

Always look sharp and take good care of your gi.

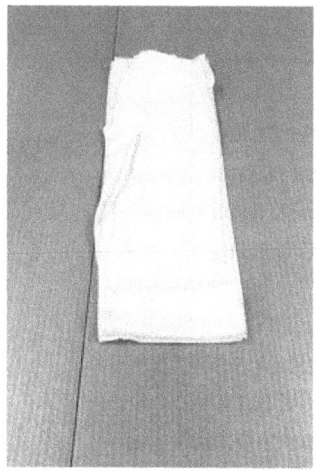

Fold the gi trousers length wise in half.

Fold the gi jacket from the left and over the right side.

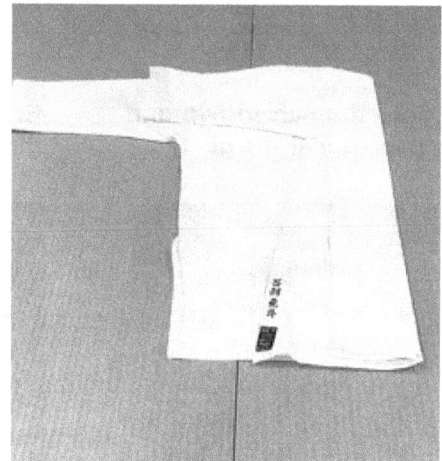

Fold the left side edge of the gi jacket to the middle.

Folding the Gi

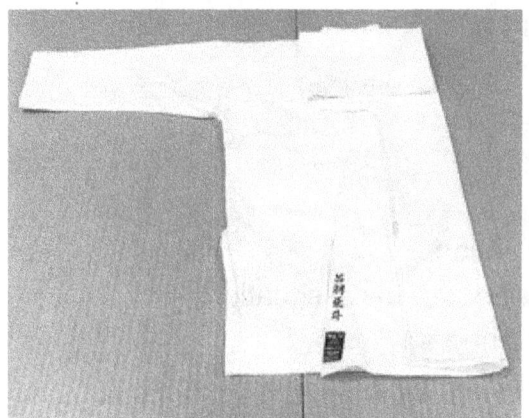
Fold the sleeve to the right side.

Fold the right side of the gi jacket to the middle.

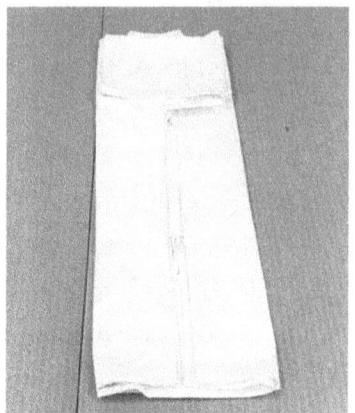
Fold the sleeve to the right side.

Place the folded gi trousers on top of the gi jacket.

Fold the gi in thirds.

Keep the folds tight.

Fold the belt in two and place under the gi.

Bring the loose end through the loop.

When arriving at home, unfold your dogi and place on a clothes hanger to air dry.

Pull firmly and tie a square knot.

Proudly carry the gi over the shoulder.

> **Note:**
> It is recommended to wash your dogi in warm water and air dry. Avoid using bleach.
>
> If at all possible have three dogis available - two for training and one for tournaments.

Students in Oregon bringing their mind to present and preparing to recite the Karate Code.

Hawaii students striving for physical, mental and spiritual strength.

THE PURPOSE OF UNIFORMS AND COLORED BELTS

The history of the gi and colored belt system is not all that mysterious, but it is interesting, nonetheless. The Okinawans originally trained in only their underwear (which is different than Western underwear), as this was the least restrictive and most practical way to learn the techniques without inhibition. At the turn of the twentieth century, when the practice was finally accepted and training was being introduced into the elementary school systems, there became a need for a uniform. It was important that the uniform accommodate the freedom necessary to perform a variety of athletic maneuvers, as well as suit the philosophy of the art.

The 'Gi' was developed for its simplicity of style and functionality. The jacket is loosely fit with large sleeves that extend to the middle of the forearm and permit free use of the arms, wrists and hands. The pant is also loosely fit with extra-wide legs, tied at the waist with a drawstring so there is no need for a belt or suspenders. The white color of the uniform denotes simplicity of style.

"Wabi" is a Japanese word evidenced throughout Japanese culture, and is a creation from the Zen tradition. Translated, wabi means "intentional understatement." This is supported by the idea that if something seems not quite complete, one must consciously try to find what may be missing. The white gi is a perfect example of "Wabi" in that it gives no indication of a student's ability. It is unadorned with awards, patches or elaborate designs which would differentiate one student from another. It simply states that all things are equal until a particular skill is demonstrated with perfection, and then the performance would speak for itself.

The history of the belt is simply this: it was needed to keep the gi jacket closed. It's really just a belt! Jigoro kano, the founder of Judo, was the first to introduce the colored belt ranking system in the martial arts as a visible indication of the student's progress and hierarchy in the dojo. The colored belt in karate more likely evolved from the Japanese, who historically used different color sashes in military and religious ceremonies to acknowledge the importance of the figures in attendance.

Kyu ranks (below black belt), also referred as "Mudansha," begin at a higher number and move down to number one. Dan ranks (black belts), or "Yudansha" and "Kodansha," increase numerically from one to ten. The rank of Shodan-ho, or provisional shodan, may be awarded to those who have the technical qualifications but display an absence of the emotional maturity required for the full shodan rank.

As for black belts, two methods of achievement are possible:

Dan Graduations - Normal black belt graduations

Shogo Graduations - Title graduations
    Renshi - Expert Teacher, typically awarded to 3rd through 5th Dan.
    Kyoshi - Senior Expert Teacher (Teacher of Teachers), typically awarded to 5th
        through 7th Dan.
    Hanshi - Master Teacher, typically awarded to 8th Dan and higher.

Tying the Belt
Method 1

Grasp the belt and drape the two ends to the side.

Place the belt over your navel area.

Bring the two ends to the front keeping the right end on top,

Loop the right end under both binds.

Hold firmly and...

...finish tieing with a square knot by placing the left end under and through the loop.

Method 2

This method is to have one even bind throughout the belt, rather than having it cross over in the back.

Grasp the belt and drape the two ends to the side.

Place the belt over the navel area keeping the short end on the right side.

Wrap the long end around overlapping the right end.

Tying the Belt

Continue to wrap until the left end comes to the front.

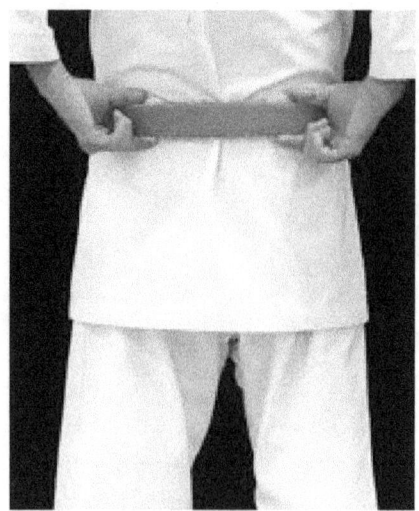

Be sure to have one even wrap in the back.

Tuck the left end under both wraps as in method one.

Be sure that the kanji is facing outward.

Loop the left end under and through the right end.

Both ends should hang evenly.

Competition Method

Place the belt over the navel area and bring the two ends to the front as in Methods One and Two.

Leave the right end a few inches longer than the left end.

Loop the right end just under the left end and between the two wraps, leaving room to loop the left end.

Tying the Belt

Loop the left end through the right loop and between the two wraps.

Pull the two ends firmly. The belt will hold more securely than the first two methods.

The colored belt ranking system in the martial arts is a visible indication of the student's progress and hierarchy in the dojo, shown here at one of our branches in India.

Chapter 5
PROMOTIONS

The purpose of having an effective promotion system is to provide students with the opportunity to set goals, for both the short term and long term. A key difference in our method, compared to what is found in most traditional karate schools, is that all the general requirements for each kyu and dan level must first be satisfactorily achieved and signed off by an examiner before students are allowed to take their exam. Many schools have quarterly or semi-annual exams and their students test in front of a board of examiners. This method is fine, however I have witnessed at some other schools that students who have not satisfactorily met their standard rank requirements are often passed. To assure that each student becomes more proactive in fulfilling their requirements, I have incorporated an examination booklet that is provided to each student. Specific days in the week are set aside for students who wish to perform and have their requirements approved.

After all of these requirements are satisfactorily met, students receive an application for testing that includes an assessment section for the student's parents and school teachers to fill out. This assessment focuses on their behavior, work ethic, attitude, etc. If all the requirements are satisfactorily met, they will be permitted to participate in the final exam, which is scheduled at the end of each month. During the exam, should any of the testing areas prove unsatisfactory, students have to wait to pass, and will have the opportunity to improve their techniques until the next examination period.

The testing process can be very stressful at times. The preparation and constant evaluation provides an opportunity for each student to apply their training under intense pressure, and to prepare for the challenges of everyday life. This testing process also assists students by giving them a chance to evaluate their own improvement and celebrate their successes.

Both children and adults have the same avenue in reaching their black belt level. In other words, youths are not held back or "penalized" due to their age. If they work hard and meet the requirements, they certainly will be awarded the rank they have achieved. At each promotion ceremony, examinees are required to pledge that they will continue to train in good faith, set a good example for their instructors and fellow students, and be a respectable person at home, school, and in their community. Should they betray their pledge, their belt will be taken away until they are once again deserving to wear it. This method may seem harsh to some parents, but if students are taught responsibility, accountability, and consequences, they come to understand why these traits are so important for growth and character development.

Ranking System

    Ranked Level
        10th Black Belt Level Judan (may designate with an aka obi)
        9th Black Belt Level Kudan, Kyudan
        8th Black Belt Level Hachidan
        7th Black Belt Level Shichidan, Nanadan
        6th Black Belt Level Rokudan

PROMOTIONS

    5th Black Belt Level Godan
    4th Black Belt Level Yondan
    3rd Black Belt Level Sandan
    2nd Black Belt Level Nidan
    1st Black Belt Level Shodan (kurobi)
    Probationary Shodan-ho

Non-Ranked Levels

10th level Probationary	Jukyu-ho	Yellow belt (kiiroi)
10th level	Jukyu	Orange belt (dai ido)
9th level	Kukyu	Blue belt (aoi)
8th level	Hachikyu	Blue belt with black stripe
7th level	Shichikyu	Purple blue (murasaki)
6th level	Rokyu	Purple blue with black stripe
5th level	Gokyu	Green belt (midori)
4th level	Yonkyu	Green belt with black stripe
3rd level	Sankyu	Brown belt with white stripe
2nd level	Nikyu	Brown belt (cha)
1st level	Ikkyu	Brown belt with black stripe

What the Color of Each Belt Represents

The different colors of belts in Karate signify the varied levels of skill and inner maturity. Although the belt colors may differ in organizations throughout the world, our standard belt colors represent the rank, and there is a philosophical interpretation of each color.

<u>White</u> is the first belt, representing innocence.
<u>Yellow and orange</u> signify the earth, and the roots and sprouts of early growth.
<u>Blue</u> represents the heavens, to which all growing things strive.
<u>Purple</u> represents the season of purification and the preparation for the growth to come.
<u>Green</u> represents the beginning of the plant's growth - strong roots have been formed and this inward strength is showing evidence of upward growth.
<u>Brown</u> represents the plateau prior to receiving the black belt. It is a reminder to the student that all future growth is dependent upon the receptiveness and fertility of the soil. It is a time for reflection on all that has come before and the importance of humility.

Each belt is more than a badge of honor. Instead, it is more like recognition of inner maturity. The awarding of a belt should never be a time for pride, but rather an occasion for self-reflection.

The ancient story was that all belts were white, and only turned black from age and the inner lessons that are learned from continuous practice of the principles of karate.

Recognition of inner maturity.

Understanding the importance of humility.

Promotions are earned.

Providing encouragement.

Chapter 6
TRAINING WITH PROPER ATTITUDES AND HABITS

"Half of our mistakes in life arise from feeling when we ought to think, and thinking when we ought to feel."
- Churton Collins

Realistic Expectations

Many people believe that the purpose of karate is to learn how to fight in order to overcome others and show superiority. However, for those who devote their lives to karate-do, the art of karate has a very different meaning. Not only is this a lifestyle, it is a way of life, and ultimately an avenue for character development that refines one's mind, body and spirit. The term "Karate-do" refers to "the way of karate," while "karate" denotes the technical aspects of karate.

Karate training extends over one's lifetime, at least for those that truly wish to learn every aspect of this unique art. One cannot learn, let alone master, all there is to know within a few months. It takes years and a lifetime to fully understand and fully know. Strong and worthy qualities come through time and effort, and these qualities must be cultivated. Karate is no different.

From the beginning, it is most important that students form worthwhile training habits which will help them develop and grow steadily. For this reason, I require prospective students to try a few classes before making a commitment. The next step, the commitment stage, is probably the most difficult for both students and parents alike. To fully understand the physical and mental fundamentals of karate, a minimum of one year of training (2 to 3 times per week), is recommended. Students will be challenged both physically and mentally, and must endure the rigorous training to win over their weaknesses. After a few weeks of training, students often find excuses. Some may look to quit if allowed. Karate is training, not playing. Those that go the distance find that they are more confident, disciplined, respectful, stronger, and have a good understanding of practice of karate. Students who successfully complete this beginner's stage often seek further understanding of karate and continue to fill their appetite with committed training.

The sensei will often challenge their student by using many training techniques, such as repetitive drills and movements that require close attention in order to be performed correctly. They may challenge students to stay in a squat position until the legs quiver, or use the aid of agility ladders for difficult footwork drills. Students will learn to develop discipline, remain focused, and meet challenging tasks without complaining or giving up.

With sports being the center stage for many throughout the world these days, it is a challenge to educate the karate student to immerse themselves in the traditional karate-do environment. Karate-do is not seasonal. They will not have a game each week to look forward to. Trophies will not be awarded for any successes or failures. Yet this special art is in itself a sport of life. The journey may not be as tangible as in sports, but it comes with failures and life-long rewards.

If you begin to wane in your training, think as though your presence in class is expected by your fellow students. You share a special spirit that echoes and touches their spirit and keeps them motivated. You are an inspiration and an important component that keeps the wheels turning smoothly. With this kind of attitude, many will reciprocate and a win-win habit will prevail.

Chapter 7
FUNDAMENTALS AS FOUNDATIONS OF KARATE

The fundamentals of karate are based on three important components. Although each has a seemingly different emphasis in karate practice, the art, competition and self-defense is dependent on excellence in kihon, kata and kumite practice. All of these integral parts provide the opportunity for every student to explore, and greatly benefit, when taught and learned correctly. Other than desire and commitment, there are standard components that need to be addressed and incorporated into each area of practice. These include form, posture, balance, the understanding of being centered, power and speed, hip coordination, focus, rhythm, timing and distance, and spirit. After a brief explanation of these important factors, I have included photos of the stances, blocks, strikes, kicks, and footwork of karate.

The Foundation of Fundamentals

*"...dishonor is like a scar on a tree, which time,
instead of effacing, only helps to enlarge".*
- Inazo Nitobe

This quote is a reflection on how the fundamentals of karate can manifest in the student. Master the small things and the performance will bear a good "scar" that grows with time. This is the philosophy and spirit of karate and the aspects of practice. With proper supervision from a qualified instructor, a student will flourish. Likewise, without good instruction, serious effort, concentration and focus, the student's efforts will be in vain. Diligence is the necessary ingredient to become proficient. Bad habits are like fleas...easy to acquire, but most difficult to get rid of.

Standard Components

Form (Katachi)
The physics and physiology of moves will be taught in practice. The instructor will point out the importance of the form in each move. With correct form, the effectiveness of each motion will be realized. In golf, correct swing form is needed to achieve accuracy, control and power in hitting the ball. Any athletic endeavor requires good form to avoid injury. In karate practice, form and precision are emphasized because techniques are useless without them, and without them a student becomes vulnerable. With proper form the movements become poetic, beautiful, and powerful, promoting self-worth, confidence and appreciation for the gifts provided them.

Posture (Shisei)
Learning correct posture, and learning to read the posture of others (and their intent), is a key component of Okinawan Karate. Western culture dictates that good posture is a reflection of self-confidence and it is presented in the way a person walks, sits and stands. Eastern philosophy believes that as a person develops good posture in walking, sitting and standing, his self-confidence then im-

proves, as well as his moral character. Either way the relationship cannot be denied.

"Pretend inferiority and encourage his arrogance."
Chinese philosopher

Balance and the Center of Gravity (Antei and Itten)

Good balance and a strong center of gravity will be learned in the fundamentals of training. Various stances are emphasized, some to enhance stability in a technique, others to enhance the ability to move swiftly in any direction. The center of gravity, two inches below the navel or at the hara (seat of emotion) shifts constantly and must maintain its integrity regardless of what the feet are doing. Leg position is influential in providing balance and support, and also absorbs the shock of an opponent's actions. "Tate sen," the vertical center of balance, should also be maintained.

Power and Speed (Chikara no Kyojaku and Waza no Kankyu)

This will be taught only after correct form and balance are achieved. This is to avoid injury and to reinforce techniques so they do not become ineffective due to lack of strength. Powerful techniques are a result of concentration and maximum force focused at a specific point. This cannot be accomplished without sufficient speed. In karate, the objective is not to slowly hit a powerful object, but to quickly strike a small target.

Hip Coordination (Koshi or Shiri)

Speed and power will be maximized with proper hip movement. If punching without emphasizing hip coordination, a loss of energy will result. If, however the power concentrated in the hips is transmitted in the execution of a technique, the result will be a powerful surge through the complete use of the body. Drive your legs into the tatami while rotating your hips to generate maximum power. Interestingly, golfers and baseball players also reach maximum power by using their hips, be it by swinging a club or bat.

Focus (Kime)

This is a critical element of training. Focus can be achieved by understanding the relationship between muscle tension and relaxation. It is necessary to remain in a relaxed state to adapt and respond quickly to constantly changing situations. Focusing on the point where a technique is executed and then immediately relaxing to prepare for the next point will enhance the level of training. Focus, as I have stated in a previous chapter, is also important to prevent injury. Students must understand their physical limitations and not jeopardize their well being by hyperextending their joints or using their breath incorrectly.

Rhythm (Rizumu)

Proper execution of combinations, or series of movements, are obtained through learning proper rhythm. The degree of focus in transitioning from one movement to the next is represented in a smooth, flowing pattern with good rhythm. This is especially true in kata practice. As in gymnastics, strength, focus and timing are critical. Understanding the timing and rhythm of a movement will provide a higher degree of effectiveness in karate practice, as well as in the display of the beauty of this art.

Timing and Distance (Hyoshi and Maai)

Precise timing and cadence, with the ability to judge distances, will be crucial factors in technique applications. The strength and power of a technique will be rendered useless if applied at the wrong time. As an opponent faces you, the ability to accurately judge distance with your safety zone and to know when to attack, counter-attack or withdraw will be crucial in determining the outcome of the encounter. You must also be in tune with your opponent's tensions and energy, and space yourself properly in order to keep him physically and mentally off-balance.

Spirit (Gei and Shik)

When we speak of spirt in fundamentals, it is not meant in a religious sense; rather, it is seen as the energy of life itself. It binds spiritual, physical and mental power, called "Ki." Karate practice will prove frustrating at times. Little things will be difficult. A kata may be impossible to memorize. The instructor may seem unfair. The fighting spirit of karate is to increase the ability to withstand frustration. It teaches self-defense skills, and more importantly, how to deal with the daily battles of life. This practice to cultivate one's mind through spirited practice and dedicated study is essential for success.

Stances (dachi)

One of the first considerations for an effective technique is a strong and stable base. A high rise structure would not withstand the strong winds if its base was weak. As in engineering, karate stances have been designed according to what techniques are to be used for a particular block, thrust, kick, or strike. Universal practice of the many stances will tone and strengthen the legs.

Students will learn how to coordinate their stances with their techniques in order to have maximum effectiveness in countering, attacking and deflecting. Stances are also designed to move from one point to another, in all directions, with minimum movement and great readiness. Stances must also be able to support the hip movements for powerful execution. If the stances wobble, other muscles will be deployed hampering the hip's trajectory. Utilizing proper stances will also make it easier to get out of the way from a powerful attacker without tripping over oneself. Correct use of stance will also provide maximum reach, weight distribution, and prevent sweeps that would unbalance you. Applying the appropriate stance for upper body techniques will show well and create an appealing and graceful kata. Several stances are also used to develop stronger muscles, willpower and fighting spirit.

It is crucial to understand that although a stance may be similar from one movement to another, relaxing and contracting the muscles at the precise moment is of utmost importance. Although stances focus on the lower portion of the body (feet, legs, knees, hips and buttocks), the hands, arms, shoulders and head must remain coordinated with each stance for maximum stability, support and effectiveness. For example a front stance taken at the moment of impact from a thrust will have a strong contraction of muscles and immediately relax for the next ensuing movement. It is also important to understand that the stances employed in kata may not be the same for kumite or in a self-defense situation. The paradox is that a stance is no stance, meaning that whatever stance comes naturally for your "kamae" (or technique) will be the best stance for that moment.

Saito-Ha Shito-Ryu Karate-Do · For The Modern Warrior

KARATE STANCES

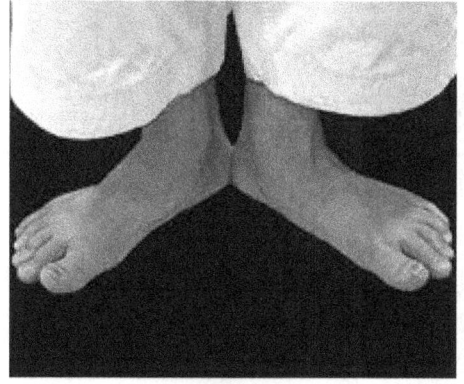
Musubi dachi

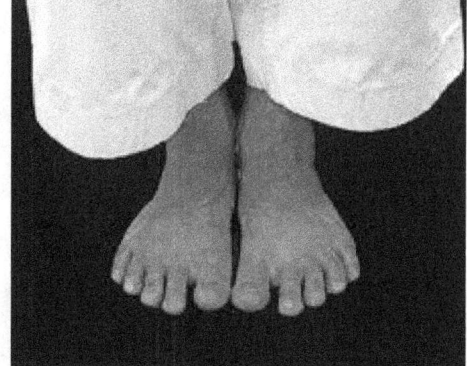
Heisoku dachi

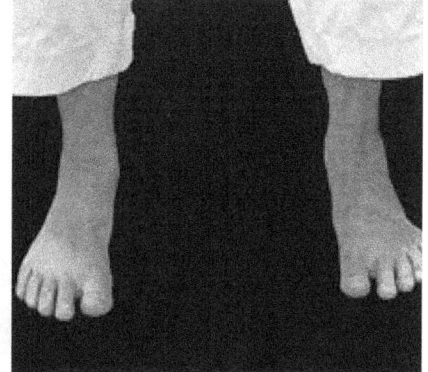
Namiheiko dachi

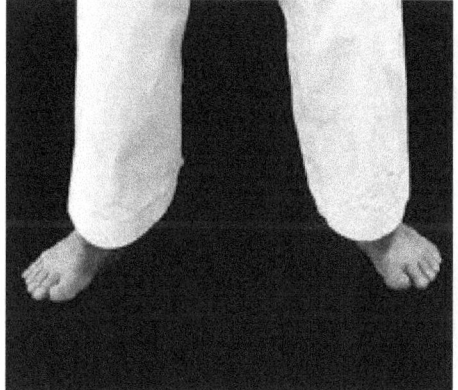
Sotohachiji dachi

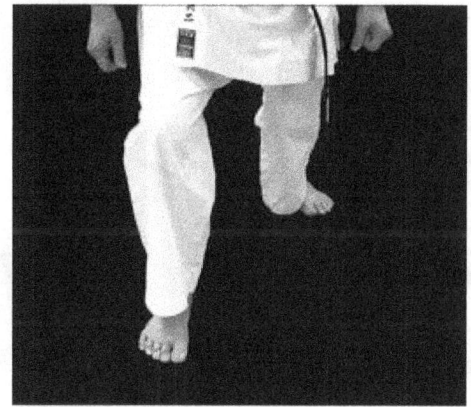
Zenkutsu dachi

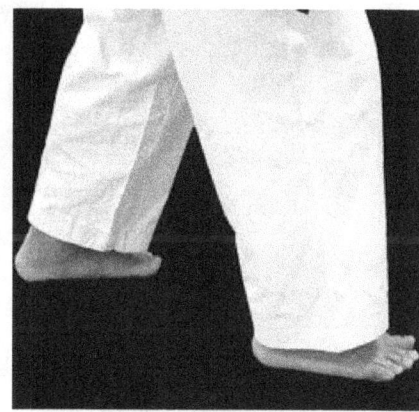
Hanzenkutsu dachi

Heiko dachi

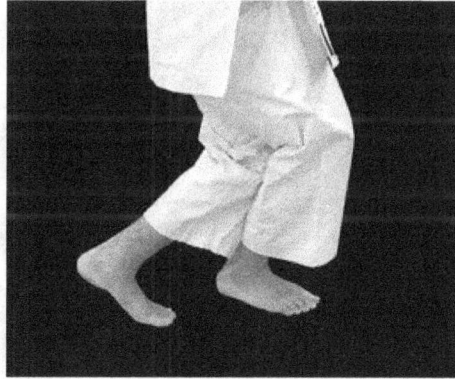
Kosa dachi

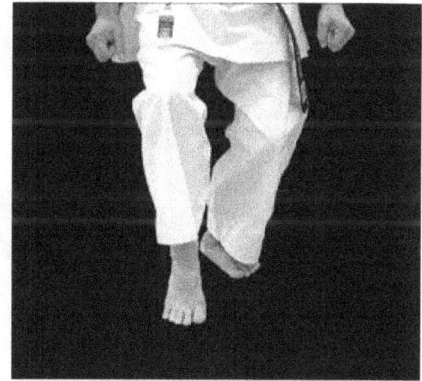
Nekoashi dachi

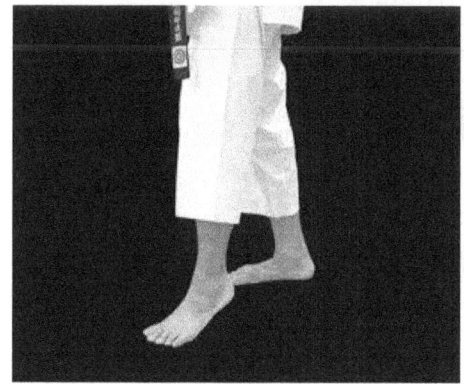
Renoji dachi

Sagiashi dachi A

Sagiashi dachi B

KARATE STANCES

 Shiko dachi

 Uchihachiji dachi

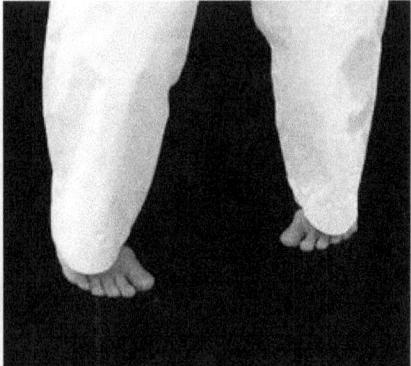 Sanchin dachi

 Kokutsui dachi

 Correct footwork is vital for every martial art.

Students learn fundamental stances and eventually incorporate them to develop the best stance for themself.

BLOCKS OR RECEPTION (UKE)

Students are taught that the karate block is more than just a block. The fact is that many blocks are intended to be used simultaneously as a block and a strike. A better definition for a block would therefore be "a reception." When that interpretation is understood, an uke will be executed not only as a block, but also as an escape, strike, thrust, lock or throw. Blocking skills will also be emphasized by "Uke no Gogenri," (Five Methods of Defense); "Raka," forcefully moving or pulling the attack downward; "Ryusui," flowing or moving the attack to the side; "Teni," shifting the body away from the attack; "Kusshin," lowering and moving the center of gravity to avoid the attack; and "Hangeki," countering and/or smothering an attack.

The fundamental methods to block will begin to take shape after a few months of intense training. Students at first might not absorb the importance of each block due to its redundancy and "difficult simplicity." Similar to learning how to read a simple sentence, the beginner may feel that it is a difficult task to do with clarity, correct intonation, and effortlessness. Yet with time and careful instruction, the result will be rewarding. A down block, for example, will have a preparatory movement where one fist is drawn to the clavicle near the shoulder, while the other fist points downward and just past the midline of the body. As one fist is drawn to the side above the waist, the other fist swings downward in a small arching motion. To augment these movements for power and speed, the feet, legs, hips, abdomen, shoulders and proper breathing are necessary for effectiveness. Correct posture, and understanding when to relax and tense, are also important elements for this block. And let's not forget focus; that is knowing when to stop the block at the precise moment, for precision, while preventing the arm or joint to extend beyond its normal limits. Once the block is mastered with all the principles that underly this simple technique, the more accomplished student will be taught to shorten the preparatory positions to increase speed. This method for developing the downward block may be used for all reception techniques.

BLOCKING TECHNIQUES - *Demonstrated by Chuck Aoto.*

Age uke (rising block).

Soto uke (Outward block).

Naka uke (inward block).

BLOCKING TECHNIQUES

Gedan harai uke (downward and sweeping block).

Shuto uke (sword hand block).

Ude uke (forearm block).

Sukui uke (scooping block).

Gassho uke (praying hands).

Hirayuki (two hand knife-edge pushing block.

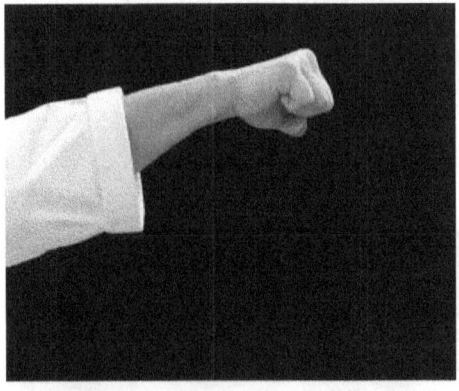
Tsuki uke (thrust block).

Hizagaeshi (knee sweeping across).

Ninoude uke (forearm inward block).

Kosa uke kaishu (crossed arm open hand block - *method A*).

Kosa uke kaishu (crossed arm open hand block - *method B*).

Gedan kosa uke (downward forearm inward block).

BLOCKING TECHNIQUES

Shotei uke (palm heel block).

Kakiwake uke (wedge block).

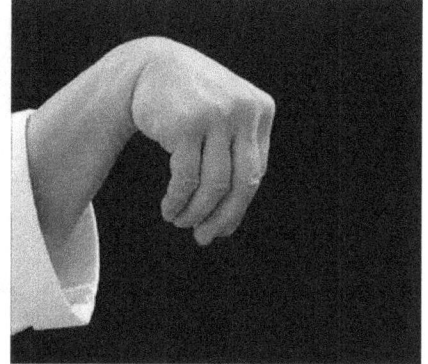
Ko uke (wrist block).

Kensasae uke (fist support block).

Hijisasae uke (two hand elbow support block).

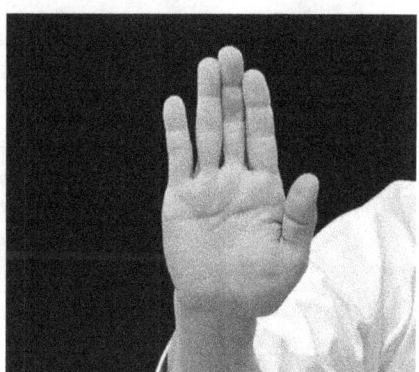
Kuri uke (inside out circle block with knife edge of hand).

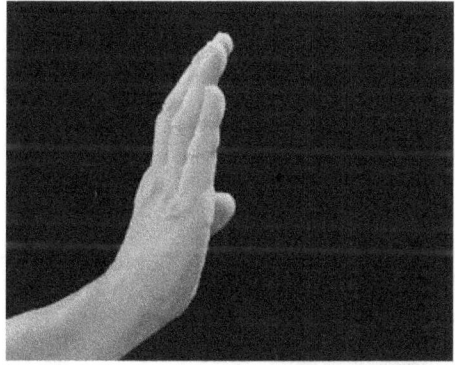
Seiryuto uke (ox hand block).

Kakete or kagi te (hooking hand block).

Katate sukui uke (one hand scooping block).

SAMPLE BLOCKING TECHNIQUES AGAINST AN ASSAILANT.

Ko uke.

Naka uke (A).

Naka uke (B).

Sasae uke.

Shuto uke (A).

Shuto uke (B).

Shuto uke (C).

Shuto uke (D).

Tsuki uke.

THRUSTS (TSUKI)

The thrust is one of the most widely used techniques in karate. For this move we can incorporate Sir Isaac Newton's second law of physics: F=ma (force equals mass x acceleration). Understanding this law of physics is essential to understanding how to maximize your thrusting power. Directing your thrust from its starting point to the target in a straight line is also an easy concept to understand.

Fundamental thrust training begins with one fist positioned just above the hip with the arm kept horizontal and parallel to the floor. The other arm extends with a thrust or block. In order to achieve the fullest potential of force, a stable stance with the proper weight distribution is required. If too much weight is placed on the rear leg, it will be difficult to rotate the hips, shoulders and forearms and power will be lost. The muscles in the legs and arms are lightly loaded but relaxed. The explosive thrust begins by pulling the extended arm, rather than only focusing on extending the punching arm. The thrust is usually intended for a forward target, however the "Tsukidome" or "retracting fist," can serve as an effective block or elbow strike to the rear. Snapping the wrist on both arms at the last moment maximizes acceleration. At that same moment the entire arm and core is tightened while quickly exhaling through the mouth. The twisting motion also serves as a deflective movement against an attack. To prevent injury, it is important not to hyperextend the arm. On impact, the index and middle knuckle are used. (Your fourth and fifth knuckles are not effective to use, and may cause injury to the fist or wrist). Keep in mind that while executing the straight punch, the uppercut and vertical thrusts are also being strengthened. A boxing type of punch is also taught for closer encounters, but is very difficult to control.

Once the basic concept of thrusting is understood and the form is correct, begin to hit a "Makiwara," (striking post), with your bare fists. Your sensei will guide you in building a firm and flexible target. By repetitive thrusting to a target that has resistance, the understanding of having all the crucial components for maximum efficiency and power will be realized. The use of the makiwara will be addressed more fully later in this chapter.

THRUSTING TECHNIQUES - *Demonstrated by Chuck Aoto.*

Proper way to make a fist.

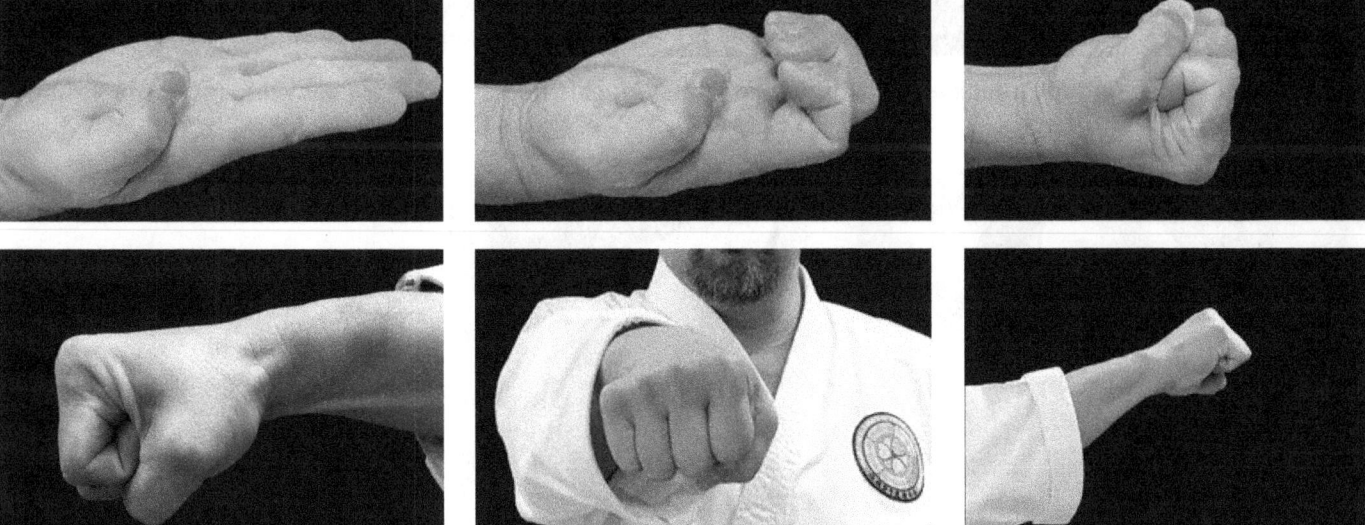

Seiken (forefist) - wrist straight. **Seiken zuki (forefist thrust).** **Age zuki (rising thrust).**

Saito-Ha Shito-Ryu Karate-Do
For The Modern Warrior

THRUSTING TECHNIQUES

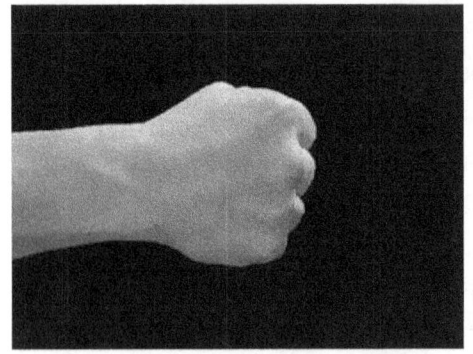
Tate zuki (vertical fist thrust).

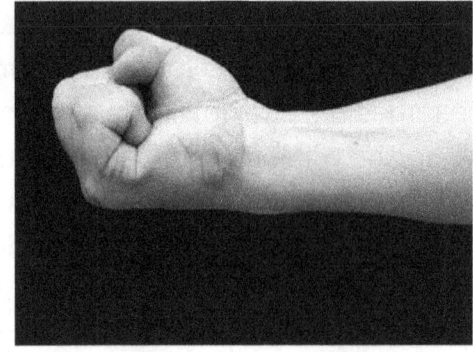
Ura zuki (uppercut).

Wa zuki (two-arm circle thrust).

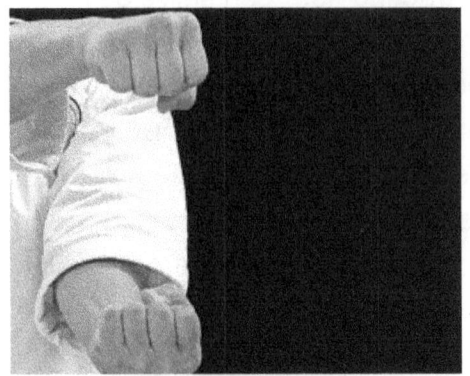
Awase zuki (U thrust).

Morote zuki (double fist thrust).

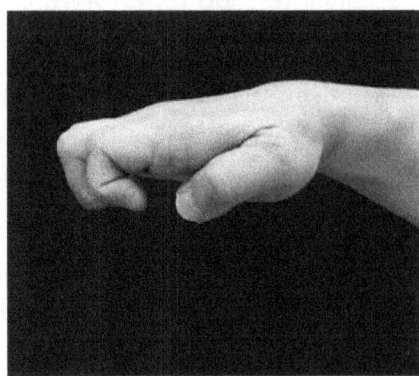
Hiraken zuki (front knuckle thrust).

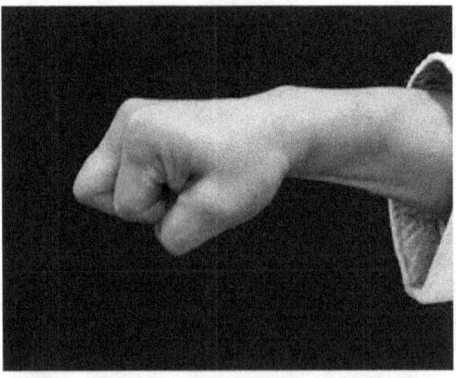
Ippon nakadaka ken (middle knuckle fist).

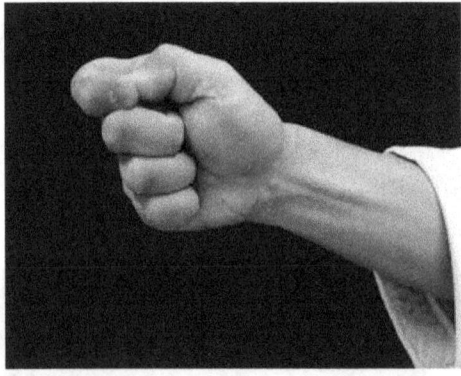
Ippon ken (one knuckle fist).

Hasami zuki (scissors thrust).

Mawashi zuki (roundhouse thrust).

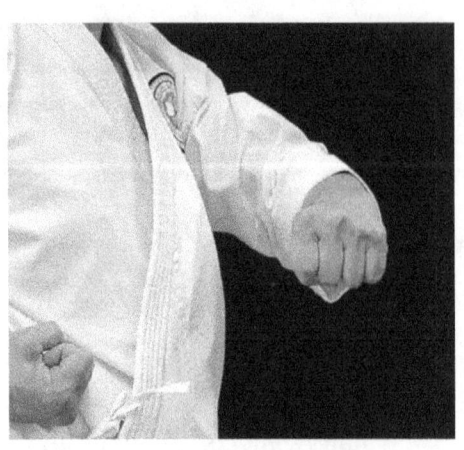
Kagi zuki (hook thrust).

Jump and thrust.

Hook thrust.

Uppercut.

STRIKES (UCHI)

There are more than 17 parts of the hands and arms that can be utilized for karate techniques. The coordination of these strikes with the withdrawing hand (hikite), proper stances, and hip movement will serve as powerful tools in karate. For a general rule, especially for the modern warrior, use a soft weapon such as a shotei uchi (palm heel strike) to a hard target like the jaw, and a hard weapon such as a tsuki (thrust) to a softer target like the throat or solar plexus.

There are many ways to use the hands as weapons, and these can prove devastating if not properly executed with the coordination of the other parts of the body such as the legs and hips. Learning to snap the wrist, turn the arm, and synchronize the elbow can also be an important factor in increasing the power and speed of each application.

The "shuto" (sword-hand or knife-hand) will prove effective if the fingers are held tightly together with the thumb pressed against the side of the palm. The outside edge of the shuto is used to strike the arm, leg, temple, neck, throat, and ribs.

The "hiji" or "enpi" (elbow) is a powerful weapon which can be used against an assailant who is very close to you, and can also be used from any direction. Targets may include the ribs, solar plexus, face, base of the spine and to the back.

To mold your hands into weapons you can depend on with minimal injury, use the aid of a makiwara, heavy bag or bucket of rice to condition your knuckles, fingers, wrists, and other parts of your hand. Applying pressure on the bones will cause the bones to adapt and become much stronger.

STRIKING TECHNIQUES

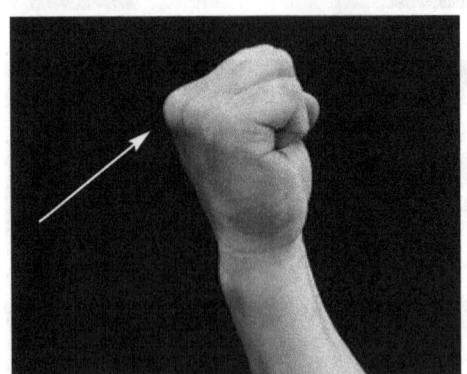

Uraken (backfist).

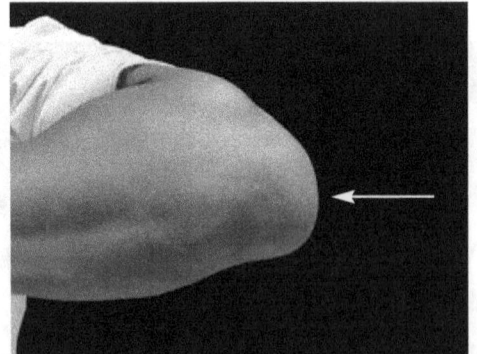

Hijiate yoko (elbow smash to the side).

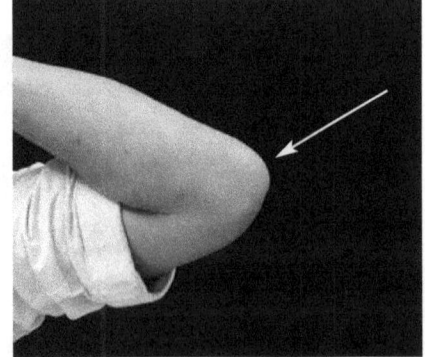

Hijiate age (rising elbow smash).

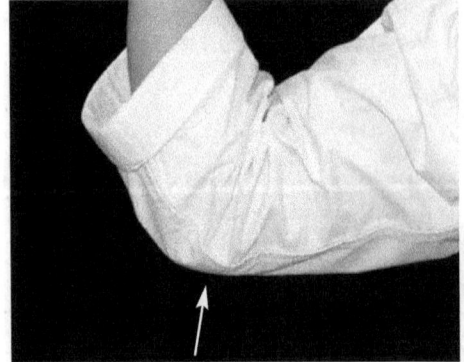

Hijiate otoshi (dropping elbow smash).

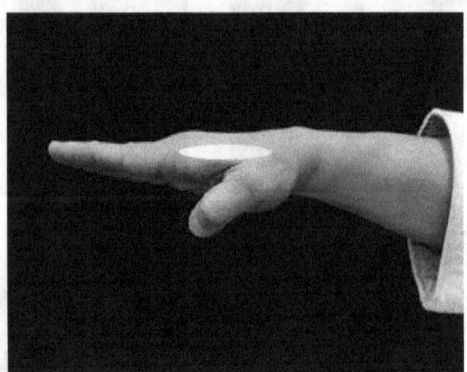

Haito uchi (ridgehand).

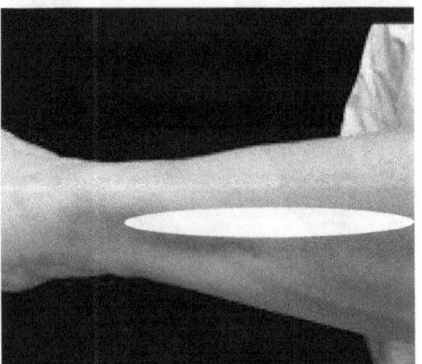

Ude uchi (arm strike).

STRIKING TECHNIQUES

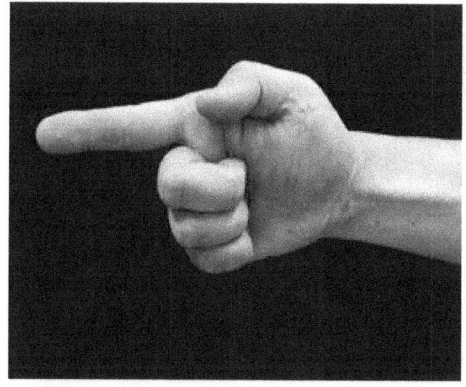
Ippon nukite (one finger spear).

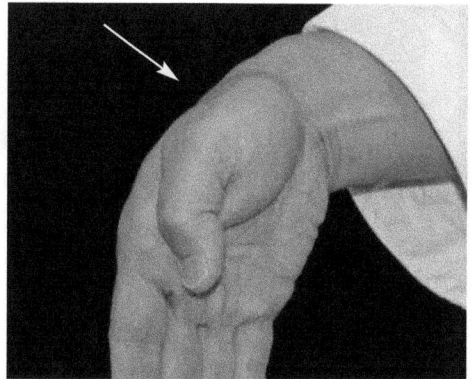
Keito (chicken beak).

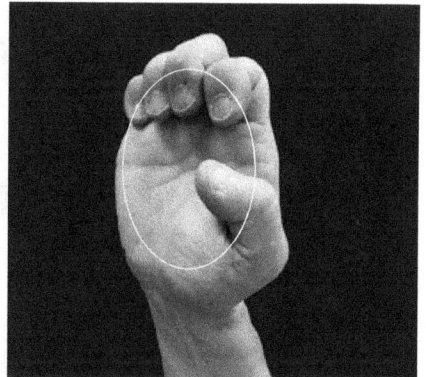
Kumade (bear hand).

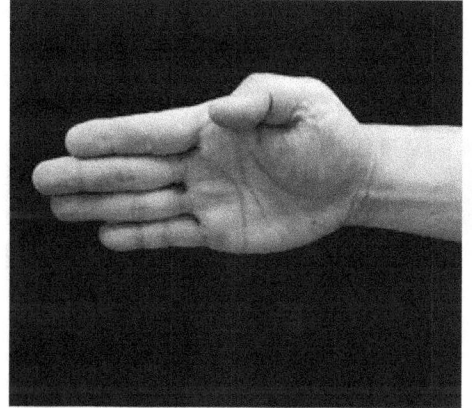
Nukite (spear hand).

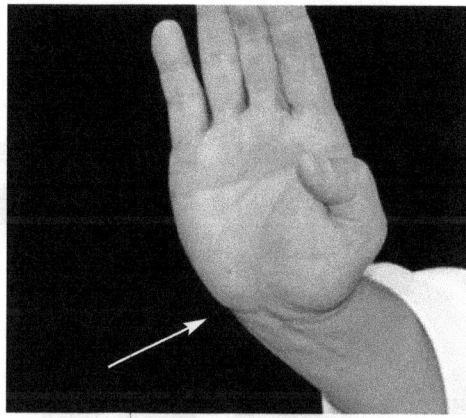
Seiryuto (ox hand).

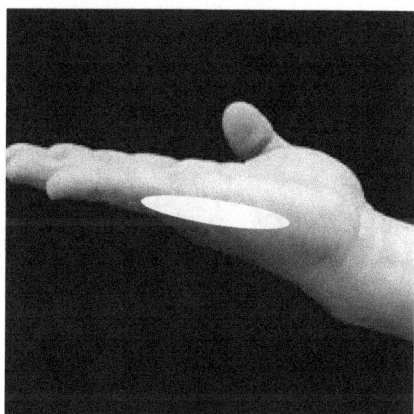
Shuto (sword hand).

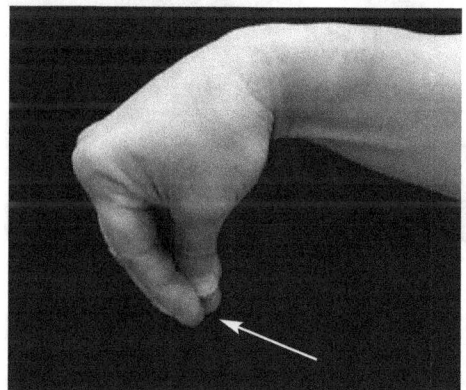
Washide (eagle hand).

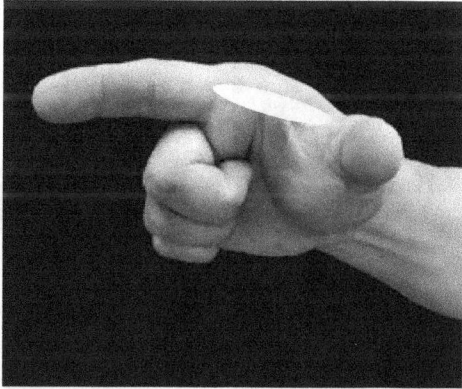
Yubi hasami (thumb and forefinger scissors).

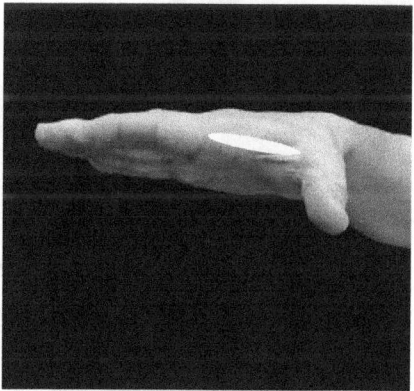
Hira basami (full hand scissors).

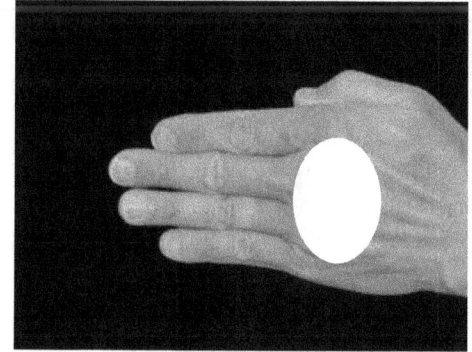
Haishu (back of hand).

Kentsui (hammer fist).

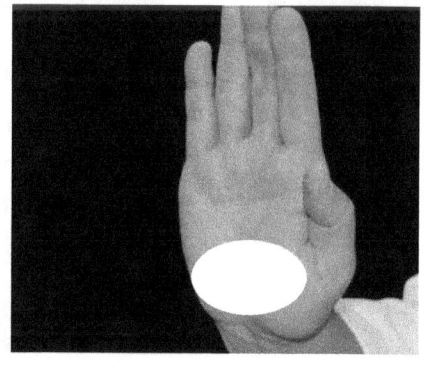
Shotei (palm heel).

Saito-Ha Shito-Ryu Karate-Do · For The Modern Warrior

STRIKING TECHNIQUES

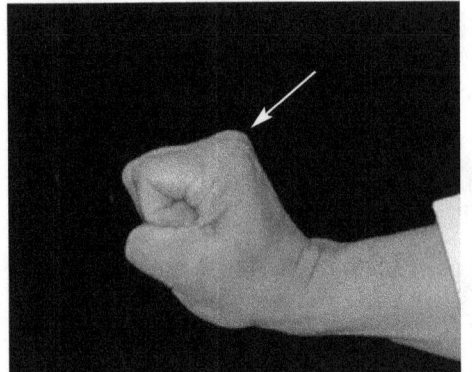
Shuho (mountain hand).

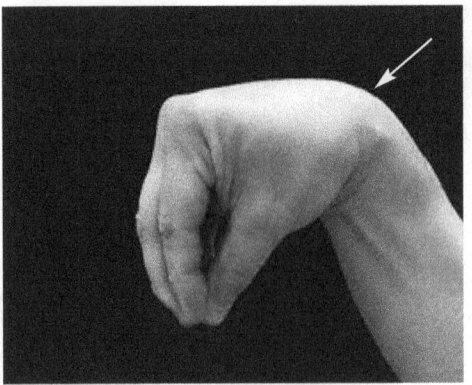
Koken (wrist).

Sample striking techniques against an assailant.

Full hand scissors.

Bear hand strike.

Ridgehand strike.

Thumb strike.

KICKS (KERI)

The kick is a strike using the leg, in unison with the knee, and foot. Properly used, kicks can serve as powerful weapons of self-defense. Some of the kicks are very simple to emulate while others require close instruction, observance, and guidance for best results. Those unable to kick high will soon learn that the higher appealing targets will be much easier to reach when the effective lower kicks are mastered. It is important to learn how each part of the foot is used for the intended target; not only for effectiveness, but also for reducing injury to your foot. There are only a few kicks that I would recommend for self-defense. One of my favorites is the front "tsumasaki geri" (kick with the tips of the toes). To execute this kick, the knee is raised lower than the waist. As the leg extends towards the target supported by moving the hips forward and slightly upward, the leg slips under the opponent's block as the toes penetrate the small "kyusho matto" (vital point target). Other effective kicks are the back, roundhouse, and side kick when delivered to the leg, joint and groin area.

When first learning the different types of kicks, instructors may place your knee in locations suitable for easier execution. For example, the "mawashi geri" (roundhouse or rotating kick) is much easier to learn if the knee is first positioned to the side of the hip while placing the foot near the buttocks. The hip is then rotated bringing the knee around, at which point the foot is released and snapped back to complete the kick. Similarly, the "yoko geri" (side kick) is easier to accomplish when the knee points slightly towards the target before snapping or thrusting the kick. Once each kick is executed properly, knee placement will be more critical in order to make it more difficult for an opponent to read the kick being executed.

KICKING PARTS OF THE FOOT

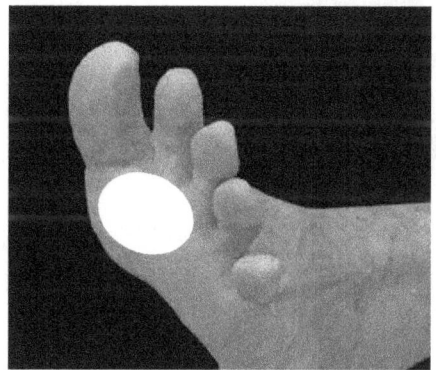

Koshi (ball of foot).

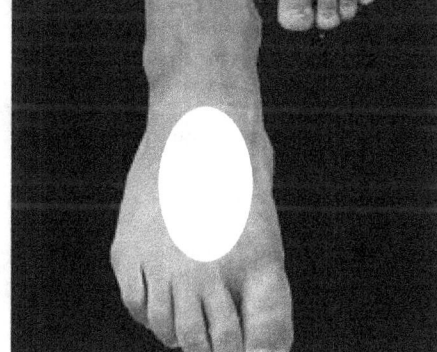

Haisoku (instep).

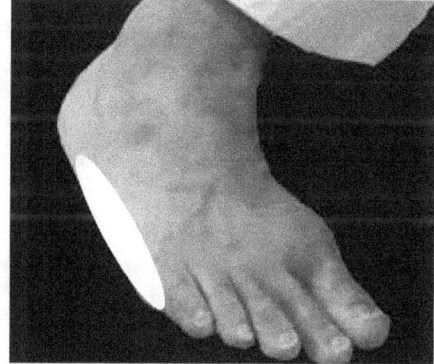

Sokuto (edge).

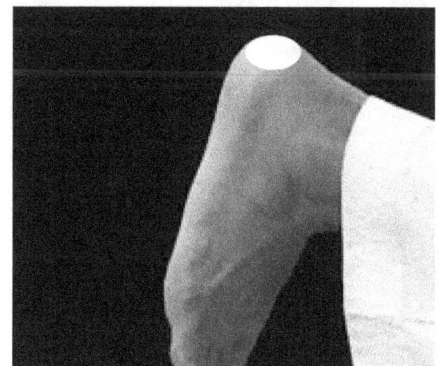

Koshu (back of heel).

Hizagashira (knee).

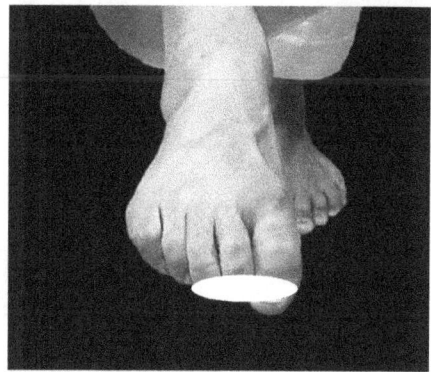

Tsumasaki (toes).

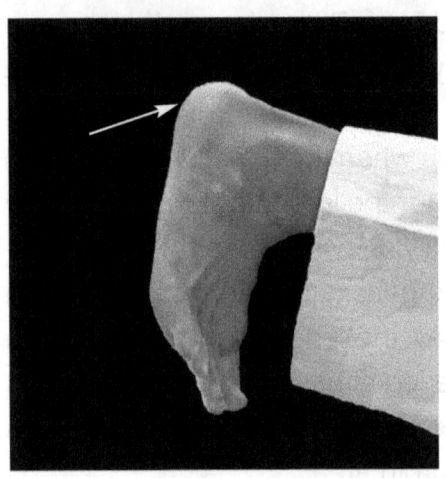 Kakato (heel).

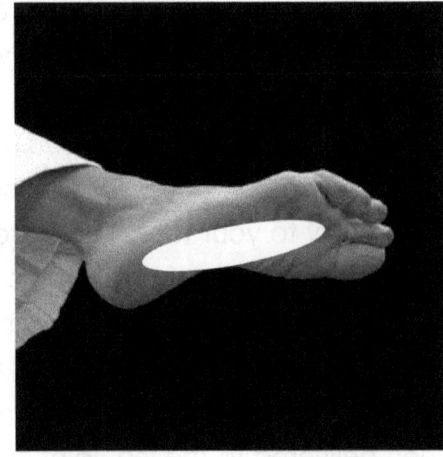 Teisoku (bottom of foot).

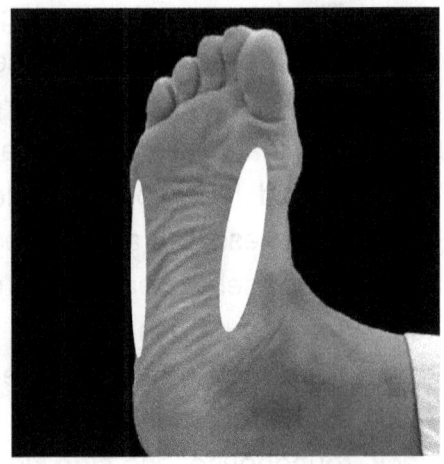 Inward or outward crescent kick.

KICKING TECHNIQUES - *Demonstrated by Crystal Hang and Benji Thai.*

 Hiza geri.

 Mae geri.

 Mawashi geri.

 Yoko geri.

KICKING TECHNIQUES

Ushiro kakato geri.

Mae kasokute geri.

Ushiro kakato geri.

Yoko kansetsu geri.

Soko geri.

Mawashi geri from ground.

KICKING TECHNIQUES

Ushiro mawashi geri.

Mae kasokute otoshi geri.

A powerful side kick (Yoko geri) is one of the major kicks taught in karate. Targets include, but are not limited to, the legs, ribs, back and head.

FOOTWORK (FUTTOWĀKU)

For techniques to be applied properly for maximum effectiveness, a vital component is having complete knowledge of footwork. Moving from point A to point B quickly and efficiently requires many hours of practice. For example, if standing in a natural stance when an attack is presented from the side, the knees and ankles are flexed to keep the center of gravity low and allow for a quick movement of the legs. The stance used for a block, strike, thrust or kick must support the technique, and then the feet must shuffle quickly for another pursuing or ready action. Remember to use gravity as a tool to move your body. When moving forward, quickly "collapse" your body over your front knee and gravity will pull you forward. Similarly, when moving backwards, relax your back knee causing your body to pull you back.

Karate engages attackers in eight potential directions, as practiced in Tenshin Happo. In Shito-ryu, when turning, the Shuri-te and Naha-te foot movements are practiced. The Shuri turn moves the foot nearest the direction of the turn, while the Naha turn uses the foot opposite the direction of the turn. Practicing both concepts equally will provide effective training and great advantages for self defense.

FOOTWORK - *Demonstrated by Michele Barnes.*

DEASHI - Rear foot steps forward. **Hikiashi -** Forward foot steps back.

Saito-Ha Shito-Ryu Karate-Do
FOOTWORK

For The Modern Warrior

Mawariashi (Nahate method) - Front foot steps across, then turn.

Mawariashi (Shurite method) - Rear foot steps across, then turn.

Yoriashi - Front foot moves forward, followed by rear foot gliding forward maintaining low center of gravity.

FOOTWORK

Tobiashi - Hop or leap to any angle.

FUNDAMENTAL TRAINING CONCEPTS OF SHITO RYU KARATE

When beginning your karate training, it will be natural for you to want to learn the flashy, acrobatic and fancy techniques often shown in martial arts movies. You may be anxious and ask your sensei when he will be teaching you these moves in order to destroy your adversaries. The reality is that training in any worthy martial arts always begins with sound fundamentals.

I have trained students in the past who followed my instructions in learning and practicing the basics for less than two months, and they have defeated black belts who thought they were proficient in learning only advanced techniques.

Mastering a handful of techniques, based on the knowledge of fundamentals, maximizes all the necessary ingredients for success. You will have more power, balance, precise timing and effectiveness. Your confidence, fighting spirit, calmness, focus and control will also be sharpened. And you will come to understand that no matter how advanced you are, training in the fundamentals will always be an important part of your karate journey.

The fundamentals will include the following training exercises and drills:

1. Tenshin Happo - Eight directions of response
2. Hijiate Goho - Five direction elbow strike exercise
3. Tenpo Gosoku no Ho - Five methods of body shifting
4. Kihon Kata Tsuki - Basic punching exercise
5. Kihon Kata Uke - Basic blocking exercise
6. Uke no Gogenri - Five methods of defense
    a. Rakka - (falling petals) Pulling or moving the attack downward with such force and precision to render the opponent's attacks helpless.
    b. Ryusui - (running water) Moving and flowing the opponent's attacks to the sides with softer and fluid motions.

c. Teni - (transposition) Body shifting away from the line of attack utilizing all eight directions of movement.

d. Kusshin - (elasticity) Lowering the center of gravity and recoiling from the opponent's attack, and then immediately unwind to counterattack, similar to the movements of a snake.

e. Hangeki - (counterattack) Meeting the opponent's attack immediately with a deflection and a counterattack.

7. Kihon Kumite - Basic engaging techniques with a partner
   a. Ippon - Single attack, straight in
   b. Nihon - Two predefined attacks, one step
   c. Sanbon - Three predefined attacks, one step
   d. Hukushiki - Walking attacks
   e. Kumite Kata - Practicing applications of kata
   f. Oyo Kumite - Applied engaging techniques with;
      a. Partner
      b. Hokei - Four attackers
      c. Mawari - Circle of attackers
      d. Jiyu Ippon - Free style, one step
      e. Jyu Kumite - slow sparring
      f. Jiyu - free style sparring

SUPPLEMENTAL TRAINING

The makiwara (which literally means "wrapped with straw"), is a training tool used to condition different parts of the body to prevent injury. It is also an important part of practice because it trains the heart and soul. The resulting pain, frustration, fatigue and test of stamina will expose what the practitioner is really "made of."

The "tate makiwara" is constructed with cedar or douglas fir, and the post is cut so the base is thicker than the top in order to give a little when struck. The "sage makiwara" is a hanging target. Many of the makiwara in Okinawa and Japan are wrapped with straw, however using foam or rope will also serve its purpose.

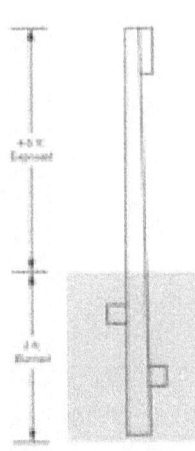

Begin by striking the makiwara with 50% of your maximum power. As your hands, elbows and feet become more conditioned, increase the power and velocity until you have reached maximum power. You will notice an increase of callous build-up in this practice, so be prudent if you are in a profession where your hands are heavily relied on (such as a dentist, or a manicurist, for example) as they could be exposed to damage.

Gyaku zuki

SUPPLEMENTARY TRAINING

Haito uchi.

Shuto uchi.

Gyaku shuto uchi.

Haishu uchi.

Hiji ate.

Sanbon nukite.

To further condition your hands, strike a rock. Place a small towel or cloth on it to prevent cuts.

SUPPLEMENTARY TRAINING

Arm conditioning drills are included in weekly dojo practices. Balance, control of the breath, relaxing and tensing the muscles correctly and staying connected with your extremities, as well as with your partner's, will increase your understanding of mutual cooperation.

Arm Conditioning
1. Forearm block.
2. Outward block.
3. Downward block.
4. Thrust while pushing out against arm.
5. Outward block while pushing out against arm.
6. Kakete against kote.
7. Kote against kakete.

Leg Conditioning
1. Shin to shin and leg to leg.

Leg and shin conditioning is painful but necessary.

SUPPLEMENTARY TRAINING

Demonstrated below are other training activities that will increase your endurance, strength and speed by engaging your arms, legs, shoulders and core. Should one of your goals be to burn calories, do these exercises three to four times per week. Keeping your weight in check will also lower your risk of some diseases including obesity, Type-2 Diabetes, and high blood pressure. As you are able to perform each of these supplementary trainings correctly, test yourself by going beyond your perceived limits until your subconscious takes over. Doing this will interface with your kata training which will help you understand the purpose and importance of kata.

Rope resistance workout best from a deep squatting position.

Pull-ups, hands face out. Chin-ups, hands face in.

Kettlebell, bridging the gap between cardio and strength training.

Ladder drills will increase your foot work speed.

Jumping or skipping rope uses your core muscles, and strengthens the body, legs, arms and shoulders.

Heavy bags develops your punching skills.

Rope climbing develops upper body strength.

SUPPLEMENTARY TRAINING

Medicine balls are good for your abs, shoulders and arms and can be used individually or with a partner.

Resistance training assists both you and your partner in understanding weight distribution, hip involvement and placement of the center of gravity.

Pushups are beneficial in building upper body strength, core, back, wrists, fingertips, knuckles and especially your fighting spirit.

STRETCHING

You may think that stretching is primarily designed for runners and gymnasts. But the reality is that all karate students need to stretch in order to have mobility, flexibility and better range of motion. Stretching is also critical to prevent strains and muscle damage.

Students should warm-up while engaging in stretching exercises. You need to get the blood flowing by jumping, moving the feet forward and back, followed by a few jumping jacks. This will help flexing the ankles and knees, then followed by the arms, shoulders and wrists. Before each class, ten to fifteen minutes of warm-ups and stretching is incorporated with your training. Be more aggressive with your initial stretching routines and less aggressive when cooling down at the end of class.

By stretching daily, your muscles will be looser, longer and leaner and when called upon for a kick or other karate activities, you will see better execution of techniques and balance.
Stretches should include, but are not limited to:

- Achilles stretches
- Ankle stretches
- Back stretches
- Bicep stretches
- Calf stretches
- Chest stretches
- Forearm stretches
- Groin stretches
- Hamstring stretches
- Hip stretches
- Neck stretches
- Shoulder stretches
- Side stretches
- Triceps stretches
- Wrist stretches.

Stretches can be done using a wall, countertop, or with your belt, both individually or with a partner.

STRETCHING EXERCISES - Demonstrated by Marissa Christensen.

Calf and Hamstring stretch   **Abductor Side Lunge**   **Cobra Stretch**

Saito-Ha Shito-Ryu Karate-Do — For The Modern Warrior

STRETCHING EXERCISES

Stride with Side Stretch — Forward Fold — Butterfly Pose

Child's Pose — Downward Facing Dog — Swan Pose

Split — Straddle Stretch — Cow Stretch

Over the Head Stretch — Three-Legged Pose — Rotated Palm Stretch

STRETCHING EXERCISES

Développer Warrior Triangle Pose

Modified Tree Pose Heel to Hip Stretch Across the Body Reach

Stretching allows techniques to be executed without compromising one's well being.

Chapter 8
THE LANGUAGE OF KARATE: KATA AND BUNKAI/OYO

"A kata is not fixed or immovable. Like water, it's ever changing and fits itself to the shape of the vessel containing it. However, kata are not some kind of beautiful competitive dance, but a grand martial art of self-defense - which determines life and death."
- *Kenwa Mabuni*

History has been documented through various means of the arts, through writings, monuments and songs. Kata is a living catalog of the self-defense strategies of dojo, and its style. Kata is the language of karate and a code in which the masters preserved their techniques. These prearranged groups of movements simulate the actions of attack and defense, using the unarmed body, or weapons against one or multiple attackers.

Basically, the kanji (Chinese written characters) for kata comes from three ideograms that form the word kata. These are "katachi," meaning form, shape or pattern; "kai," meaning to cut or dissect; and "tsuchi," meaning earth or soil.

These katas have been passed from generation to generation, and to the 21st century, by masters who taught them to either their eldest son or to a student they trusted. Initially, the kata would be practiced with a partner exchanging blocking, kicking, striking, grasping and throwing techniques. However, as the numbers of attacks and defenses became too difficult to remember, several of the movements were weeded out to make it easier for the students to remember and practice. An additional problem that surfaced was the need to rely on a partner who, for whatever reason, could not be present to practice. So kata became a solo creation that a student could perform at any time. Many of the names of kata come from either the masters who created them, the places where the kata was perfected, the words that encouraged the spirit of the kata, or the number of moves in the kata, which might have spiritual significance.

As I have stated in Chapter 1, consideration for the creation and development of the kata styles came from the attire, hairstyles, stature and culture of that time. Another interesting thought is that the movements were probably based on linguistics. Incorporated within the language are cultural compositions and mental processing that formulates ideas resulting in creative and ingenious works. For example, in the Chinese language one ideogram represents one word, concept or idea. You have several components in one character, but it forms one word. This is unlike Hiragana and Katakana, two of the key systems in Japanese writing, where several characters form one word. In English you have several letters that shape a word. So based on this understanding, we can acknowledge that the language spoken affects the thought process of the creators of the kata.

Now let's transmit that consideration into the formation of a kata. The Chinese kata, for example, combines many techniques in one continuous movement. In comparison, the same kata developed by an Okinawan or Japanese master will have several separate movements. This observation isn't to say that one way is better than the other, but it is interesting, and opens for great discussion on how language may frame one's perception and thought.

Another example of language differentiation is in the simple translation of words. "uke" translated into English means "block," yet "uke" in Japanese actually means "to receive." So does one accept that the blocks taught in karate are primarily for that purpose alone, or does one broaden their understanding of reception to determine how an "uke" technique will be employed? "Hiji sasae uke," or "morote uke," as another example, is often translated as a "support or augment block." The question is, are you supporting the arm to just block, or are you supporting the block with a strike or thrust? And are you placing great emphasis on one block, or combining a block with a strike, thrust, grasp or throw? I urge you to consider these points carefully.

Shito-ryu Karate incorporates the most katas within the style, since it was developed by the influence of both Naha-te and Shuri-te. Over 60 katas are incorporated within the Saito-ha Shito-ryu Karate-do program.

Teaching kata, even in modern times, has been proven to be the most effective way to transmit the technical, physiological and other vital components of karate-do. With self-discipline, hard training and one's own creative efforts in practicing kata, the knowledge and spirit of "Bugei" (martial arts) will be received.

Several karate masters have changed the original names of katas to better fit into the language and culture of Japan. This is a respectful reasoning and explanation of why this occurred, however, I think there was underlying political pressure that caused these changes to be made. Some of the variations of the kata names from Okinawan to Japanese names are: Pinan to Heian, Patsai to Bassai, Kushanku or Kosokun to Kanku, and Naihanchin to Tekki - to name a few.

Kata is a formal exercise with a glossary of detailed patterns that students engage in to perform the movements until they eventually become instinctive. Kata is not intended to simulate a mock fight, but as a vehicle for the transition and flow from one movement to another, teaching the student proper form and position while encouraging them to polish their self-defense techniques. Kata is also the essence of karate that aids students to attain a higher spiritual awareness through its practice while developing confidence, motivation, discipline, and control. This understanding translates into an ability to achieve the wholeness and balance that enables greater strength in dealing with any type of adversity. It aids in controlling the impulses that fly between the mind and the body.

This balance is achieved as kata is practiced over and over again, until the mind and body become one. The movements are as natural and automatic as breathing. Kata is the backbone that shapes karate's form, meaning and beauty. These katas have been preserved for hundreds of years, and it is vital that they be practiced correctly to maintain the integrity of the art.

With proper kata practice, students learn to avoid fighting and to never defend in anger, but with unyielding determination. Each kata begins and ends with a bow. Kata should be performed with spirit and strength, and never with arrogance. The practice of kata includes breathing, stances, posture, focus and repetition.

Western culture is much more centered on rapidly achieving goals and moving on to the next level without taking the time to commit to a complete understanding of that which they are striving to achieve. Karate and the study of kata are ongoing and ever-evolving, they are practiced in order to attain goals that are below the surface. The visible accomplishments are obvious, the mental and spiritual components are less tangible.

The practice of kata must be taken very seriously. It is fruitless to memorize a series of movements without understanding that all the movements are interrelated, not random. Focus intently on every motion, every flick of the hand, move of a foot, or glance of an eye. As kata is religiously and repetitiously practiced, the appreciation of its form will be learned. Practicing alone or in front of other students provides the ability to learn discipline and gain confidence. Once the first kata is fully understood, the next will become easier with the advancement of proper training.

Kata is also what I call "meditation in motion." As you immerse yourself in the performance of kata, concentrating on perfectly delivering each of the movements properly and enjoying the freedom of expression, for that moment, you have released yourself from all the things that weigh heavily on your shoulders. The child that tests you to your limits. The driver that cuts you off in traffic. The raise that you were promised that never came through. The neighbor's dog that keeps barking throughout the night. These situations can bring your stress level to boiling and send your blood pressure skyrocketing. Certainly this is not a good thing for your health and state of mind.

Anger is not a bad thing. It is an emotional signal that tells us that there is a problem that needs to be dealt with instead of ignored. Keeping this emotion bottled up is unhealthy and may have consequences. When stress hormones like adrenaline and cortisol are not released, there is a greater risk for diseases to creep in and destroy your longevity. Some bottle up their emotions, while others explode in uncontrollable rages, throwing things, yelling obscenities, and even destroying relationships.

Kata practice can definitely release a lot of stored anger in a <u>positive</u> way. I underline positive because studies have shown that outbursts of anger, even when recommended in controlled therapy circles, still places pressure on your heart and cardiovascular system. Kata, employed as a vehicle to wear down adrenaline, is a very easy solution for diffusing anger. Tensho is one of the katas I recommend. It is truly a meditation in motion that will allow you to vent stored-up frustration and anger.

Movement of the body, proper breathing, and even audible breaks (maybe listening to the calming sounds of lapping waters or chattering dolphins), will allow your state of mind to rest and your body to become calm, cool and collected.

So kata, simply put, is an arrangement of movements with a strict set of rules for precision, and can be seen as poetry in motion. Each kata is a cultural inheritance bequeathed to a student. Practicing them seriously will assist you in fighting your own internal demons, will act as an aid in sharpening your self-defense skills, and in their practice you will be preserving these special treasures for future generations to enjoy.

Ingredients of Kata

Enbusen

Each kata has a prescribed order and pattern or "enbu," (demonstration or presentation), "sen," (line) which follows part of, or all of, an eight-directional line of movement (as in Tenshin Happo), and the performance is executed as close to that practice line as possible. This road map in itself becomes a challenge, and when met, results in greater awareness, focus and positive self-development.

Kishin no Yoi

The kata performance should always be preceded with "ki," (spirit) "shin," (mind) "no," (of) "yoi," The kata performance should always be preceded with "ki," (spirit) "shin," (mind) "no," (of) "yoi," (prepare), or the "correct mind and spirit attitude that is vital before combat." Whenever possible, execute each kata as an opportunity to share your strong spirit with your fellow students. The repetitious and concise practice of each kata will lead to a deeper meaning and understanding of karate.

Bunkai

"Bunkai," ("having been cut into many parts," or "analysis"), is the intellectual and analytical process of understanding the deeper applications of each kata movement. There are hidden techniques, "kakushite," embedded in the kata, but with thorough study, maturity and practice, these techniques will surface for you to incorporate in your training. The creators most likely had a certain movement(s) in the kata for a specific application. However, since there is no solid evidence of what each movement represented, it was left to the interpretation and analysis of each master. Many of the thought processes that concluded with the kata applications are plausible, yet others are so far fetched that one has to chuckle with the wild imagination employed. Nevertheless, the study of kata and its applications are a great opportunity for instructors and students alike to share their thoughts and maintain the integrity of this treasured art.

Oyo

"Oyo," (practical application and physical enactment) is the demonstration of self-defense scenarios using kata techniques, and is a way for the techniques to be analyzed. It is important that both the "tori," (executor, or the one who completes a technique) and the "uke," (person who "receives" the technique), coordinate each of the movements precisely and vigorously. This mutual cooperation is vital in understanding that both the tori and the uke are responsible for their individual roles, and when these roles are synergized great understanding can be accomplished.

Kokyu and Tai no Shinshuku

Correct and controlled breathing should always be understood and practiced while executing kata. This is called "kokyu," (breathing, respiration) and, in principle, no movement should be made without proper breathing, and no breathing should be made without movement. It is important to breathe using the "Tanden," or "Hara," (one's center of gravity) to allow one's ki to manifest to its highest level. When audible breathing is used, it must be synchronized with each movement.

Kokyu is also demonstrated with proper "Tai" (body) "no" (of) "shin" (expansion) "shuku" (contraction), or body expansion and contraction. Slower movements will provide the opportunity for you to hear each breath through your nose and mouth. Quicker movements are supported by active exhalation with more passive inhalation. After each forceful exhalation, held air will be replaced with relaxation. When all of these components are synchronized, maximum power can be achieved in each technique while maintaining readiness for the body to receive a blow without harm or injury.

Kiai and Kime

"Kiai" (spirit convergence) and "Kime" (focus) together are the perfect synchronization of all the technical and physical aspects of a technique, done with total mental commitment and the intent of the movements, harmonizing with spirit, and maximizing the effectiveness of one's technique. This is what makes the kata come alive.

You will come to develop your own kiai, but to begin, you might shout "eh ah." Be sure to release your compressed energy using your core muscles. The kiai also shares your spirit with others, including the sensei, who welcomes your positive energy.

Chakugan and Metsuke

"Chaku" means to "notice or observe" and "gan" means "to fix ones eyes upon, or correct eye vector." "Me (eyes) tsuke" (to attach to) means "to focus one's eye on." In kata practice, Chakugan is not focusing on one spot but rather gazing to ascertain the correctness of each movement, both physically and mentally. Many instructors teach their students to look at the opponent's eyes. Eyes can be deceiving, so I instead have students gaze at the throat and heart area while staying aware of the entire body and surrounding environment. To stimulate the peripheral vision, I instruct students to gaze slightly to one side of the target. By doing so, the information and intentions of your opponent will be ascertained.

Waza no Kankyu

"Waza (technique) no (of) kan (slow) kyu" (fast). Also referred to as speed control, this is an important element of kata practice. The correct velocity for each movement needs to be incorporated to define the purpose of the technique. Also, the proper relation between the fast and slow movements must be defined throughout each kata. Directly related to "waza no kankyu" are rhythm and timing. Rhythm and timing are achieved through drills with timing changes. Instead of looking robotic, a speed-up from one thrust to the another, followed by a brief pause, will assist you in effectively performing a kata. This crucial element of kata will also give pause between combinations in order to achieve maximum effectiveness for the ensuing movements.

Chikara no Kyojaku

Another ingredient of kata is "Chikara (power) no (of) kyo (strong) jaku (weak)." This means that the correct use of power must be obtained by properly relaxing and contracting the muscles to maximize the full potential of each technique. You certainly would not use the power of a jet engine in a Piper Cherokee. Applying physics and applying the proper use of power will keep you balanced and provide you with ultimate strength. To achieve this important ingredient of kata, you must let go of the ego.

Keitai no Hoji and Shisei

"Keitai (shape or form) no (of) hoji (keep or maintain)" means to maintain correct posture and body form at the beginning, during, and at the end of each movement of the kata. "Shi (style) sei (body)" means considering every aspect of the body and its alignment and positions. "Shisei" relates to stance, posture, wrist and arm position, leg and ankle position, vertical line, head positioning, and even moral character. As in aerodynamics, each part of the aircraft must be assembled accurately for smooth and safe operation. By taking time to shape each technique properly, you will learn to identify and achieve excellence in movement.

Jushin no Antei

"Jushin (center of gravity of the body) no (of) antei (balance or stability)" means to maintain correct center of gravity. When transitioning from one stance to another, there should be stability, and the level of the hips should be maintained properly to the end, even if the required stances change heights. The shock on impact should penetrate the target rather than dissipating back to the executor of the technique due to poor centering and balance.

Zanshin

"Zan (remain) shin (mind)" is maintaining correct vigilance and awareness after each technique and at the end of each kata execution. It is the state of mind where you are not focused on any object - rather it is the calm before and after a storm. This practice is crucial for self-defense as it teaches you not to assume that you have totally rendered your opponent helpless.

Summary

The points listed in this chapter are very important components for students to understand and practice in order to receive full value from each kata. Once a kata is learned, execute each movement as your sensei sculpts it with you, without interrupting the main intent of the movements and bunkai. Kata will become an integral part of your overall karate-do training as you seek to understand its language and code, and that will unveil the true gifts within you.

As you become proficient in kata and have tucked away vital information in your brain, use it in assisting your fellow students. By doing so you will be able to put this useful information into practice while securing it into your mental catalogue.

Each ingredient can also be directly utilized in your daily activities. "Zanshin," (perfect finish) can teach children to be responsible and efficient in their duties. For example, after eating a meal at home and before leaving the table, they should take their dishes to the dishwasher, clean the table, and then push their chair in. For parents, before signing off on their child's homework paper, they should make sure that it is completed with excellence. When children work, before placing their stamp of approval on the finished product, adults should inspect their work to ensure it has been completed to the highest standards. Adults also can, and should, apply zanshin in their daily lives.

Another different example is using the principles of "chikara no kyojaku" and "keitai no hoji" and "shisei" while lifting heavy objects. It is important to position the body correctly, maintain good posture and form, and breathe correctly in order to achieve the task without injuring yourself.

To efficiently progress in kata, practice in the "multiple of four" approach. First, extract the integral parts of the kata and practice it slowly, making sure that each stance, posture, preparatory position, and execution of each movement is correct. Next, perform the entire kata slowly with proper focus (kime), relaxing and contracting your muscles correctly with proper breathing, making sure the transition from one technique to another is smooth and deliberate. Note the kiai points. Next, practice the kata with power and speed. Lastly, perform the kata with correct rhythm, timing, speed and power.

At times new katas are formulated to enhance the evolution of bunkai, fitness, and creativity. I was inspired to create the "Futen no Kata" an eiku (oar) kata for Tony Mendonca and Rumi Kosugi (two of my faithful students), five advanced basic katas named "Saitoshi Shodan to Godan" in honor of my father, and more recently "Makoto," in memory of my friend Glen Makoto Uemura who was a member of the 1st Special Forces Group that was deployed in Vietnam.

KIHON KATA

In order to refine the basic blocks, strikes, thrusts and kicks, basic katas are taught to all beginners. Students quickly understand that power is generated by the legs, hips and core, rather than the muscles in the arms and upper extremities. Repetitive training techniques develop muscle memory, and practicing long enough will ensure that eventually that movement will no longer require much thunking. As this process is realized, students practice more intensely because they understand that by doing so, more space in the brain is available for higher learning.

Students who have difficulties in focusing and staying attentive on one thing will learn through kata practice to stay in the present. Once the wheel of kata is in motion, they have no choice but to go with the flow until the kata has ended. What matters in kata is how one has illuminated a positive attitude in executing the techniques as best as they were able to, in that moment. There is no room for excuses or going back to something already done, only learning from past experiences to purge negative and selfish thoughts, and, of course, the ego.

From the very first kata, a glimpse of "Mushin" (no mind), or "to have no conscious thoughts," will begin to take root. Responding naturally without using a conscious thought process will determine the outcome in a dangerous situation.

KIHON KATA NIJUGO - *Performed by Abbey Jones.*

1 Musubi dachi and kiotske.

2 Rei.

3. Kaishu Kamae.

4 Left foot steps to soto hachiji dachi and pull fists to sides.

5. Nigiri kamae.

Saito-Ha Shito-Ryu Karate-Do For The Modern Warrior

KIHON KATA NIJUGO

6 Right jodan age uke.

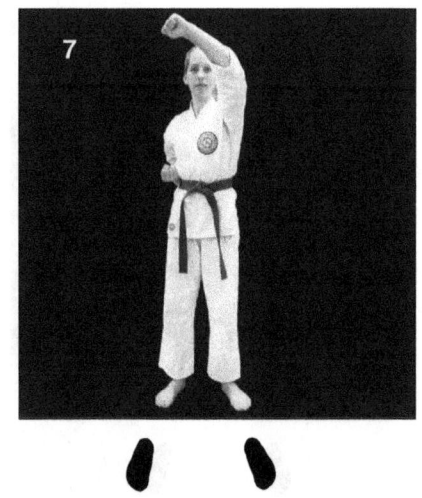

7 Left jodan age uke.

8 Right chudan yoko uke.

9 Left chudan yoko uke.

10 Right naka uke.

11 Left naka uke.

13 Right gedan harai uke.

13 Left gedan harai uke

14 Right chudan shuto uke.

KIHON KATA NIJUGO

15 Left chudan shuto uke.

16 Right age hiji ate.

17 Left age hiji ate.

18 Right yoko hiji ate.

19 Left yoko hiji ate.

20 Left foot steps to Shiko dachi and right chudan zuki (kiai).

21 Left chudan zuki (kiai).

22 Squat lower and right choku zuki.

23 Left choku zuki.

Saito-Ha Shito-Ryu Karate-Do
For The Modern Warrior

KIHON KATA NIJUGO

24 Left foot steps to soto hachiji dachi and yoko uke kamae.

25 Right mae geri.

26 Left mae geri.

27 Right mawashi geri.

28 Left mawashi geri.

29 Left kizami zuki (kiai).

30 Right kizami zuki (kiai).

31 Pull fists to sides.

32 Nigiri kamae followed by closing salutation.

The next series of Kihon Katas add to the understanding of the importance of the foundation taught in karate. Various stances are practiced in the execution of the blocks, strikes and thrusts while emphasizing correct hip usage, posture and breathing. Correct spirit and attitude are also the common denominator that will help each karate-ka foster perfection, no matter how complex the movements are.

Too often students become anxious and wish to move on to more advanced katas, but with patience and maturity, they will come to understand why the Kihon Katas are so important to learn and practice. The honing of each Kihon Kata is the very essence of Shito-ryu karate-do and with constant practice, progress to a high level of skill will be realized.

KIHON KATA ZENKUTSU DACHI DAI ICHI - *Performed by Braxton Shoemaker.*

1 Rei.

2 Announce kata and kaishu kamae.

3 Soto hachiji dachi and pull fists to sides.

4 Nigiri kamae.

5 Left gedan harai uke.

6 Right chudan zuki.

Saito-Ha Shito-Ryu Karate-Do For The Modern Warrior

KIHON KATA ZENKUTSU DACHI DAI ICHI

7 Right gedan harai uke.

8 Left chudan zuki.

9 Left gedan harai uke.

10 Right chudan zuki.

11 Left chudan zuki.

12 Right chudan zuki (kiai).

13 Left gedan harai uke.

14 Right chudan zuki.

15 Right gedan harai uke.

KIHON KATA ZENKUTSU DACHI DAI ICHI

16 Left chudan zuki.

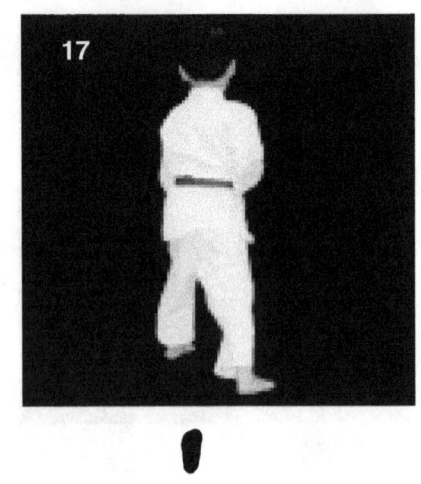

17 Left gedan harai uke.

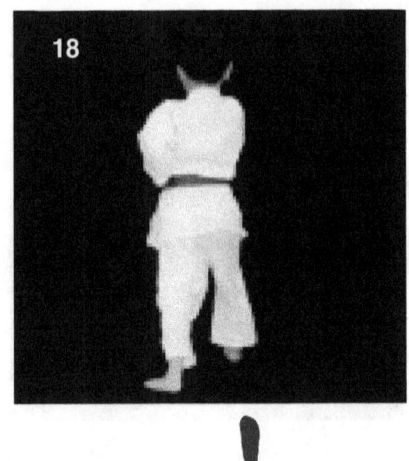

18 Right chudan zuki.

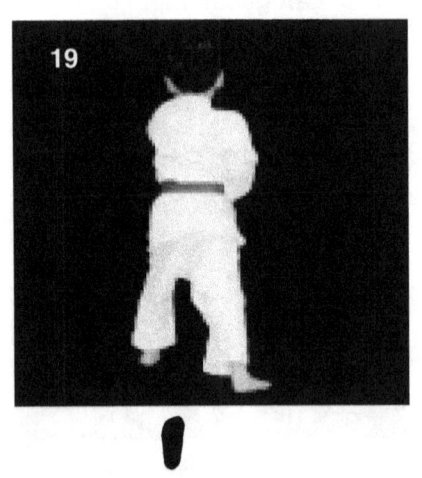

19 Left chudan zuki.

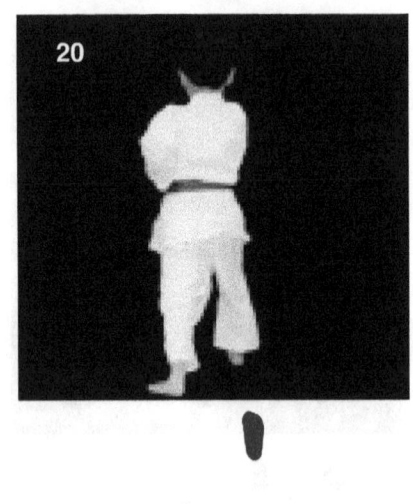

20 Right chudan zuki (kiai).

21 Left gedan harai uke.

22 Right chudan zuki.

23 Right gedan harai uke.

24 Left chudan zuki.

Saito-Ha Shito-Ryu Karate-Do For The Modern Warrior

KIHON KATA ZENKUTSU DACHI DAI ICHI

25 Soto hachiji dachi and pull fists to sides.

26 Nigiri kamae.

27 Rei.

KIHON KATA TSUKI - *Performed by the author.*

1 Sparring Kamae

2 Reverse thrust

3 Vertical thrust

4 Uppercut

5 Uppercut

6 Hook thrust

7 Round thrust

8 Lunge thrust

9 Double U thrust (kiai).

After completing 1 - 9, repeat same on other side.

PINAN KATAS

After the Kihon Katas are taught, the five Pinan Katas are introduced. These katas were created by Itosu "Ankoh" Yasutsune and continue to be practiced worldwide by Shito-ryu, Shotokan, Wado-ryu and Shorin-ryu, and in some Korean styles of martial arts.

Historians have theorized that Itosu created the five Pinans from either the mysterious Channan Kata, Kushanku Kata or both.

Itosu was a well-educated man who worked as a scribe to Sho Tai, the last king of the Ryukyu Kingdom, until the monarchy was formally annexed and dissolved by Japan in 1879 to form Okinawa Prefecture. Placed in charge of Okinawa's physical training program, Itosu introduced karate to the Shuri Jinjo Primary school in April of 1901. He also went on to teach at Shuri Dai-ichi Middle School and the Okinawa Prefectural Men's Normal School in 1905.

Since the primary focus for teaching these katas was discipline and physical fitness, Itosu taught beginners and children without exposing the dangerous techniques the kata contained. Keeping each kata short also made it easier to teach children. This introduction into the educational system of Okinawa by Itosu was a clever way to unveil the secrecy of karate, which eventually gained popularity and public acceptance.

Students practicing in the courtyard of the Shuri Castle, led by Shiroma, Shinpan, who trained with Kenwa Mabuni under Itosu and Higashionna. He also called his style Shito-ryu.

There are many teachers, and students alike, who question the importance of the five Pinans. One of the main reasons, in my opinion, (excluding styles that do not have Pinans in their syllabus), is that they lack the knowledge of bunkai and oyo. They haven't explored the many methods of self-defense techniques hidden in the movements and are practicing the more simple blocks, kicks, thrusts and strikes. Yet if movements are dissected, analyzed and performed with a partner, chokes, throws, joint locks, releases, etc. are unveiled. Aside from the self-defense aspect of these katas, executing each movement correctly and with enthusiasm has very positive health benefits. This is part of our history and we should make a dedicated effort to preserve what the earlier masters created for us.

Roxy McPherson has matured into a fine young lady through her Pinan practice, her supportive parents and her faith.

Saito-Ha Shito-Ryu Karate-Do — For The Modern Warrior

PINAN SHODAN - *The 1st of the Pinan Series performed by Michele Barnes.*

1 Musubi dachi and kiotske.

2 Rei.

3 Announce kata and kaishu kamae.

4 Soto hachiji dachi and pull fists to sides.

5 Nigiri kamae.

6 Left nekoashi-dachi, left chudan yoko-uke, at the same time, right ken pulls to the front of the forehead (back of the fist facing forehead) and elbow pointing to the opposite side.

7 Left nekoashi dachi, right chudan kentsui uchi while left ken pulls to the right shoulder.

8 Soto hachiji dachi, left jodan yoko barai & right ken hikite to right hip.

Saito-Ha Shito-Ryu Karate-Do

For The Modern Warrior

PINAN SHODAN

9 Right nekoashi dachi, right chudan yoko uke, at the same time, left ken pulls to the front of the forehead (back of the fist facing forehead) and elbow pointing to the opposite side.

10 Right nekoashi dachi, Left chudan kentsui uchi while right ken pulls to the left shoulder.

11 Soto hachiji dachi, right jodan yoko barai and left ken hikite to left hip.

12 Right nekoashi dachi, right chudan yoko uke.

13 Right chudan mae geri.

14 Right foot pivots and turns the body to shomen, left nekoashi dachi left chudan shuto uke.

15 Right nekoashi dachi right chudan shuto uke.

16 Left nekoashi dachi left chudan shuto uke.

PINAN SHODAN

17 Right zenkutsu dachi, and right chudan yonhon nukite and left ken hikite to left hip and (kiai).

18 Left nekoashi dachi left chudan shuto uke.

19 Right nekoashi dachi right chudan shuto uke.

20 Right nekoashi dachi right chudan shuto uke.

21 Left nekoashi dachi left chudan shuto uke.

22 Left zenkutsu dachi right chudan yoko uke and left ken hikite to left hip.

23 Right chudan mae geri.

PINAN SHODAN

24 Right zenkutsu dachi left chudan gyaku tsuki.

25 Left hiji otoshi drawing right foot back to hanzenkutsu dachi.

26 Left chudan mae geri.

27 Left zenkutsu dachi right chudan gyaku zuki.

28 Right zenkutsu dachi right chudan hijisasae uke.

29 Reset the rear foot, left zenkutsu dachi left gedan uke.

30 Right hanzenkutsu dachi right jodan ageuke.

31 Zenkutsu dachi right gedan uke.

PINAN SHODAN

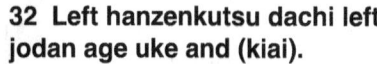

32 Left hanzenkutsu dachi left jodan age uke and (kiai).

33 Soto hachiji dachi, pull fists to sides and nigiri kamae.

34 Nigiri kamae followed by closing salutation.

PINAN SHODAN OYO (ENACTMENT OF THE BUNKAI) - *The author assisted by Robert Burstein gives a sample demonstration of the many parts that have been cut and analyzed (bunkai) of this kata.*

Saito-Ha Shito-Ryu Karate-Do
PINAN SHODAN OYO

PINAN NIDAN - *The 2nd of the Pinan Series performed by Chuck Aoto.*

1 Musubi dachi and kiotske.

2 Rei.

3 Announce kata and kaishu kamae.

4 Soto hachiji dachi and pull fists to sides.

5 Nigiri kamae.

6 Left nekoashi dachi, left jodan uchiotoshi with large circular motion with right fist hikite to waist.

7 Right han zenkutsu dachi and right chudan zuki.

8 Right zenkutsu dachi and right gedan harai uke and left fist hikite to the left waist.

PINAN NIDAN

9 Right hanzenkutsu dachi and right jodan uchiotoshi with large circular motion.

10 Left zenkutsu dachi and left chudan zuki.

11 Left zenkutsu dachi and left harai uke.

12 Right hanzenkutsu dachi and right jodan age uke

13 Left hanzenkutsu dachi and left jodan age uke.

14 Right hanzenkutsu dachi and right jodan age uke (kiai).

15 Left zenkutsu dachi facing 45°, and left gedan harai-uke.

16 Right hanzenkutsu dachi and right chudan zuki.

Saito-Ha Shito-Ryu Karate-Do
PINAN NIDAN

17 Right zenkutsu dachi facing 45° and right gedan harai-uke.

18 Left hanzenkutsu dachi and left chudan zuki.

19 Left zenkutsu dachi and left gedan harai uke

20 Right hanzenkutsu dachi and right chudan zuki.

21 Left hanzenkutsu dachi and left chudan zuki.

22 Right hanzenkutsu dachi, and right chudan zuki (kiai).

23 Left shiko dachi facing 45° and left gedan shuto barai and right kaisyu at suigetsu.

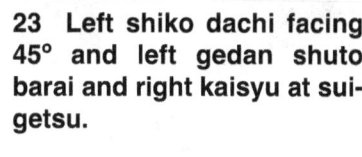

PINAN NIDAN

24 Right shiko dachi facing 45° and right gedan shuto barai and left kaisyu at suigetsu.

25 Right shiko dachi facing 45° and right gedan shuto-barai and left kaisyu at suigetsu.

26 Left shiko dachi facing 45° and left gedan shuto barai and right kaisyu at suigetsu.

27 Sotohachiji dachi, pull fists to sides and nigiri kamae, followed by closing salutation.

PINAN NIDAN OYO (ENACTMENT OF THE BUNKAI) - *The author assisted by Robert Burstein gives a sample demonstration of the many parts that have been cut and analyzed (bunkai) of this kata.*

Saito-Ha Shito-Ryu Karate-Do

For The Modern Warrior

PINAN NIDAN OYO

PINAN SANDAN - *The 3rd of the Pinan Series performed by Ken Frownfelter.*

1 Musubi dachi, kiotske.

2 Rei.

3 Announce kata in kaishu kamae.

4 Soto hachiji dachi.

5 Nigiri kamae.

6 Left nekoashi dachi, left chudan yoko uke and right ken hikite to the right waist.

7 Heisoku dachi, right chudan yoko uke and left chudan harai uke.

8 left chudan yoko uke and right chudan harai uke.

9 Right nekoashi dachi, right chudan yoko uke and left ken hikite to the right waist.

Saito-Ha Shito-Ryu Karate-Do
PINAN SANDAN

For The Modern Warrior

10 Left chudan yoko uke and right harai uke.

13 Right Zenkutsu dachi chudan yonhon nukite with left ken hikite to left waist (kiai).

11 Right chudan yoko uke and left harai uke.

14 Left kokutsu dachi with right nukite lowering to gedan gluteus area slightly bending the elbow with left ken hikite to left waist.

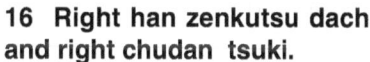

16 Right han zenkutsu dachi and right chudan tsuki.

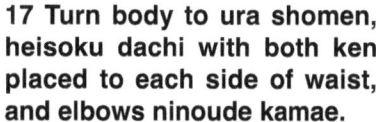

17 Turn body to ura shomen, heisoku dachi with both ken placed to each side of waist, and elbows ninoude kamae.

12 Left nekoashi dachi, left chudan yoko uke.

15 Shiko dachi and left chudan yoko barai.

PINAN SANDAN

18 Nami heiko dachi and right ninoude uke.

19 Shiko dachi and right chudan zuki quickly returning fist to ninoude kamae.

20 Nami heiko dachi and left ninoude uke.

21 Shiko dachi and left chudan zuki quickly returning fist to ninoude kamae.

22 Nami heiko dachi and right ninoude uke.

23 Shiko dachi and right chudan yoko barai leaving arm out, simultaneously chambering left ken to waist.

Saito-Ha Shito-Ryu Karate-Do   For The Modern Warrior

PINAN SANDAN

24 Left hanzenkutsu dachi, and left chudan zuki (kiai).

25 Namiheiko dachi while maintaining left chudan zuki.

26 Left foot moves counter clockwise to shomen, soto hachiji dachi and left hiji ate to rear and right ken goes to left shoulder area with age tsuki.

27 Yoriashi to the right side, sotohachiji dachi, and right hiji ate to rear and left ken goes to right shoulder area age tsuki.

28 Soto hachiji dachi, pull fists to sides and nigiri kamae, followed by closing salutation.

PINAN SANDAN OYO (ENACTMENT OF THE BUNKAI) - *The author assisted by Robert Burstein gives a sample demonstration of the many parts that have been cut and analyzed (bunkai) of this kata.*

PINAN YONDAN - *The 4th of the Pinan Series performed by Teguh Hendry Santoso.*

1 Musubi dachi, kiotsuke.

2 Rei.

3 Announce kata in kaishu kamae.

4 Soto hachiji dachi and pull fists to sides.

5 Nigiri kamae.

6 Left nekoashi dachi, left chudan yoko kote uke.

7 Right nekoashi dachi, right chudan yoko kote uke.

8. Left zenkutsu dachi, gedan kosa uke from right chest area with right arm on top.

Saito-Ha Shito-Ryu Karate-Do

For The Modern Warrior

PINAN YONDAN

9 Right nekoashi dachi, right chudan hiji sasae uke

10 Heisoku dachi, both ken pulling to right waist.

11 Left jodan yoko barai with left chudan mae geri to left side.

12 left zenkutsu dachi, right chudan hiji ate into left shotei of hand.

13 Heisoku dachi, both ken pulling to left waist.

14 Right jodan yoko barai with right chudan mae geri to right side.

15 Right zenkutsu dachi, left chudan hiji ate into right shotei of hand.

16 Left zenkutsu dachi, right jodan sukui uke, and left kaishu at front of forehead.

Saito-Ha Shito-Ryu Karate-Do

For The Modern Warrior

PINAN YONDAN

17 Right chudan mae geri.

18 Right kosa dachi, left ken osae uke, right jodan uraken uchi and left ken hikite to left waist (kiai).

19 Left nekoashi dachi, left chudan yoko uke.

20 Right chudan mae geri.

21 & 22 Right hanzenkutsu dachi, right and left nihon zuki.

23 Right nekoashi dachi, right chudan yoko uke.

24 Left chudan mae geri.

123

PINAN YONDAN

25 & 26 Left hanzenkutsu dachi, left and right nihon zuki.

27 Left nekoashi dachi, left chudan sasae uke.

28 Right nekoashi dachi, right chudan sasae uke.

29 Left nekoashi dachi, left chudan sasae uke.

30 left hanzenkutsu dachi, morote kaishu extending to shoulder level.

31 Right hiza geri while pulling ken to sides of body (kiai).

32 Left nekoashi dachi, left chudan shuto uke body.

PINAN YONDAN

33 Look sharply to the right side (45°) in preparation for the next movement, yoriashi, right nekoashi dachi, right chudan shuto uke.

34 Left foot pulls back (45°), pull fists to sides, sotohachiji dachi and nigiri kamae, followed by closing salutation.

PINAN YONDAN OYO (ENACTMENT OF THE BUNKAI) - *The author assisted by Robert Burstein gives a sample demonstration of the many parts that have been cut and analyzed (bunkai) of this kata.*

Saito-Ha Shito-Ryu Karate-Do
PINAN YONDAN OYO

For The Modern Warrior

Saito-Ha Shito-Ryu Karate-Do
PINAN YONDAN OYO

For The Modern Warrior

Saito-Ha Shito-Ryu Karate-Do For The Modern Warrior

義 礼 勇 名誉 仁 真 忠義
Integrity Respect Heroic Courage Honor Compassion Honesty Sincerity Duty Loyalty

Kata practice on the island of Kauai is always exhilarating.

PINAN GODAN - *The 5th of the Pinan Series performed by Logan Mendonca.*

1 Musubi dachi, kiotsuke, and rei.

2 Announce kata in kaishu kamae.

3 Soto hachiji dachi and pull fists to waist.

4 Nigiri kamae.

5 Left nekoashi dachi, left chudan yoko uke, right ken hikite to waist.

6 Light chudan gyaku zuki, left ken hikite to waist.

7 Heisoku dachi, left ken moves across body to waki kamae (palm down), right ken hikite to right waist.

8 Right nekoashi dachi, right chudan yoko uke, left ken hikite to waist.

9 Left chudan gyaku zuki right ken hikite to waist.

PINAN GODAN

10 Heisoku dachi, right ken moves across body to waki kamae (palm down), left ken hikite to left waist.

11 Right hanzenkutsu dachi, right chudan hijisasae uke.

12 Left zenkutsu dachi, pull ken to sides, gedan kosa uke (closed fists).

13 Kaishu jodan kosa uke.

14 Flip hands to right side, right kote uke with left hand shotei on top of right hand.

15 Nami heiko dachi, left chudan yoko barai with right ken hikite to right waist.

16 Right hanzenkutsu dachi, right chudan zuki (kiai).

Saito-Ha Shito-Ryu Karate-Do
PINAN GODAN

17 Shiko dachi, right gedan harai uke, left ken hikite to left waist.

18 Left hanzenkutsu dachi, left chudan yoko barai from right shoulder.

19 Right zenkutsu dachi, right hiji ate into left shotei.

20 Right kosa dachi, right jodan uraken uchi with left ken under right elbow.

21 Right renoji dachi (standing tall), rotate upper body toward the left while keeping right Jodan uraken uchi (90°) kamae.

22 Jump bringing knees as high as possible, and landing simultaneously with both feet.

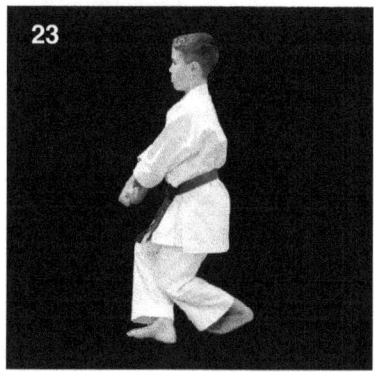

23 Right kosa dachi, gedan kosa uke.

PINAN GODAN

24 Right zenkutsu dachi, right hijisasae uke.

25 Left nekoashi dachi, left gedan harai uke, with right jodan yoko uke at 90°.

26 Slightly pull left foot back, right nekoashi dachi, right gedan harai uke, with left jodan yoko uke at 45° (kiai).

27 Pull left foot back, pull fists to waist in soto hachiji dachi and nigiri kamae, followed by closing salutation.

PINAN GODAN OYO (ENACTMENT OF THE BUNKAI) - *The author assisted by Robert Burstein gives a sample demonstration of the many parts that have been cut and analyzed (bunkai) of this kata.*

Saito-Ha Shito-Ryu Karate-Do
PINAN GODAN OYO

Saito-Ha Shito-Ryu Karate-Do
PINAN GODAN OYO

For The Modern Warrior

SEIENCHIN

"Seienchin" or "Seiyunchin" means "Calm in the Storm." Higashionna is given the most credit in bringing this classical kata to Okinawa from China. While several katas use quick and snapping movements, Seienchin is a unique kata that emphasizes low shiko stances with circular blocking, grasping, pulling, throwing and locking techniques. This kata has no kicks and is designed to strengthen the arms, legs and body for close-quarter self-defense. Seienchin is also Saito-ha Shito-ryu's signature kata, helping students who practice it find themselves. It is a kata that flows with beauty and strength, harmonizing the spirit and mind, and creating a greater sense of well-being in your life.

SEIENCHIN - *Performed by Kelsey Kitts.*

1 Musubi dachi, kiotsuke.

2 Rei.

3 Kaishu kamae.

4 Uchihachiji dachi and roll ken to nigiri kamae with both fists to side of body.

5 Right shiko dachi at 45° with both hands kaishu slowly moving to gedan position.

6 Breath in as both hands are raised to the chest with fingers pointing by the chin.

Saito-Ha Shito-Ryu Karate-Do
SEIENCHIN

7 Breath out and slowly form fists and morote gedan harai uke.

8 Right kaishu chudan yoko-uke with left hand kaishu placed at suigetsu with palm up.

9 Quickly execute right ka-kete.

10 Slowly draw right hand to chest while executing left nukite 45° while breathing out slowly.

11 Left shiko dachi at 45° with both hands kaishu slowly moving to gedan position.

12 Breath in as both hands are raised to the chest with fingers pointing by the chin.

Saito-Ha Shito-Ryu Karate-Do For The Modern Warrior

SEIENCHIN

13 Breath out and slowly form fists and morote gedan harai uke.

14 Left kaishu chudan yoko uke with right hand kaishu placed at suigetsu with palm up.

15 Quickly execute left kakete.

16 Slowly draw left hand to chest while executing right nukite 45° while breathing out slowly.

17 Right shiko dachi at 45° with both hands kaishu slowly moving to gedan position.

18 Breath in as both hands are raised to the chest with fingers pointing by the chin.

SEIENCHIN

19 Breath out and slowly form fists and morote gedan harai uke.

20 Right kaishu chudan yoko uke with left hand kaishu placed at suigetsu with palm up.

21 Quickly execute right kakete.

22 Slowly draw right hand to chest while executing left nukite 45° while breathing out slowly.

23 Right foot lifts side of left knee while placing right ken into left shotei at chin level.

24 Right foot steps forward to heiko dachi while rolling top of ken inside left shotei and extend arms to chudan level.

Saito-Ha Shito-Ryu Karate-Do

SEIENCHIN

For The Modern Warrior

25 Right foot steps back to left heiko dachi and extend right open hand to jodan level.

26 Right chudan hiji ate into left shotei.

27 Right foot steps 45° to uchi-hachiji dachi and right ken sasae uke.

28 Left foot steps forward 45° to left shiko dachi and left gedan zuki directly from kensasae uke.

29 Left foot steps back 45° to right shiko dachi and right gedan harai uke.

30 Left foot steps forward 45° to uchihachiji dachi and left ken sasae uke.

SEIENCHIN

31 Right foot steps forward 45° to right shiko dachi and right gedan zuki directly from kensa-sae uke.

32 Right foot steps back 45° to left shiko dachi and left gedan harai uke.

33 Left foot steps back to right shiko dachi and right shotei uke placing left hand in front of forehead.

34 Right foot steps back to left shiko dachi and left shotei uke placing right hand in front of forehead.

35 Step forward to right uchiha-chiji dachi and right chudan naka uke inside of left shotei.

36 Yoriashi to right heiko dachi and right jodan uraken-uchi (kiai).

SEIENCHIN

37 Right foot steps to left uchi-hachiji dachi, 45°, right harai uke and left chudan yoko uke.

38 Left chudan kakete.

39 Right step forward 45° to right shiko dachi, right jodan ura zuki, right uraken uchi and left kaishu to suigetsu with fingers pointing up.

40 Right gedan harai uke and hikite.

41 Right foot steps back to left shiko dachi at 45° and left gedan harai uke.

42 Right foot steps forward to right neko ashi dachi, left hiji ate and right chudan age hiji uke.

SEIENCHIN

43 Right foot steps back, right hiji ate and left chudan age hiji uke.

44 Left foot steps to right uchi-hachiji dachi, 45°, left harai uke and right chudan yoko uke.

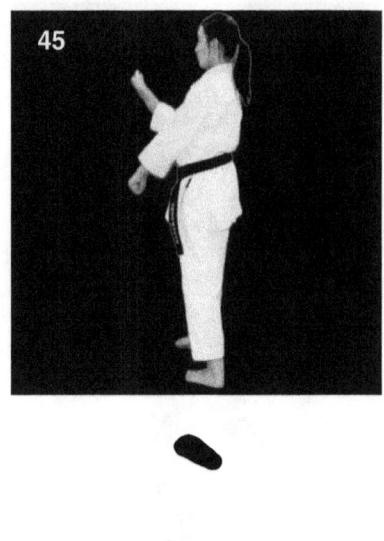

45 Right chudan kakete.

46 Left step forward 45° to left shiko dachi, right jodan ura zuki, left uraken uchi and right kaishu to suigetsu with fingers pointing up.

47 Left gedan harai uke and hikite.

48 Left foot steps back to right shiko dachi at 45° and right gedan harai uke.

Saito-Ha Shito-Ryu Karate-Do
SEIENCHIN

For The Modern Warrior

49 Left foot steps forward to left neko ashi dachi, right hiji ate and left chudan age hiji uke.

50 Left foot steps back to right neko ashi dachi, left hiji ate and right chudan age hiji uke.

51 Left chudan shotei uke in an arching motion positioning to side of elbow.

52 Right yoriashi and right jodan uraken uchi placing left kaishu in front of suigetsu (kiai).

53 Step back with right foot to neko ashi dachi with kaishu hands extended to chudan level.

54 Morote chudan hiji uke to sides and slightly upward and forming a peak with the fingers.

SEIENCHIN

55 Left foot steps back to musubi dachi and kaishu kamae.

56 Followed by closing salutation.

SEIENCHIN OYO (ENACTMENT OF THE BUNKAI) - *The author assisted by Matthias Gattey and Skyler Jackson gives a sample demonstration of the many parts that have been cut and analyzed (bunkai) of this kata.*

Saito-Ha Shito-Ryu Karate-Do
For The Modern Warrior

SEIENCHIN OYO

SEIENCHIN OYO

Saito-Ha Shito-Ryu Karate-Do

For The Modern Warrior

SEIENCHIN OYO

SEIENCHIN OYO

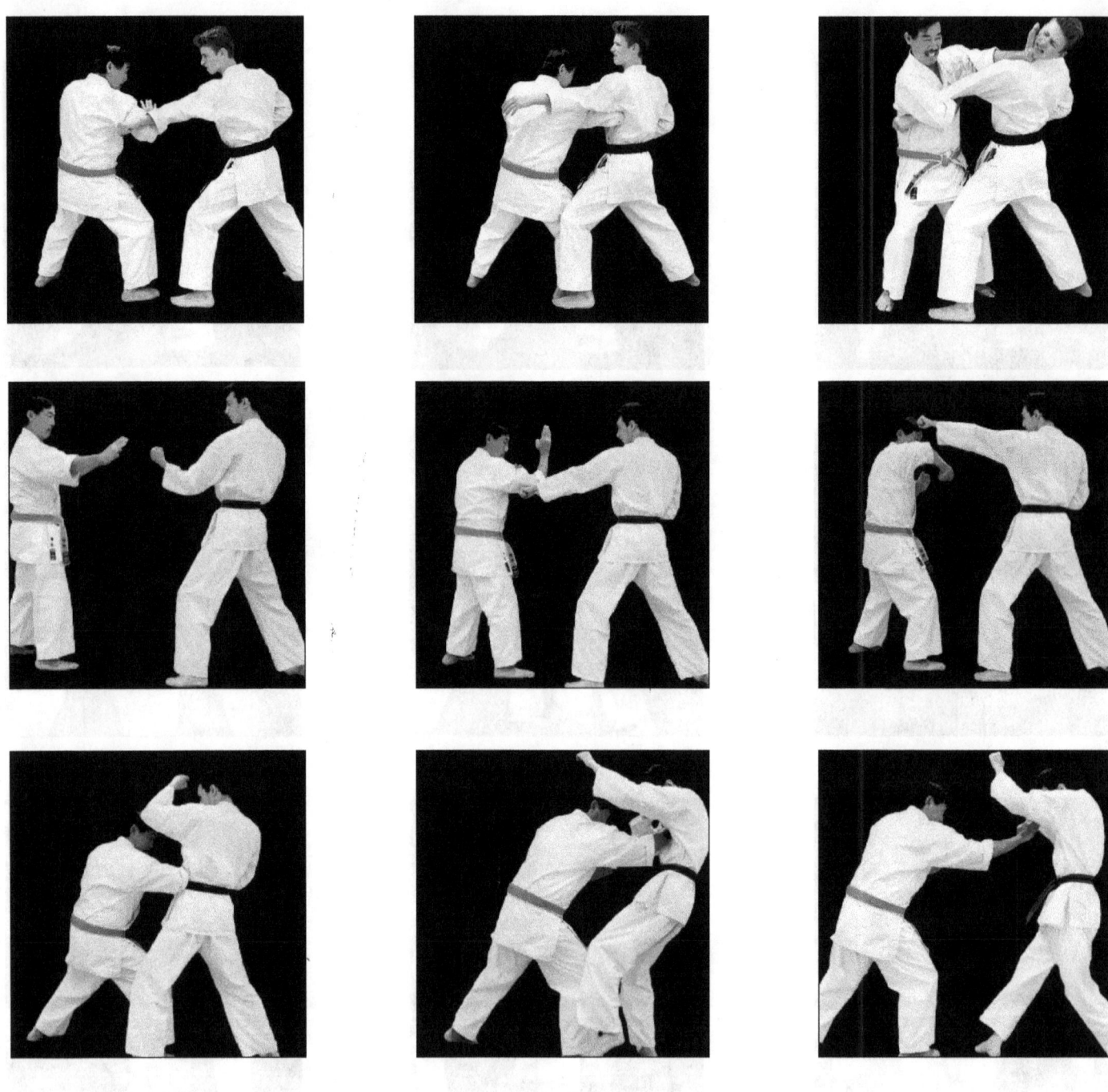

Chapter 9
KOBUDO

From the beginning of time, man has learned to use weapons for hunting and self-defense. From hurling stones to spears, and then from bows and arrows to muskets... and now in the 21st Century, with the use of bombs, lasers and smart weapons, man has devised many different ways to better defend himself.

The Okinawans also developed their own weapons, especially for the use of defending themselves against those that subjugated them as early as in the 1400s, and later in the 1600s. Since the Okinawans were forbidden to possess any traditional war-fighting weapons, they had to cleverly create weapons from their farm tools and other makeshift implements. Everyday tools such as the boat oar, crutches, rice grinder handles, sickles, and even-shoulder-carried poles were converted to become weapons.

We coin these weapons, as well as others, with the name "Kobujutsu" (old martial arts) or "Kobudo" (old martial ways). The use of these weapons was easy to master for those that already had a foundation in karate. The complete freedom of the ryuku martial arts allowed practitioners to move to the front, back, left, right, up and down resulting a very effective method of attacks and defenses. In order to manipulate each weapon, several masters devised patterns of movements, called kata, for their own practice as well as a method to teach others.

There are several organizations today that continue to preserve the old weapons of Okinawa, despite the fact that many of these weapons are no longer practical in the modern era. It is my belief that those serious in preserving the martial arts directly related to karate should dedicate some time to the study and practice of kobudo.

The use of the more popular weapons are included in the following pages. The weapons which are not often seen are illustrated below.

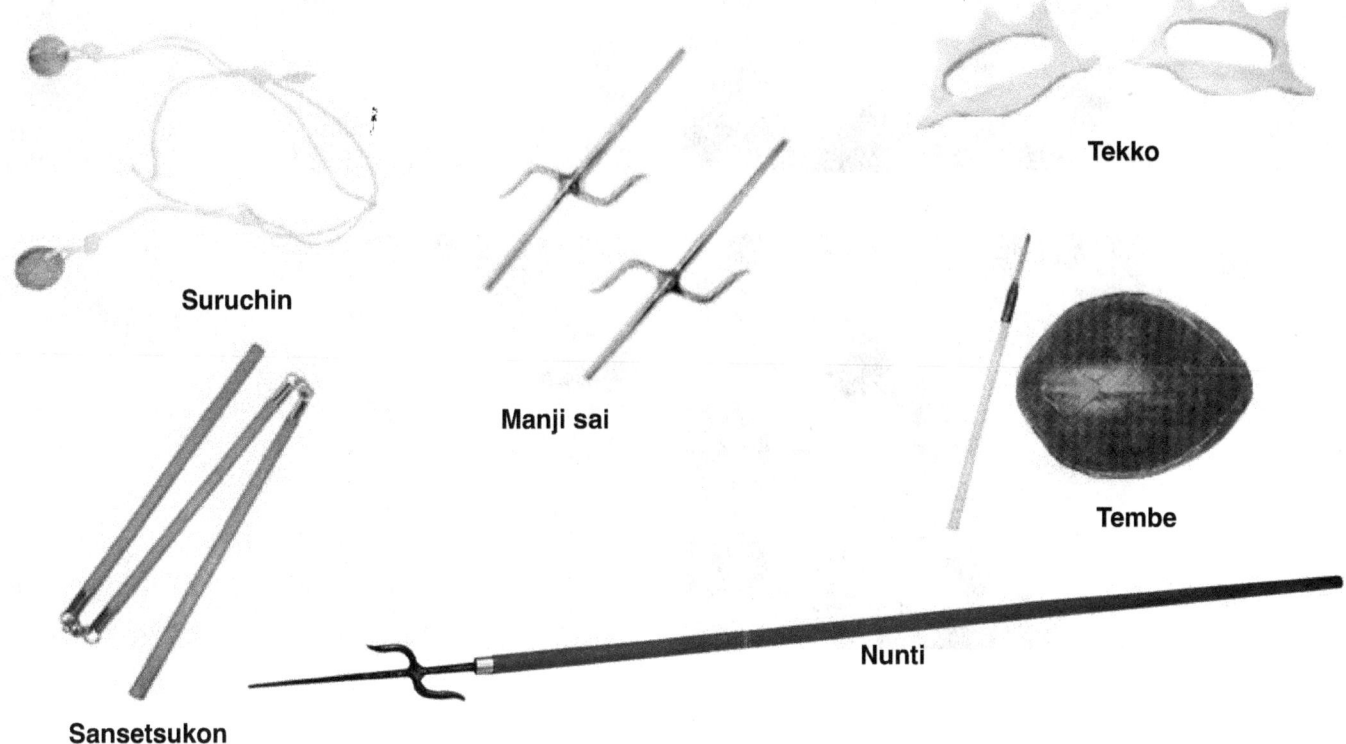

KOBUDO

The more well-known Okinawan weapons practiced with today.

The **"Roku Shaku Bo"** is a solid staff constructed from a hard wood, measuring approximately six feet in length. One could also customize the size according to their height. With the "Tenbin" (shoulder carrying pole) commonly used for carrying buckets of water, farm grains or supplies, Okinawan martial arts masters cleverly developed a staff for use as a self-defense tool. One could easily drop the buckets they carried to defend themself using the staff to block and attack.

KOBUDO

The **"Nunchaku"** is a classical Okinawan weapon constructed of two wooden sections joined by rope or horse hair. It was generally used as a horse bridle. This weapon can be used to thrust, squeeze as a vice, block, and flail to keep the attacker at bay. Nunchakus were also constructed with three or four wooden sections.

KOBUDO

KOBUDO

The **"Sai"** is a weapon constructed of a metal shaft and handle with two curved prongs that act as hand guards. The typical length is 18 to 21 1/2 inches, and when held, should extend past the elbow to ensure it will protect the entire forearm. A pair of sai were used, and at times a third one was tucked in the belt. The sai were effective as blocking, striking and trapping weapons. They were thought to be used as a farming tools, but I think that they were made for self-defense since any blacksmith could make one, due to the simple design.

KOBUDO

The **"Eiku" or "Kai"** is an Okinawan boat oar that was used at times as a weapon. It was not a weapon used by the Japanese warrior class, but more with the Okinawan Kobujutsu weapons arts.

KOBUDO

The **"Kama"** is another classical weapon constructed with a sharpened straight or curved blade attached to a wooden handle. Farmers used this tool to cut grass or grain, although the weapons grade kama was constructed differently to withstand the powerful attacks of other weapons, such as the "Bo." When two of these weapons are used, it is called "Nijugama." When it is attached to a "Kusari" (metal chain) with a "Fundo," (heavy iron weight) at the end, it is called the "Kusurigama."

KOBUDO

The **"Tonfa"** is another Okinawan weapon. It evolved from an ancient Chinese crutch used to aid in walking. Some believe that it was a handle from a mill grinding stone that could easily be removed and be used as a viable weapon. A pair of tonfa was used to block, thrust, pull and strike. Some law enforcement groups use the expandable tonfa baton today.

KOBUDO

Chapter 10
REFLEXES APPLIED TO KARATE

This section examines some of the reactions that occur during karate practice. Technically, reflexes are the result of involuntary activity. When surprised with an attack, the startle reflex, an unconscious defense response to sudden stimuli (such as a loud "kiai" or when startled), a variety of movements will occur. The eyes blink, the head will jerk away, muscles tense, the arms can flail wildly, and the response is to try to evade in an erratic manner. Through training, however, involuntary responses may be replaced with voluntary responses. In other words, the individual may respond with an appropriate block, well-timed thrust, kick, or strike, or may use passive means to avoid being hit altogether.

Transmission of the Reflex Signal

These principals are fairly well known, but this mechanism contains two important points.

First, a chemical reaction helps pass a charge from one nerve to the next. It is commonly known that temperature greatly affects how chemicals interact. Warmer temperatures quicken reactions and colder temperatures slow them down. It's been proven that human reflexes are significantly faster during warm conditions. Therefore, it is wise to wear warm clothing while waiting to spar, especially at tournaments. If the body is cold, expect to have slower reaction times.

Second, a proper amount of stimulation is necessary before the nerve will fire. Touching a lukewarm stove will not cause the hand to jerk away. Enough heat must be present in order to cause the response. It is a psychological law that if many small stimuli are applied rapidly, they will compound until the nerve fires. This is called "summation." Let's use the example of heat on a scale of 1 to 10. And, let's assume that 8 is hot enough to make one jerk his hand away from the stove, but 6 is not hot enough to cause the same response. But, however, several 6s in quick succession would create enough stimulus to cause one to jerk his hand away.

This law may be applied in kumite, which has a high, or cortical, level of reflex. If perfectly prepared to counterattack, the nerves to one's appendages become loaded with small impulses. Then, when the time is right to counter an opponent, a faster than usual response is possible.

Spinal Level Reflexes

These reflexes are virtually automatic and occur instantly. Most of these reflexes are protective in nature:

"Golgi Tendon Reflex": Sensory nerves working with the tendons control this reflex. A good example of this is when one tries to bicep curl too heavy a weight to lift. Rather than defy physics and risk injury, the reflex will have the person simply drop the weight.

Stretch Reflex: The "myotatic reflex" is the stretch reflex. This reflex is a response of a muscle trying to stretch beyond its present length. This protective response prevents any muscle damage. It is important to gently and slowly stretch the muscles before doing strenuous karate training in order to prevent the risk of muscle tears or other damage.

Rebound Reflex

Another interesting phenomenon regarding spinal level reflexes is called the "rebound reflex." Reflexes fatigue rapidly. This means that immediately after a reflex ends, a second reflex is much more difficult to elicit. This explains why someone who is faked even slightly out of position is "frozen" for just a split second while the real strike is delivered. Therefore, it is quite effective to use the same strike that was used as a fake.

Low Brain Level Reflexes

These are subconscious functions of the body. They deal with such things as arterial blood pressure and respiration.

High Brain or Cortical Reflexes

The brain is where the ultimate reaction to stimulus processes. It is the area where sight, sound, and touch can be interpreted for the stimulus to react. This level of reflex is abstract in a sense, because thought elicits a response, such as a block or a strike.

When one begins to learn karate, each move must be interpreted and purposefully performed. Soon, patterns begin to form on the subconscious level. Reactions are faster than thoughts. This is why reactions must be carefully controlled. That is, one won't punch until ready, but when ready, the punch may be controlled on a subconscious level with focus, control, power and speed. The process of learning to control each subconscious reflex in the proper form is key. This process never ends and is a difficult task. All of these memorized reactions must be continually altered and then put into proper form and learned again on a subconscious level. The ultimate goal is to have automatic levels of good form and response.

Sebastian and Matthias Gattey begin their jump, and then the subconscious level of their performance takes over through constant practice.

Muscle Spasm

Muscle spasms, or cramps, result from any locally irritating factor such as severe cold, lack of blood flow to the muscle, over-exercise of the muscle, receiving a sharp blow, lactic acid build up and dehydration. These may cause pain, which causes a muscle contraction, which creates more pain and increases the contraction. A small irritation may, in this way, cause a full-blown muscle spasm.

Counter-flexing the muscle may completely cure the pain of a muscle spasm. Our tournament physician also recommends drinking pickle juice, which I have found from personal experience definitely works.

Chapter 11
KUMITE

Kumite is the study of strategy, over the years, to achieve the spirit of the warrior.

"Today is a victory over yourself of yesterday..."
- Miyamoto Musashi

Kumite, or sparring, is a method of training which allows students to apply techniques to actual fighting situations. During karate's early development, kumite existed only in secrecy. The masters placed heavy emphasis on fundamentals and kata training. Not until the late 1920s did sparring become formally introduced into karate training. Though it seems to contradict the basic premise of karate, in that its true purpose is to avoid aggression at all costs, the basic purpose of kumite is to provide a useful tool in creating more controlled and passive attitudes. This training becomes a testing ground for both the physical and mental components of the individual's nature. Through realistic confrontation, the dual forces of true nature, the positive vs. negative, or the soft vs. hard, may be explored.

A karate instructor has the critical role of promoting and instilling the components of control, discipline, and respect into a student's training. These components prevent negative attitudes from forming and aid in avoiding injury. Through this training, weaker students will learn to enjoy the challenges of kumite and will gain strength and confidence. Stronger students will learn to have compassion and understanding for their training partners, and also learn self-control.

When the art of kumite is mastered, there will be an overall sense of calmness when facing a storm. Techniques are polished and relaxed. The spirit is strong. There is a heightened awareness of an opponent's motives, and one will have developed the innate ability to react accordingly. There is no concern for winning or losing, and no fear. There is never a sense of antagonism toward the opponent. The mind is in a state of "mizu no kokoro," or "mind like water"; non-aggressive, like a calm pond reflecting the moon on its surface, able to direct the proper responses both offensively and defensively without over-thinking. This is the ultimate goal of kumite training.

To augment this advanced level of ability, one must use active and passive strategies. Active strategies may involve feinting, physical contact such as pushing or pulling, or stomping and shouting "kiai." These tactics are designed to conceal the true intent of your actions and cause the opponent's physical and psychological balance to falter. Passive strategies may include subtle body movements, shifts in directions and body positions that will cause an opponent's focus to be undermined. You may choose to invite your opponent to attack you by purposely exposing a target area and setting him up for a surprise counterattack. An understanding of "kyo" or "void" is also vital, and will add to your success in kumite. I have elaborated on "kyo" in the next chapter.

Before beginning any sparring practice, it is customary that partners bow to maintain an ambience of seriousness and commitment toward each other. The bow is also employed to acknowledge that control will be maintained and the ego will be pushed aside. Once the drill is completed, it is again customary to bow to your partner, symbolizing your appreciation for training with him.

It is also important to note that all of the levels of sparring may be practiced in slower motion or softer sparring, especially for those with physical or age considerations.

Basic Sparring (Kihon Kumite)

In basic sparring, a predetermined offensive technique is announced by the attacker and is used to target a specific area. The attacker, or "semete," begins from a front stance and down block position and steps forward executing a thrust or kick with every step. The defender, who is the "receiver" or "ukete," will identify the technique used (such as a face thrust) and attempt to successfully block the attack in a specific stance, and then execute a strong counter-attack. Basic sparring includes ippon kumite (single attack sparring), nihon kumite (two predefined attacks sparring), sanbon kumite (three predefined attacks sparring, hukushiki (walking attacks sparring) and kumite kata Sparring (applying kata techniques). Skills of positioning, posturing, distancing and timing are learned in these methods of sparring.

Tracey Raggi and Alexandria Elesky practicing basic sparing.

Students also learn the effectiveness of various thrusts, kicks, strikes and blocks. These methods of sparring provide confidence, releasing fears that cause one to lose a battle before it even begins. Once students are proficient in kihon kumite, they will begin the following oyo kumite stage where the applications are not predefined and the level of sparring is more intense and challenging.

Semi-Free Sparring

This level of oyo kumite includes "Hokei" (four attackers), "Mawari" (circle of attackers) and "Jiyu Ippon" kumite (one-step free sparring). The instructor will identify the attacker(s) and defender before the drill, and students may move around freely. The semete may use any accepted technique and the

Andreas Gattey and Elise Gattey practicing pre-arranged sparring.

This method of sparring provides the opportunity for students to sharpen their distance and timing.

ukete must respond in precise fashion. The ukete must reflexively respond with a decisive block and/or counter-attack, thus developing timing, distance, control and psychological skill. This is more complex and sets the stage to learn to respond instinctively, as opposed to calculatingly.

Stance is a critical element to be effective at kumite. There must be balance and the ability to move quickly in any direction. The weight of your body should be on the balls of your feet. Body position will determine how an opponent will design an attack. It is wise to keep a well-balanced posture with

Countering an attack with precision and control is also very important in sparring.

the front arm bent, fist higher than shoulder level and approximately 14" in front of the shoulder. The head should be held straight. The other arm should be placed so that the fist is positioned past the sternum with the elbow close to the side of the body. This protects the center of the body while keeping the weapons of the hands and arms near the opponent. Do not stare into your opponent's eyes; rather gaze at his heart and throat area. Eyes should be in a meditative state, contemplating the whole body and movement of an opponent. The distance and space maintained from the opponent is a crucial element in determining the outcome of the match. Proper breathing techniques will enable the mind to relax and focus. This sparring exercise teaches students to recognize and seize opportunities, take advantage of targets presented to them, and to have the courage and confidence to act accordingly, thus preparing for the final level of sparring.

Free-Sparring (Jiyu Kumite)

Jiyu kumite is the final oyo kumite training stage. This is the type of sparring students look forward to participating in because it is an immediate approach to self-defense, free from the restraints of basic kumite drills. Students will begin to develop their own fighting style and identify the techniques that will work for them. Smaller students will learn to shift and sidestep an attack in order to keep their larger opponents off balance. Larger students will learn to use sweeping techniques and strong counter-punches. To be successful in jiyu kumite, students need to continue their practice in basic sparring and semi-free sparring until all the ingredients for success are understood and executed. By doing so, if attacked, the response will be immediate and the results rewarding.

It is also important to note that all of the levels of sparring may be practiced in slower motion or softer sparring, especially for those with physical or age considerations.

Dojo Kumite and Tournament Kumite

For a more realistic approach to sparring, I personally enjoy "Dojo Kumite." During my earlier days of training, instructors were not concerned with lawsuits, insurance mandates and parent intrusion. We learned to spar without safety gear and hit each other with great intensity. We didn't pause each time we delivered an effective technique, rather we kept sparring until the sensei commanded us to stop. We also learned to "grin and bear" the bruises and pain and without complaining or relying on pain pills. Bengay ointment or Salonpas patches were all we needed!

Dojo kumite is a most realistic approach to self-defense because it teaches participants to endure the challenges of attacks with a greater fighting spirit. Attacks are not limited to certain target areas, and the use of elbows and open hand techniques (such as palm strikes) are often used.

"Tournament kumite," or "point sparring", on the other hand, is still effective, but students need to be aware that if attacked, there will be no referees to award a point when an assumed effective blow is delivered. An assailant is often very resilient to attacks allowed in tournament play, so students must train with dojo kumite to learn to prepare for any possible attacks. Positive realizations that can be attained in tournament kumite are effective approaches to timing, cardio endurance, distancing and self-control drills.

Kaitlin Hausman sharpens her sparring skills by hitting the target correctly to avoid injury.

Jade Elardi also uses a target to sharpen her kicking techniques.

Yakusoku Kumite is essential to enhance clean techniques and to control one's emotion.

Chapter 12
KYO

Often, even from well-trained karate students, we hear such remarks as, "I knew he was going to attack me, but I couldn't do anything about it. He was just too fast for me."

Or you'll hear someone say, "I can't figure it out; I just didn't see him coming." What do these comments really tell us?

We have all experienced that at times when we were attacked and the technique(s) executed by our opponent penetrated right through our defense. But there were also times when our opponent seemed to know exactly when the attack was coming and easily defended against it, no matter how well executed the technique may have been. Does this lead us to conclude that our hope for success, especially in kumite, is a mere 50-50 chance?

We are often told that with sufficient training one can know exactly when the opponent will strike, as well as when to strike an opponent. What is this source of knowledge? Is it an intuitive or an instinctive response? Can it be reduced to theoretical knowledge, which may then in turn be used in practical application? Are we able to read the state of mind a person is in?

Sources of Knowledge

When following the path of karate training and research, I have found there to be three basic sources of knowledge: the teachings of martial arts masters, the combat stories of Budo warriors, and the personal study and experimentation.

Knowledge can be acquired by observing a true master who embodies both knowledge and ability. A good teacher will emphasize four important principles of attack: "sen sen no sen" (seizing the initiative just before the opponent makes a move for attack); "sen no sen" (seizing the initiative at the precise moment an opponent attacks); "go no sen" (seizing the initiative just after the initial attack; and kyo (void) or "kyo no tsuku" (strike at the kyo). The implications of these principles are enormous. To be accomplished in kumite one must not only know the moves of an opponent, but must also be able seize each opportunity in order to raise your percentage for success.

The second source of knowledge is found in the combat stories of past Budo warriors which impart hints and suggestions for victory. For example, Miyamoto Musashi, also known as the "Sword Saint," engaged in as many as 60 duels throughout Japan, and to many, never lost a fight. In his book Go Rin No Sho, (The Book of Five Rings), he refers to "go no sen as tai no sen." He explains, "When the enemy attacks, remain undisturbed but feign weakness. As the enemy reaches you, suddenly move away indicating that you intend to jump aside, then dash in attacking strongly as soon as you see the enemy relax." Others have frequent references to expressions like "Kyo o tsku" or, "Kyo o tsukareru." Kyo is translated in various ways to mean "void," "non-substance," "empty," or, in this context, "an unguarded moment" or "an opening." Thus, "Kyo o tsuku" can be translated as "Strike at the kyo." These explanations are good, but are nevertheless not sufficient enough to allow one to know exactly when such a moment occurs.

The third source of knowledge is acquired by personal study and experimentation. Aside from considering a practitioner's ability to master the many techniques, experimenting and studying the psychological and physiological aspects of kumite are also valuable. I have already touched on this in

Chapter 9 during my discussion on reflexes. Understanding how reflexes occur, one can learn how to create kyo, or a void, in an opponent. This may be accomplished by visual perception (with the eyes), auditory perception (through hearing) and tactile perception (by touch). A quick faking movement, a loud "kiai" or stomping the mat, or a quick touch to an opponent's leg can act as a useful tool of combat. While many students use these tactics randomly, a conscious and deliberate execution of these will cause their opponent to react, thus creating an opening, and an opportunity to break through their defense. Another interesting thought is in the saying, "myo wa kyo-jitsu no kan ni ari." The secret lies between exhaling and inhaling between attack and defense. When startled, one inhales in preparation to flee or fight. After one exhales, and just before inhaling, therein lies a moment of rest, and an opportune time to attack.

    Strive to understand the complete meaning of kyo. The ability to recognize when a person's state of mind is empty, blank or off guard has great benefit in kumite. And in turn, if we can understand the same concept when applied to ourselves, we learn to be more prepared if attacked. When an opponent is not focused, empty, distracted, or in between breaths, they're in kyo. This then becomes the opportune moment to strike. In comparison, when we see our opponent is focused, takes in air and holds their breath, and is mentally prepared, we know this is not the best time to strike. Being successful in creating an opening for an attack will be rewarding, but understanding when <u>not</u> to attack is the true essence of karate-do.

Kaysavan Ragunathan of India, understands kyo and knows exactly when to deliver an effective technique.

Chapter 13
SELF-DEFENSE

"Karate ni sente nashi"
"There is no first attack in karate".
- Gichin Funakoshi

Karate originated as a form of self-defense for citizens of Ryukyu Kingdom, especially during the invasion of Japan's Shimazu Clan of the Satsuma Domain in 1609. Because the Okinawans were not allowed to have weapons, they trained their bodies to be like steel, their hands like swords, and their legs like bamboo posts in order to defend themselves against the Samurai. They developed the use of farm tools as weapons to complement their own physical strength and ability to protect themselves. I'm sure the Okinawan karate practitioners were quite proficient in defending themselves, however I also find it odd that there are not many stories or accounts of actual encounters where karate was actually used, especially from those subjugating them. My conclusion is that since the Okinawans were peace-loving people and treasured their life, they avoided fighting by not provoking their enemy. They learned to "fight to avoid fighting," the same philosophy that I personally embrace today.

Observing nature, we see that predators single out and attack the weak, the young, and the old. It is the same in our society. Human predators look for signs of weakness and insecurity in their victims - a "sure thing." And to these predators, who are mostly males, females and children look like easy marks.

However, for those who study karate, the would-be assailant makes several faulty assumptions. He believes he is more physically superior than his intended target. Relying on this presumed advantage, the male thinks he can easily control and victimize his subject. For females then, the elements that will protect you are a blend of distance, timing, speed, force, mental preparedness, and an unyielding fighting spirit. These elements, properly combined, produce powerful blocks, strikes, kicks, thrusts, and a willingness to escape from harm's way.

Self-defense can be defined as "the right to prevent suffering force or violence through the use of a sufficient level of counteracting force or violence."

It is universally accepted that one can defend themself from harm under appropriate circumstances, such as against injury attempted by another. But specific laws and rules vary from country to country and from jurisdiction to jurisdiction, so it is wise to be familiar with what constitutes as appropriate action when provoked or attacked.

I have taught self-defense tactics by providing courses for armed-forces members, law enforcement officers, hospital staff, veterinary personnel, YMCA and YWCA members, and also for numerous other civic organizations. Teaching techniques that may be applied with sufficient force can assist many in dealing with compromising situations. Of course, being able to talk your way out of a bad situation, or being able to retreat to safety, is the best solution. At times, however, especially when there is an immediate threat of physical harm to you or your family, the use of lethal force may be justifiable.

One cannot attend a couple of self-defense classes and expect to be able to defend themselves if attacked. What I'm conveying here is that it will take more than a few hours to perfect workable techniques. Not only do the physical movements require constant practice, but lessons on mental preparedness are also crucial and need weekly rehearsing. My suggestion is to get a group of your friends and acquaintances together who are serious in practicing self-defense and arrange an ongoing class with a reputable karate instructor.

When it comes to children, it is important for them to be aware of dangerous, suspicious, and inappropriate behavior. They must learn to report uncomfortable signs and observations to their parents, teachers, or proper authorities. Karate training will assist them in staying focused and better in-tune to their surroundings. They will be taught how to maintain a safe distance from uncomfortable situations. Their karate training will also provide them with the confidence and proper self-defense techniques to use against bullies in school, and simultaneously will teach them how not to be a bully as well. They will also be taught to be cordial and not afraid to share pleasantries, even with strangers.

Sets of prescribed routines have been developed for the purpose of defending oneself against an opponent or multiple opponents. These include the "henshuho" techniques, "wazas" and "bunkai/oyo" of the kata. Techniques include defense from the positions of sitting, laying down, walking and standing against grappling, choking, pinning and weapons attacks.

It is also important to understand and practice passive deception. Psychologically, one may control the outcome of a situation, be it aggressive behavior or a physical threat. It is very helpful to deliberately confuse attacker(s) by providing incorrect information to them and concealing true intentions. The ability to control the attacker's mind using words and physical body language may save one's life. For example, communicating to an aggressor that you are recovering from a heart problem, or simply by agreeing with him, may lower his level of aggressive behavior. Playing with your hair, to keep your hand near the aggressor's face. Pulling out a handkerchief, blowing your nose, then dropping it to the ground may distract him. In other words, using any ploy to confuse, distract and diffuse the situation creates the opening to flee or fight.

No matter how proficient one becomes in mastering self-defense techniques, it is always better to avoid a fight if at all possible. Always remember that running away is an effective and useful technique.

I would like to share a personal story of my first encounter in which I practiced self-defense. I attended Sunset Beach Christian School, a private elementary school, on the North Shore of Oahu, Hawaii. Upon graduation, I began my high school studies at Kahuku High School, "Home of the Red Raiders," about 6 miles north from our home. At the time I was already involved in the martial arts, and word got around that I was quite proficient in karate. Almost immediately, one of my classmates had it in for me and wanted to prove to his other buddies that he could "take me." He began giving me "stink eye," and whispered things to his friends in an attempt to intimidate me. Not wanting to have this type of negativity distracting me from my studies, I simply approached him and asked him if he wanted to settle his grievance with me. He raised his voice to gain attention from his friends, but I whispered to him to calm him down, and gave him the opportunity to resolve his issue with me after school. I asked him to meet me behind the agriculture building, alone, where we would be able to settle this once and for all. He agreed. After school, I got on the bus and went home. The next day, before class started, I walked up to him and asked him why he never showed up. He put his head down a bit, shrugged his shoulders and never said a word. From that day forward, he respected me and we eventually became good friends. He never found out that I didn't show up either. This was my first great lesson on how to avoid a fight through proper karate-do training.

SAMPLE OF SELF DEFENSE TECHNIQUES

"No matter how proficient one becomes in mastering self-defense techniques, it is always better to avoid a fight if at all possible."

Kailey Kitts uses various techniques against Steve Schiffman. Palm strikes, knee kicks, stomping on the foot and throwing techniques can prove useful against an assailant.

SELF DEFENSE

Saito-Ha Shito-Ryu Karate-Do

For The Modern Warrior

Michele Barnes demonstrates other effective methods in escaping an assailant's attack.

SELF DEFENSE

Lisa Pickart demonstrates other effective methods in escaping an assailant's attack, and Kelsey Kitts demonstrates a fairly simple over the shoulder throw.

SELF DEFENSE

Sam Manuel is no match against Passage, the tiger.

Grants Pass Public Safety officers improving their self-defense tactics.

Chapter 14
COMPETITION

Those with a competitive spirit will enjoy tournaments. There are smaller dojo competitions as well as worldwide tournaments - those with over 3,000 athletes - where skills may be tested against the most talented "karate-ka" (karate student).

There is much to be gained by competing in well-organized reputable tournaments. The student learns to be physically and mentally prepared, understands discipline at a deeper level, and ultimately develops more depth in character. It is a forum to measure the success of the training program they have endured. The experience of competing with other dojos will test the depth of awareness a student has achieved. There are literally hundreds of tournaments held each year in the United States alone. As in finding a worthy dojo to attend, similarly it is important to seek information of tournaments before deciding to participate in them. Understand their rules of engagement, who the players are, what kind of schools are invited, how their officials are selected and how organized the event is. Check to see if the event will be in a safe environment; if there will be certified medical personnel on-hand with adequate first-aid equipment and supplies, if there will be ambulance service and even if security will be provided. Do the promoters have a good track record, and are they affirming healthy "Budo-based" (positive ways for preventing conflict) techniques and attitudes?

Tournaments that are worthy of participation are those that embrace the principles of classical Karate-do and structure their competition accordingly. Then you know that rules are clearly defined, and that officials and coaches are trained and certified and will display respect, courtesy and professionalism.

The safety of the athletes is always a priority. Every aspect of the event should be a class act. Baron Pierre de Coubertin, founder of the International Olympic Committee wrote, "It is necessary to maintain in sport the noble and chivalrous character which distinguished it in the past, so that it shall continue to be part of the education of present day peoples in the same way that the sport served so wonderfully in the times of ancient Greece. The public has a tendency to transform the Olympic athlete into the paid gladiator. These two attitudes are not compatible."

Competition often times places a financial burden for many who just don't have the funds to travel, pay for lodging, food, and registration fees. For this reason, I have created a competition for kata which I named "Cyber Kata Competition." Participants from all over the globe now have the opportunity to compete with others without having to travel from their own dojo. The Competition Director decides what the age and experience level the competition will be. Instructors then submit videos of the competitors, from two different angles, to the Chief Referee. Appointed judges then score the athlete's performance and submit their technical and artistic score to the referee. A nominal fee is charged for processing and mailing the awards to the winners. Cyber Kumite Competition is still in the developmental phase, but holds great promise in the future of karate competition.

During my days of competition, trophies were awarded only to the first, second and third place winners, as reminders of true achievement. In recent years, however, regardless of an individual's effort or level of skill, all participants receive ribbons or awards. Not only does this diminish the value of true accomplishment, it also sends a risky message, especially to children. As children are exposed to the realities of life, they will start to find themselves disappointed when they do not receive anything for their efforts. Awards in life's competitions are not guaranteed, but if one keeps trying and does not give up, they will eventually receive "medals" for their successes. The journey to the winner's podium will be difficult, but it is attainable if one keeps trying with desire, discipline, correct attitude and good coaching. For this reason, I believe that organizers of tournaments should be mindful when it comes to presenting awards.

Renzo Marchini (aka) and Nico Yardas (ao) both executing great techniques at the Oregon State Championship. Nico received the point for the face thrust.

Matt Collins executing an effective uramawashi geri to score three points at the Saito Cup in Oregon.

John Isabelo preparing to score on his opponent in a tournament in Hawaii.

TKFI Competition Team headed by Tony Mendonca in Reno, Nevada.

U.S. National Team - Number 1 in team points at the World Cup at McMasters University in Canada.

Ubiratan de Souza Lima from Brazil (TKFI Director of South America), wins the Gold.

Winners at the Grants Pass Invitational Championship, held at the Performance Art Center, at the Grants Pass High School.

Saito Karate-do Classic at Grants Pass High School.

THE OLYMPIC DREAM

Ever since I can remember - as early as in the 1960s - instructors would often remark that karate was soon going to be an Olympic sport. Four years later still nothing, and then four more... until decades had passed without even a consideration from the International Olympic Committee. Not until I began taking an interest in competition as an organizer and director did I come to realize why karate had not been accepted as and Olympic sport.

The JKA (Japan Karate Association), the largest and most powerful karate organization at one time, could have been instrumental in getting karate into the Olympics. Instead, many of the pioneers who were sent out to teach Shotokan in countries throughout the world had a "fraternal" attitude, so those not practicing Shotokan or JKA karate would not be accepted into their tightly-knit society. Many instructors, mainly Hidetaka Nishiyama, (who later founded the International Traditional Karate Federation), ostracized other Okinawan and Japanese styles and wanted to have world domination for sports karate. But as history has revealed, his objective backfired. Political arrogance and not accepting other viable karate styles or organizations kept karate away from being accepted to the Olympics.

In 1990, the WKF (World Karate Federation) emerged as the world-governing body of karate, and became a member of the International Olympic Committee (IOC). Presently, it has 191 member countries and over ten million members. It is headquartered is in Madrid, Spain, and the president, at this time, is Antonio Espinos. WKF discussions are now held with the intent of molding karate into an exciting sport with more public appeal. This led to changes in rules, officiating gestures and terms, and point management in kata and kumite competitions.

Finally on August 3, 2016, the IOC approved karate for inclusion in the 2020 Summer Games in Tokyo, Japan. But then once again, partly due to the exclusion of other karate styles, grievances from other viable organizations, and again more political posturing, karate has been excluded from the 2024 Olympic Games in Paris, and possibly the 2028 Olympic Games in Los Angeles.

In my 23 years of service to sport karate, I have concluded that, instead of having the common denominator as the athlete and the betterment of the sport, too many organization leaders are motivated by personal vendettas against each other, power, ego, money and "name recognition." However, this is slowly changing for the betterment of sport karate, especially here in the Pacific Northwest. The older generation sensei, myself included, are taking a step back and allowing their senior instructors to be more proactive in the competition arena. I am witnessing a more cohesive working attitude that is appreciated by all the participants. Instructors are more supportive of each other and are not allowing personal differences to result in banning athletes from participation in a competition. The quality of officiating is rising to a higher standard and ensuring fairness to all competitors. I hope this is also happening throughout the rest of the United States, as well as universally, in this sport.

Tony Mendonca at the United States Olympic Training Center.

I truly hope that karate does become an Olympic sport, but only with the principles and precise techniques taught in the dojo. Meanwhile, I will be content in teaching students how to be great competitors in the competition of life.

CAGE AND ULTIMATE FIGHTING COMPETITION

In recent years, promoters have used the martial arts to attract a breed of fighters to engage in a fighting style that resembles the battle of the gladiator. Personally, I do not wish for any of my students to participate in this type of competition where the goal is to beat the opponent by a knockout, tap out, or by having the referee stop the match due to perceived severe injury. I'm certain some participants in this sport have had several concussions, and probably some even severe brain damage. Yet as long as the promoters are raking in the money and drawing in thousands of spectators, this type of competition is not going away.

I would hope that our karate students are saner than that, and wish to not jeopardize their well-being just to appease their ego. An interesting subject for discussion would be ascertaining what causes our society to enjoy congregating in masses to watch men and women destroy each other.

COMPETITION IN LIFE

Competition in life begins even before birth. Hundreds of white squiggly cells swim to win the opportunity to fertilize an egg. From that moment competition is unavoidable.
- You compete with your siblings to establish a pecking order.
- You compete to acquire friends.
- You compete to be accepted to a team or group.
- You compete for grades to receive honors and scholarships.
- You compete for higher ranks in the military.
- You compete in college and universities with your classmates in hopes to secure a high paying job.
- You compete for jobs and contracts.
- You compete with others for a mate.
- You compete for votes.
- You compete to be selected for high paying salaries in professional sports.

And the list goes on. But you can see that competition exists in almost every aspect of your life.

The famous Chinese strategist, Sun Tzu, in his book The Art of War, understood the importance of the principles and ethics that must guide a nation in competition. Especially in war (as in sports and business as well), victory should leave a positive and lasting impression on everyone concerned. In other words, to achieve a lasting victory, those that have been conquered must be treated with dignity and respect. To ruthlessly conquer will only cause revolts, conflict and anger.

In sports, for example, Japanese baseball teams will allow the opposing team to catch up if they are way behind, in order to save embarrassment. In karate competition, champions in Japan who have won their share of gold medals, are asked to retire in order to provide others the opportunity to share the podium. It is a wholesome way to preserve respect and honor. Perhaps more sports, relationships and businesses can be encouraged to incorporate respect and honor for others in order to have a win-win outcome.

In my opinion, although we value the importance of setting goals to win or to accomplish something, it is the process of reaching and attaining your goals that will leave a positive impact on yourself and others. Sadly, Western culture historically has carelessly pushed others aside to obtain their goals. I think that initially Americans took Herbert Hoover's 1928 successful presidential campaign speech of "rugged individualism" and "self reliance" to heart, and that restored American confidence and hope. Unfortunately, many lost sight of including others happiness and success in their victories, and the competition for power and wealth has turned some to greed and selfishness.

I wish not to be misunderstood... I am not condemning people who have an entrepreneurial spirit and become successful in what they do. I do caution, however, when their personal goals are their only ultimate reward. To take unfair advantage of others destroys the intended spirit of America.

To be successful in competition, I often discuss in my workshops and seminars, Stephen R. Covey's "<u>7 Habits of Highly Effective People</u>." Using my own acronym "PEFWUSS," I am able to echo these important HABITS:

• Habit 1: Be Proactive®

Take responsibility for your actions in life. Too often, blame is placed on everyone except yourself for bad decisions and poor choices. If you wish to be successful you must stay focused and disciplined, set realistic goals and be an active participant in what you do. Don't allow yourself to keep reacting to variations of external circumstances. Take the bull by the horn, take charge, and assume responsibility of your choices in life.

• Habit 2: Begin With the End in Mind®

Don't leave it up to fate to dictate what you are going to do. Instead, have a clear vision of your future goals. Prepare accordingly by having all the necessary tools in order to make your journey a reality.

• Habit 3: Put First Things First®

Prioritize! Don't allow distractions to steer you off your course. Keep things in proper order of importance to bring you to your vision much quicker.

• Habit 4: Think Win-Win®

Like the Japanese baseball team who is way ahead and allows the other team to score, thoughtfully find ways to share your victory with a positive attitude in order to build great relationships with all concerned.

• Habit 5: Seek First to Understand, Then to Be Understood®

Don't jump to conclusions and interrupt those who are trying to share a problem or concern with you. Instead, listen carefully and gather as many details as possible before providing advice.

• Habit 6: Synerize®

Trust those that you feel that can assist you in reaching your goals. Their contributions spotlight their strengths and expertise and will help you tremendously. This is better than just trying to do everything yourself. A perfect example of synergy was when the Walt Disney Company and the Amateur Athletic Union (AAU) facilitated the magical creation of ESPN's Wide World of Sports Complex in the Walt Disney World Resort, in Bay Lake, Florida.

The AAU is one of the largest, non-profit, multi-sport organizations in the world. It has over 700,000 members and 150,000 volunteers across 41 sports programs in 55 U.S districts.

The Walt Disney Company's mission is to entertain, inform and inspire people around the globe. They are the world's premier entertainment company. Understanding the importance of sports, they thoughtfully came up with the idea of building a major sports complex to host championships, practices and training programs. They had the marketing skills and funds, but wanted (and needed) the AAU's sporting experience to assist them in finalizing their plans. It was through using each other's strengths, they synergized and made this vision a reality. I count myself as fortunate to have been a part of this creation.

• Habit 7: Sharpen the Saw®

Just as a tool that does the job it was intended to, you need to keep positive habits in good working order and use them. Good habits need to be reinforced with repetition. They have to be repeated often in order to make them so powerful that they will reward you (and others) along your life's journey.

Competition in life is knowing how to compete. You have to decide who can help you in becoming a strong, positive and successful competitor. Competing with the right components, you will be rewarded with lasting happiness and contentment by treating your opponents with dignity and respect.

Wholesome karate competition assists students to prepare for the many competitions in life with confidence, fortitude, hope and vision.

Kata practice provides the opportunity to focus on what lies within us.

Chapter 15
CONSIDERATIONS FOR PARENTS

A young tree with many branches, but weak roots, will not withstand the test of nature. It is the same with children. To grow strong and endure, they too must have a solid foundation. Through discipline, governed by love and consistency, parents provide their children with the balance that is necessary for healthy growth.

By enrolling your children in the practice of karate-do, you are strengthening their foundation. From their practice and study they will learn many important values that relate directly to life, and this will enable them to face life's many challenges.

In the practice of karate-do, your children will learn the many aspects of dealing with conflict. Psychologically, they will be taught to be aware of their environment, to interpret body language and signals, to keep their emotions in check, and to prepare for the unexpected.

The underlying foundation of their training will be based on discipline, respect, honor, courage, and self-control.

Karate training will further their understanding that they alone are responsible for their actions, and that they alone have the choice of becoming successful or facing failure in life.

The training provided in karate is not pain-free. Students learn to lick their minor wounds and tolerate painful muscles after rigorous training. Life hurts - emotionally and physically - but suffering does not need to require pharmaceutical intervention that can lead to addiction of drugs. Karate will teach students to increase their pain tolerance and deal with pain holistically by using natural remedies.

Parents have a great responsibility in raising and teaching their children. They too should understand "Shu•Ha•Ri," as discussed in Chapter 2. A wheel turns smoothly on a well-balanced axle, yet if too tightly placed, it becomes choked and function is lost. Parents often are either too lenient or too strict with their children, and so striving to find balance is endless. The assistance that you give your child can rebound adversely, depending on how much help you provide. The support parents may need in voicing and teaching the critical fundamentals of positive growth can be shared by a responsible karate teacher. Once you have found such a sensei, the parent must learn to trust him and not attempt to micro-manage their instructions. Working as a team as a united front will ensure positive outcomes.

Parents should allow their children to understand, and feel, guilt and shame. In my adolescent years, my parents taught my brothers and me how to be responsible at home, at school, and at play. Whenever our actions were associated with wrongdoing, we felt guilt and remorse that our responsibility fell short of their expectations. Whether someone witnessed our wrongdoing or not, we felt embarrassed and ashamed that both our reputation and our parent's reputation would be tainted. In other words, we felt guilt due to what we had done, and felt shameful for doing it. This natural part of life which keeps society moral and decent is fading away, for young and old alike. Without guilt and shame there is little motivation to avoid wrongdoing.

Parents and teachers need to reprimand children when they misbehave or make mistakes. Importantly though, these rebukes need to be balanced with nurturance so that children do not associate it with who they are, but rather what they did. Children need to be held accountable for their actions, acknowledge their mistakes, correct the behavior, apologize for their shortcomings, and then move on. Dwelling on mistakes, or constantly reminding them of past mistakes, creates unhealthy guilt and shame and can have the adverse effect of teaching them to shun these feelings altogether. Then emotional disorders may ultimately occur often leading to depression, self-hatred, anger toward others and anxiety. The practice of instilling healthy attitudes toward guilt and shame manifests into children becoming productive and valued members of the family and the community.

Spirituality is another topic for discussion. Many kids who were raised going to a place of worship, Sunday school, or youth group often drop out after high school because they feel they were unfulfilled with lessons of genuine spirituality. While not true in all cases, there is a growing number of our children who disrespect spiritual authority altogether and either are unable or unwilling to stand for truth, even when it is taught to them. I believe that the prime cause of a child's spiritual deficiency begins at home. Parents are failing their children by word and example, and by putting other things first. In my opinion, parents should not deny their children spiritual training that will provide them with hope, duty, commitment to their moral compass, truth and faith. As in all areas of training, learning and applying spirituality and morality should not be secondary to any other distraction (like sports, electronic devices, social media, or whatever pop culture fad is happening at the time).

I believe all humans have a strong spiritual aptitude and that their presence in the world is significant, and that everyone can contribute to creating wholesomeness and joy in the world. I feel it is important to teach children to feel reverence and respect for our planet and for our solar system and see all the natural beauty they hold. Just as the world turns with precision and harmony, so can we do our share in connecting and sharing with our fellow brothers and sisters. Not all things in life work out as we hope, however with proper guidance and training, children learn how to make the most of what they have.

Parents must set a good example not only for their own children, but also for other children they interact with and their parents. When parents use foul speech, dress inappropriately, and use immoral behavior, stumbling blocks for their children are created. Other children's parents are put on the spot when witnessing this behavior as well. Don't sit idly by and allow yourself to become too complacent by not inspecting your daily actions. Influence and encourage your children with positive behavior, preparing them to feel capable when faced with the many worldly ills that lie ahead. Be the person who sets positive examples for your children, and others, to follow.

Another important consideration is commitment. Children need to be committed to their training program. If you are their parent or guardian, you will need to honor commitment by bringing your children to classes regularly and on time, and also by meeting their financial obligation. The majority of students attending my honbu dojo have to commit to a two-year program. We provide many positive and difficult challenges to our students, but with that comes strict guidelines and firmness they may be unused to in the teaching realm. Once students understand and accept the clarity of dojo training, etiquette, and manners, they are able to reach their goals through hard work, effort, and commitment. Students who do not honor commitment often find excuses to stop attending classes, especially when faced with difficulties. It is so disappointing when students are allowed to drop out without having learned the important life lessons of commitment, perseverance, and patience, and all the rewards and benefits that come from hard work.

Another consideration involving commitment that should be addressed is when children take interest in sports or other school activities when already committed to a karate training program. We encourage students to investigate and participate in other interests, and as a parent you should do so as well. However, parents should remember, and stress to their children, that their first commitment was to their karate practice. If they do decide to pursue another interest, ideally they should wait until their karate commitment has expired. Another option is to permit them to participate in other activities only if they are willing to balance their time equally with karate, while also taking into account the time needed to complete their homework and family duties as well.

To instill and maintain a positive spirit in your children, ask them to demonstrate what they have learned in class. Work with them on their promotion requirements (such as the terms, history, community service, and responsibilities) at home. Schedule a time for them to practice at home for a minimum of 15 minutes each day, or even better, several times a day. It is important that children feel they have your interest and support in their training.

Teach children to fight the habit of procrastination, because if not addressed and corrected they will experience high levels of stress that will follow them into their adult years. By helping them to stay motivated and accomplish tasks in a timely manner, you will keep laziness from creeping into their daily lives and becoming a habit that will be hard, if not impossible, to break.

Children learn to have great respect for their instructors, sometimes more so than their parents or teachers in school. When your children's behavior is less than favorable, remind them that their sensei will be very disappointed to hear about it!

In Hawaii, adults are called "Uncle" or "Aunty," even if they are not related. This special familial and cultural relationship provides a setting for mutual respect. Similarly, the dojo environment nurtures this type of respect where the teacher equally respects the students and trains them as if they were their own children.

Should you decide to watch your children's classes, remember that in the dojo they are in the "custody" of their instructor on the mat. Your children will learn to listen and follow their sensei's instructions, rather than constantly look over their shoulder and listen to your comments from the dojo observation area. If you have difficulty not engaging with your children when they are on the mat, it is best for your children that you leave the dojo. Or better yet, sign up for classes and train with your children on the mat!

"Your children are not your children.
They are the sons and daughters of Life's longing for itself.
They come through you but not from you,
And though they are with you yet they belong not to you.
You may give them your love but not your thoughts,
For they have their own thoughts.
You may house their bodies but not their souls,
For their souls dwell in the house of tomorrow,
which you cannot visit, not even in your dreams.
You may strive to be like them, but seek not to make them like you.
For life goes not backward nor tarries with yesterday.
- Khalil Gibran

Lastly, I will leave you with a few troubling observations, and some positive recommendations that will help to arm your children with the necessary tools to build a hopeful future for themselves.

Of late I have been noticing that some children, especially boys, seem to be clueless on how to navigate and survive in their daily lives without parental influence. Parents shield them from experiencing problems, thus not allowing them the opportunity to solve them on their own. So, in essence, these children have become overly dependent on their parents. To avoid this conundrum, parents should teach their children the necessary skills of problem-solving, and then let them try, on their own, to correct the problem without constant interference. Parents who think they are helping their children by constantly stepping in are <u>not</u>, in reality, helping at all. This behavior only stunts their children's growth, both emotionally and developmentally. Children must be allowed to learn their lessons from trial and error. By doing this sooner rather than later, children will have a much better chance negotiating the realities of their lives.

Another personal observation I've had is that, in this day and age, many parents want to be their children's best friend. Although this may seem plausible and "modern" these days, it is not beneficial to convey that you and your children are equals. As a parent, it is your duty to set boundaries and follow through during this "structure and rules" period in their life. When you are successful in setting healthy boundaries with your children, you will find they actually do want, need, and enjoy having a defined structure and rules in their lives. This helps them to feel safe. So no matter how difficult it may be, parents need to be strong and unyielding at times in order to instill inner strength in their children. Only then will they truly be able to weather the storms that lie ahead.

In addition, parents need to trust the instructors that are teaching their children in school and at the dojo. At times your child may face disciplinary action due their bad behavior. It is best if you do not come to their rescue, coddle them, or tell them dismissively that either the teacher (or they) "must be having a bad day." Children need to be held accountable so they see what they have done in order to change their behavior. At the same time, it is important that parents never make light of children's negative behavior when it is brought to their attention. This removes the lesson that needs to be taught at that time, and is done just so the parent feels better because the situation makes them feel uncomfortable. The lesson is all that is important.

Three generations of the Hatch family leave a positive mark on the residents of Southern Oregon.

Jeffrey, MaryJo, Tony, David and Riley.

With the rise of the "stranger danger" warnings taught to children these days, parents instruct their children not to speak to strangers. While I agree that children should not allow a stranger to get physically close to them, I believe when someone says "Hello" or "Good Morning" in public, children should return the same courtesy without assuming that all strangers are bad. As parents, and in the dojo, we can properly teach children how to assess a situation and be prepared how to act should the need arise.

Another important life lesson is teaching children how to work and earn money so they may purchase certain items they want, such as a special toy or a bicycle. A child shouldn't come to expect these special things to flow into their lives just because they've "been good." Aside from their daily chores, which is an obligatory family contribution, children should learn to ask their parents for additional work in order to earn the money necessary to make their special purchase. By having "skin in the game" they learn to value their item(s), appreciate what they have earned, and strive to take good care of these purchases.

Parents are always welcome to assist in the fun games for our "Lil Dragon's" classes.

OTHER CONSIDERATIONS FOR PARENTS

The benefits you are receiving when enrolling you or your children in a karate school:

- Someone to look up to.
- A personal therapist.
- Someone to help guide you through life.
- The comfort of having someone in your corner 24/7.
- Someone to remind you to always seek the best for yourself and to always choose the better path.
- A personal trainer who will help you with: workouts, diet, strength, flexibility, and weight loss.
- A guiding light for the entire family who will teach you humility, patience, respect for yourself and others, courtesy, listening skills, and discipline.
- Someone to teach you to be accountable for your actions.
- Someone to teach you to stand up for yourself and others.
- Someone to hug you when you are feeling sad, help you up when you have fallen, and stand by you - even if no one else in your life will.
- Someone who will share not only their martial arts knowledge, but also their wisdom of life.
- Someone who will invest their all into you, even when you don't believe in yourself.
- The ability to see that you are never alone. Your dojo is your family, through thick and thin, and are all better together.

If you still believe you are paying too much for this hobby, consider this: Would a doctor, lawyer, plumber, carpenter, dentist, chef, mechanic, dressmaker, shop owner, or therapist offer all of these services in addition to their standard services?

Chapter 16
YOU THE STUDENT

For you who are interested in karate, or who are already training at a dojo, it is important to understand that a proper attitude is required. Having a positive attitude will determine your willingness to learn. Be aware that having preconceived thoughts about karate may have influenced you with false teachings and beliefs. You will learn that skills take time to learn and must begin with sound fundamentals. You will not be taught how to swing the "Nunchaku" or engage in acrobatic movements as you might expect. Instead, you will learn how to achieve a positive attitude that will motivate you to learn life's lessons and will arm you with successful techniques to "win over" yourself. To pave the way to success you need to stay motivated, despite the challenges you are confronted with. To believe otherwise will certainly send your practice in a downward spiral leading to unsatisfied results.

The sensei will begin by uncovering your attitudes on learning. He will then use this information to help you shape a more positive attitude toward learning. The student must let go of their ego and other obstacles that prevent them from learning with motivation and gratification.

We incorporate "Direct Teaching" and "Cooperative Learning" methods in our dojo. In the Direct Teaching method, our instructors teach the required materials and constantly review what is learned. When using the Cooperative Learning method you will see groups of students working together or one-to-one mentoring. Both methods encourage all students to work towards a common goal. We also will provide opportunities for less confident and shy students to break through their obstacles, and this is achieved by having them lead warm-ups or demonstrate techniques for others in their class.

For those who sign up and have already had some martial arts training, it is important to remain humble. Rather than bringing forth excuses during your training based on your previous training methods, take whatever you have learned and simply incorporate it with your new beginning. Do not fault yourself if your previous teacher wasn't teaching you properly, and just be appreciative that you are now learning correctly.

Remember to acknowledge where you are in your training. Don't worry about how others are fairing or make excuses to appear "cool." Stick to your training habits, but make sure they are good ones. Stay focused in accomplishing one thing at a time. Be conservative in learning new things, but aggressive in trying to reach your goals. Let go of your ego, and accept the results of your daily training. Not everything goes according to plan, but with a healthy attitude, you'll unleash the courage to press on without inner tensions.

I have discussed the need for commitment in a previous chapter for parents. I cannot overly stress the importance of being bound to your study of karate. Your determination to learn all that is offered should never be altered by compromises. Unlike many sports, karate is not seasonal. The life-learning skills taught in karate go hand-in-hand with your training, and are so vital in arming you with the necessary behavior and devotion to achieving your goals. Another important requirement of commitment is to be on time. Doing so demonstrates that you are diligent and dependable and therefore can be trusted. I teach my students to follow this simple and easy to remember edict; "To be early is to be on time, to be on time is to be late, and to be late is disrespectful and rude."

At times in life you may be picked on, bullied or made fun of. When someone repeatedly displays aggressive behavior or cruelty toward you, it is important to look at and clearly see what you are "advertising on your billboard." If you are not happy with what you see, perhaps you should change your "advertisement." Instead of displaying, "Pick on me. I lack confidence, I hate it here...," try exuding "I am confident, I smile and keep my head held high so I can share the sunshine with you, I love life....". Difficult as it may seem, it is possible to restore and display the many positive traits you already possess. Karate training will certainly help with self-confidence and body language.

Other thoughts for you to consider and practice:

Do not speak in a foreign language in company of those who do not understand your tongue.

Do not be too hasty to speak, especially when your parents or your Sensei is speaking to you. Hear them carefully and ponder their message.

Associate yourself with good people. It is better to be alone than to be ruining your reputation by keeping bad company.

Always keep your promises if you wish to be respected by family, friends and acquaintances.

Maintain a healthy attitude, have a willingness to learn, commit to your goals, and your actions will keep you on a path of productive practice that will let you experience the richness of karate-do.

Karate is not seasonal. The life-learning skills taught in karate go hand-in-hand with your training, and are so vital in arming you with the necessary behavior and devotion to achieving your goals.

Chapter 17
EXAMINING THE SENSEI

"It is not the way of the warrior to be shamed and avoid death."
- Samurai Mototada, Torii (1600)

This statement should hold true with all sensei. Although sensei of today do not subscribe to the austere code of honor of the samurai, nor commit ritual suicide ("Seppuku") when shamed or dishonored, they should take the stricter path they have pledged to follow. Their conduct should be beyond reproach. They should always be very serious in their teaching of karate and maintain only the highest standards in their instruction.

Who better to guide students, polishing them to become a shining being? None other than the sensei, the one who has found the path that leads to excellence, and can better define it for students to follow. So, in general terms, a sensei is a teacher.

A sensei should provide their students with inspiration. Students will come to respect their teacher and feel comfortable enough to confide in him in times of need. Sensei should never use their students as tools to satisfy their ego or to prove how superior they are to them. On the contrary, a sensei should teach students to discover their strengths and weaknesses so they may grow and flourish in the martial arts and life.

Good sensei walk a defined line which is based on sound principles and clear understanding. Many students entering the dojo will, for the first time in their lives, be in an environment governed by tradition, respect, formality, and discipline. I was raised in Hawaii with a close connection to Japanese traditions and upbringing, so it was not foreign for me to embrace the rigid instructions taught in the dojo. However, many parents today have brought forth a more modern approach to discipline, respect, and formalities and so influence their children to train and yield with caution. Good or bad, these elements are to be considered and must guide each sensei's actions. For example, if the atmosphere is overly strict and rigid, it will be self-defeating as students may not understand this kind of training regimen, at least not right away. I have a few suggestions that all sensei can incorporate in their practice to achieve balance and strengthen their ability to teach more capably, thoroughly, and accurately.

Just as parents guide and direct their children to ensure healthy growth, a sensei must do the same with their students. To accomplish this, one must have the desire to teach and have the proper attitude at all times. With these critical prerequisites, sensei will find themselves constantly striving to improve their own skills. Obviously, sensei who pursue their own growth will greatly enrich their students' abilities to grasp the intricacies of karate. Students will notice the added confidence in their teacher and will respond with a surge of positive, flowing energy. Training will be extremely rewarding when this occurs.

For students to grasp the underlying morality of karate-do, the aspects of discipline, etiquette, and honor must be an integral part of the program. The sensei who comes across as a remote, cold drill sergeant running a regimented boot camp will fail. Many students, especially the younger ones, will quickly quit such a program and enroll in any of the numerous upbeat and entertaining exercise programs, or "McDojos," offered today.

Dojos should also not overplay Eastern culture and traditions, as this tends to minimize wholesome communication when over-emphasized. This results in misunderstandings with students. For example, it is always respectful for students to be mindful of their sensei's presence and bow. But sensei should never demand that a student fall on their knees and bow. There are also karate instructors that force their students to be subservient and carry their bag or briefcase. Good students should be aware and attentive to their instructor's needs and offer to assist whenever possible, without being told. It is a matter of respect.

It is especially important in the beginning and intermediate classes that the environment be firm yet sensible. Classes are enjoyable when the presentation of each lesson is varied and changing. By doing so, students will find classes exciting and will not become bored. A sensei should watch for signals from students that indicate they are pleased with the skills they are performing. Too much time should not be spent assisting one student while others are waiting for the next command. Instead, they can continue to practice on their own while helping others. Remember, the beginning of any venture is usually the most tentative stage since students are more insecure and unsure of themselves. Although they may be learning techniques and katas, they haven't had the time necessary to absorb the deeper meaning and purpose of karate. Teachers must be patient, kind, understanding, and, most of all, encouraging. Students respect teachers who bring these qualities to their teaching, and then students are willing to accept firm guidance.

This is not to say that teachers should not strive to bring these same qualities to their advanced classes and students. Variation, stimulation, and enjoyment are keys to any good teaching program. But as students increasingly advance and begin to grasp the broader picture and the deeper significance of karate-do, the harder they will be willing to work and discipline themselves to arrive at each successive plateau. Nevertheless, students, no matter what the rank, are human beings first, and, as such, need encouragement, respect, and kindness.

Karate teachers who have immersed themselves in learning and maintaining the integrity of this treasured martial art are rooted in the tradition of righteousness. You would never hear about the true samurai who uses his sword to purposely make his adversary suffer, no matter what evil he has committed. If he had to draw his sword against his enemy, the intention was to maintain his worthiness of honor by ending their life with precision and mercy. To use his sword with the intention of making his enemy suffer would make him a lessor man than his enemy.

Similarly, the karate instructor has to teach students to avoid stooping lower than their adversaries. Matthew 5:38-42 says, "an eye for and eye, and a tooth for a tooth." But it continues to say, "that ye resist not evil: but whosoever shall smite thee on the right cheek, turn to him the other also." In karate one must perfect their skills to the highest level in order to understand this. For the average layperson who learns karate only for self-defense, the immediate goal is different so the teaching might become different. Instructors may instruct students to spit at their adversary or kick sand in his eyes to impair his vision when being attacked. These underhanded methods may prove useful in escaping from harm's way out in the real world, but may also lead to negative behavior and a self-centered attitude in everyday living. If you are teaching students to take advantage of another person by using dishonest means, no matter how much it may help it will make it very difficult for them to fully understand and then empower the influence of righteousness.

Sensei who train with other sensei take advantage of an excellent method of improving technical and teaching skills. By training together once a month, teachers can share ideas, problems, and any pertinent matters necessary to strengthen themselves and aid in their personal growth. This type of training also creates a sense of community that is vital to the organization.

Sensei who make no effort to train together use the excuse that, because they are actively teaching, they do not have to train. The very possible end result of this thought process will be that students will sense that their sensei's teaching lacks depth, and then they will become bored and drop out. Worse, injuries will occur more frequently, especially when students become stronger and more developed. Teachers who do not train usually have to prove their abilities in an unprofessional manner to retain some semblance of respect from their students. Their own lack of control and confidence is readily seen by the students. When such teachers are threatened in sparring, what control they do have is lost and injuries result.

Good teachers do not cater to their stronger students just to improve their dojo's tournament records. Worthy sensei understand the needs of all their students, including those who need delicate attention. The good sensei will give these students the extra encouragement and support they need. Talking to students on a one-to-one basis is an excellent way for teachers to learn the true personalities of their students and determine their inner needs. A compassionate sensei always has a welcoming ear to listen carefully. This individual contact also enables sensei to structure their classes in a manner which better meets the needs of the students.

I fault no sensei for making money from teaching, selling DVDs, books or using other revenue generators. I do caution sensei that operate their dojos to make huge amounts of money, and who do not provide instruction based on sound fundamentals in techniques, moral guidance and positive karate principles. I have often seen instructors water down the very concepts of karate-do that need to be taught to all they instruct, such as patience, discipline, fortitude, commitment and perseverance. Then, in essence, that dojo becomes merely a playground and promotions become prizes rather than deserving achievements.

Wise sensei should, at times, test their students by taking views diametrically opposed their own just to see their student's reactions. Whatever the method, the true sensei always will work with each student's well-being in mind.

Questions should always be welcomed. Students should be taught to keep their questions on the subject at hand, as this will maintain coherence. It should be made clear if the teacher wishes students to raise their hands. If a question is asked of students, many will respond by raising their hands, rather than immediately answer what is asked of them. Often, even in school, students will raise their hands in response to a question asked, but have no idea what the answer is. Teaching and permitting students to respond effectively and immediately to questions prepares them for mental, physical or spiritual attacks.

Students need to have fun in their training. Games should be devised in the dojo to encourage students to enjoy their karate training. For example, a fun activity is the "Sumo Challenge." A round ring is defined by a thick rope, and the objective is to have two opponents push, pull or throw the other out of the ring, or have them fall while inside the ring. The use of bosu balls is another favorite activity for the younger students. They learn to stay balanced on the balls, otherwise, they are told, they will fall into the "shark-infested waters below." These fun methods of training increase productivity and confidence, and also instill courage and a willingness to try something new.

Effective sensei should expand the dojo's activities to include beach training, hikes, picnics, pot-lucks, fishing, Karaoke, and other enjoyable functions that the entire family may participate in. These activities also promote greater friendships among the students and lead to mutual support and encouragement. This spirit adds vitality to their karate training.

Respect can be seen as mutual regard for personal qualities, abilities and achievements by both the instructor and student. Sensei need to be humble. At times students may perform a technique better than their instructor. This should always make instructors proud, and they should praise their student's ability rather than find criticism in their performance. We can all find areas that need improving, but at these times it is always best to just mutually enjoy their accomplishments with them.

Students who lose concentration or are unwilling to train with your higher expectations may frustrate you. Instead of giving them push-ups or "time-outs," they should be asked to go to the front of the class to demonstrate the technique being taught. By doing this, a sensei might be pleasantly surprised with the outcome!

Sensei should also use training tools such as mitts, heavy bags, jump ropes, ladders, rings, kettle bells, and foam rollers, to name a few. These tools will give immediate feedback to students and provide them the opportunity to fine-tune their techniques.

Instructors should plan wisely before deciding to teach part-time, or deciding to make it a full time commitment. To be successful, the latter choice will involve sound business planning. With all the financial, legal, and teaching responsibilities, the quality of karate taught to students should never be watered down. I have observed sensei that become more interested in increasing their profits than with providing their students with the kind of training they deserve and expect. It is very easy to be swept by this type of practice if their state-of- the-art dojo has an operating expense of several thousand dollars each month. Remember, students will do whatever is required of them. If they fall short of their full potential, it is the instructor that has denied them the ability to achieve excellence due to their greed, ego, and other shortcomings.

At times, students may fall into unexpected hardship and are not able to pay for their tuition. Rather than provide lessons at no cost, it is more mutually beneficial if they are allowed the opportunity to come up with another arrangement; perhaps trading their service to the dojo for attendance in their karate classes. In this way a sensei is keeping value in their instruction and teaching their students to work out a win-win situation, rather than teaching them to expect anything for free. If the dojo doesn't require lawn or garden maintenance, you might ask them to provide a few hours a month of community service.

Instructors will often join organizations related to the sport of karate. Healthy organizations can serve their members in many ways. Some of these ways include instilling a sense of family, and imparting knowledge in kata (Bunkai/Oyo), kihons, kumite and self-defense techniques. Organizations benefit each other by instilling a sense of mutual respect between members, acknowledging rank acceptance offering homologation from other instructors, as well as many other benefits. But a troubling occurrence I see becoming more prevalent today is that sports organizations are slowly undermining non-sports organizations. They are demanding dan ranks in their requirements to grant official's licenses. They impose fees for members, fees for coaches and officials, and fees for mandatory clinics and certifications. Instructors who consider sports organizations to be more beneficial than organizations that lean more to the traditional values of karate will often stray from their commitment to the organization they once pledged allegiance to.

"All people have the spirit - it is just a matter of careful guidance. It is just like jade in a matrix - if you throw it away, it's just a rock, but if you cut and polish it, it is a gem."

- Gaoan

"Karate helps you make quick decisions without hesitation. Constant practice keeps your decisions the correct one."
D. Saito

Chapter 18
NUTRITION

Growing up in Hawaii under merely adequate conditions, we ate whatever was served to us. If we complained, we didn't eat. Nevertheless, my mom was a masterful meal preparer. For example, she would slice one steak into very small pieces, mix it with vegetables, and serve it with rice to feed all 8 of us. We enjoyed oxtail stew, miso soup, shoyu chicken, omelets made with tuna and green onions, lots of fresh fish my dad would spear, and of course spam musubi. My brothers and I quickly acquired a taste for takuan (pickled daikon radish), natto (healthy fermented soybeans), and furikake (a dry Japanese seasoning). Occasionally she would make rice balls with an umeboshi (pickled plum) in the middle, wrapped with seaweed. At times we were treated to maki sushi, a rolled sushi with seaweed on the outside and rice and fillings on the inside, and inari sushi, a fried tofu "pocket" filled with sushi rice. Our garden provided us with a multitude of fresh vegetables. There were lots of guavas, papayas, lilikois, mountain apples, mangos, bananas and pineapples to enjoy. We seldom had sodas and we drank lots of fresh milk.

Going outside the home to eat was a treat with so many ethnic foods to try. Hawaiian luaus offered kalua pork, poke, poi, and lau lau. Our Filipino friends offered pancit, chicken adobo, and lumpia. Chinese foods included chow mein, peking roasted duck, and sweet and sour pork. Korean friends served bulgogi chicken, and kimchee, and our Portuguese neighbors shared kale soup, Portuguese sausage, malasadas and Portuguese bread. We were health-conscious but loved eating all the delicious foods, and did not worry about all the warnings about food, in general. We tried to be conscious of balancing our meals with enough of each food group to keep healthy. We all sat and ate together, especially at supper time. This special time helped with healthy digestion. With daily walks, swimming, surfing, cycling and a year-long list of outdoor activities (plus the fact we lived in a favorable climate) we were quite active and therefore healthy. Now I'm not saying that Hawaii has the best or most nutritious foods, but did you know that presently Hawaii has the highest life expectancy in the United States for those over 65?

Many of our youngsters today are not eating healthy foods. With both parents working outside the home, they are likely too busy to take the time to plan healthy meals for their family. Whatever the excuse, diabetes, obesity, anxiety, and numerous health problems are on the rise.

Not everyone has favorable genes, and they may therefore have medical conditions that make it tougher to maintain a vibrant lifestyle. Interestingly, Dr. Hyla Cass, M.D., says, "You may think that feelings of anxiety - excessive worrying, irritability...jitteriness...panic attacks...upset stomach - start in your brain. The truth is that 80% of emotion-related signals begin in the gut."

So what can you do to eat healthier in today's busy schedule? Eliminate toxic foods such as meats and grains which contain antibiotics and herbicides. Avoid highly-processed foods such as sugar-spiked sodas, ice cream and candy. Consume fermented foods that contain good bacteria for your gut such as natto, pickles, sauerkraut, miso, kimchi, yogurt and kombucha. Eat high-fiber foods such as beans, avocados, pears, apples, and whole grain breads. Have healthy snack foods such as mixed nuts, carrots, and red bell peppers. And most importantly, drink lots of water. Don't compromise your immune system by causing stress and anxiety with poor nutrition!

Eating healthier will keep you training with a positive attitude and spirit. You'll feel a surge of energy, have a better attitude and carry yourself more positive manner.

Panko breaded fresh mahimahi.

Duck with takuan and natto.

Spinach salad with apples.

A hearty meal with eggs, veggies, meat and fruits.

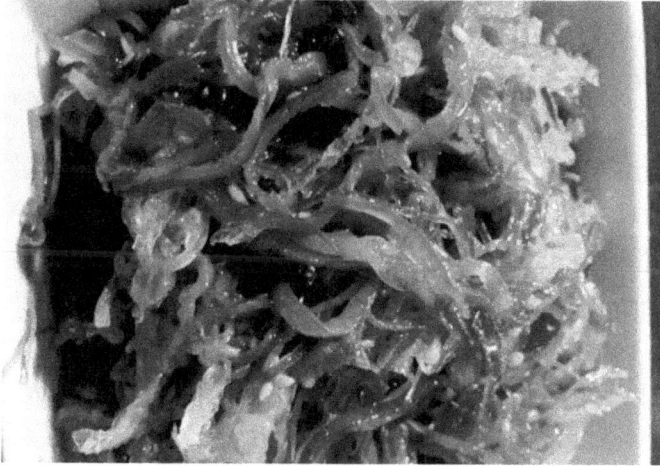
Seaweed salad.

Tasty sukiyaki dinner.

A sample menu of what the author eats. Breakfast also includes oatmeal with blueberries. Lots of fruits and nuts are enjoyed for snacks. An occasional hamburger and spam musubi fulfills the Hawaiian appetite.

Chapter 19
LIVING LIFE TO ITS FULLEST POTENTIAL

My dad, Toshio, lived on Maui but visited Japan in June 1941 because of his mother's illness, and later on her death, in August of 1941. At this time, war with Japan appeared to be imminent, but my dad managed to obtain passage aboard a ship and then returned to Hawaii in October of 1941. The following year, on November 7, 1942, my dad was arrested by the U.S. military and sent to Sand Island Detention Camp on Oahu where he spent almost one year. Then, under the evacuation order of October 30, 1944, he was detained at Tule Lake Internment Camp, in Newell, California where he joined some 18,000 other American Japanese internees. He spent nearly 4 years in that barbed-wired stockade with turrets manned by soldiers armed with machine guns. It was like the prison camps in Germany. From Tule Lake, my dad was sent to Texas, then to Seabrook Farms, New Jersey, where he worked in a frozen food factory as a contract laborer. He finally returned to Maui, and then moved to Oahu where he and my mom Clara raised me and my five brothers.

Why do I include this horrific experience that my dad and many others suffered this unthinkable atrocity? Well, when I began to ask my dad lots of questions about his experience, I came to see that I didn't really understand what had occurred and caused these Americans to be treated unjustly. The important lesson that he left with me was that no matter how wrongly he was treated, not for a moment was I to blame the government. Nor should this experience ever be used to as an excuse to complain, protest or have thoughts of retribution. Instead, I was taught that as a Japanese American I needed to place American interests first, and strive to become a productive citizen with outstanding character. He would often simply say, "Shoganai" and that is; if something is out of your control, it is better to accept it, learn from it, move on, and live life to its fullest potential.

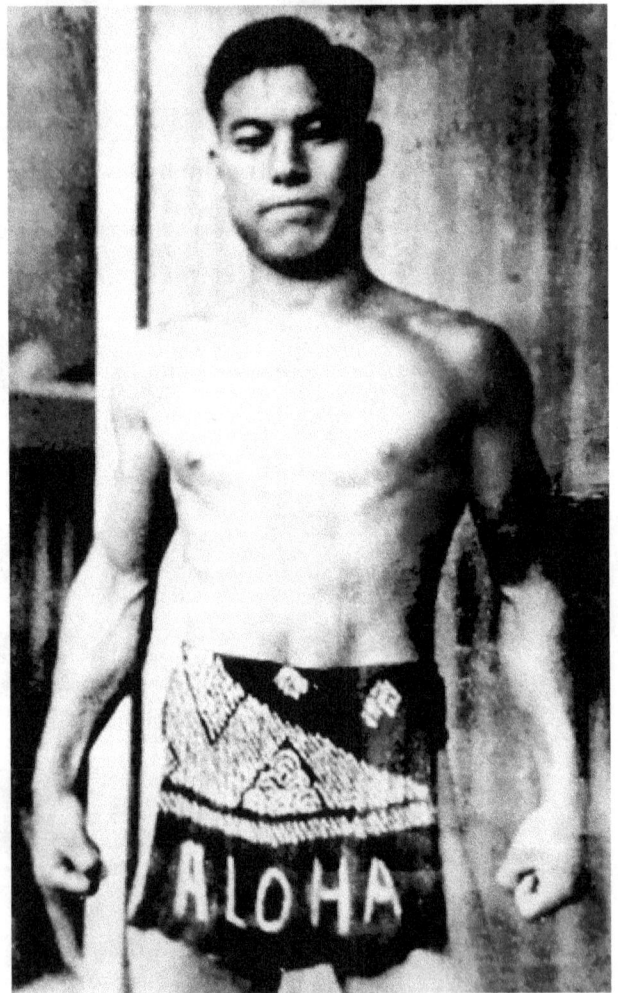

Toshio Saito, the best dad ever.

Moving to Sunset Beach, located on the North Shore of Oahu, I continued to learn many life lessons from both of my parents. My dad worked tirelessly as a carpenter to make ends meet, my stay-at-home mom was totally dedicated to our family, and they both worked hard to make sure my brothers and I had the best upbringing possible. They enjoyed teaching us the importance of pulling our share of work, and more, while keeping things simple. Although both parents made tremendous sacrifices by putting our needs first, they made a point of keeping humor alive in the house. Even with one brother in and out of Shriner's Hospital due to medical issues, and another brother who suffered with mental challenges, they never complained nor asked for help.

Mom took the time to teach us how to wash clothes and how to carefully use the clothes wringer to squeeze the water out without getting our hands in the way, which would result in losing a finger. She taught us how to iron, sew, and cook - and how to do each task with perfection.

My dad taught us how to be innovative. He taught us how to make our own bows and arrows and how to manicure bonsai trees. After purchasing our first home, he had a vision of building an addition on the bottom of our raised house. After drawing up some plans, we began to dig the dirt below only to find a huge boulder in the way. We laughed with tears when I suggested that we dynamite the huge obstacle, jokingly of course. After weeks of using the jackhammer on it, we determined that the rock was impenetrable. I would have given up by that point, but not my dad! Instead, he suggested we dig a deep hole beneath the boulder and sink it to provide enough clearance for his remodeling project. I was called to duty in the Air Force on the mainland so had a good excuse to leave this monumental task to my dad and my brother Burt. So on the weekends, they started to dig. And dig they did...for over a year! After one very rainy night, the water softened the dirt that was holding the boulder and it finally gave way, and that huge obstacle finally sunk into the hole below. Fortunately, my brother wasn't down in the hole scooping dirt into the bucket that would be hoisted for emptying by my dad when the rock gave way. My dad's new creation provided our family, my students, and many others with two bedrooms, a bathroom and a living room gathering place to enjoy.

I was very fortunate to be able to witness and learn what brought joy to my parents. They lived their lives simply and always completed the projects and tasks they expected of themselves. They were not driven to live beyond their means, and they enjoyed the things God had provided for them such as a happy family, great friends, and a beautiful community to live in that was surrounded with lots of love...all this with the backdrop of the beautiful Pacific Ocean. They lived life to its fullest potential and taught us to do the same.

Toshio Saito, author's dad, and brother Burt beginning their long digging process.

Sinking this huge boulder took over a year of strenuous work.

APPENDIX

Attendees of Tomohiro Arashiro's enjoyable kobudo workshop in Grants Pass, Oregon.

APPENDIX 1
THE FOUNDING AND FIRST LAUNCHING OF SAITO-HA SHITO-RYU KARATE-DO

July 2, 2008
Albany New York

In support thereof by the following endorsements:

Tsukasa Mabuni & Japan Seito Shito-ryu Shihan Kai - Japan

Dr. Chuck Aoto, sensei - Oregon
Tomohiro Arashiro, Kyoshi - California
Brian & Lisa Ash, sensei - Montana
Ivano Di Battista, Shihan - Italy
Robert Brace, PhD., Professor, OHSU - Oregon
Joseph Bunch, Hanshi - Hawaii
Ceci Cheung Shihan, PhD., Scientist OHSU - Oregon
Ray Dalke, Hanshi - Oregon
Fumio Demura, Hanshi - California
William Dometrich, Hanshi - Kentucky
Chief Lee Donohue, Sr, Hanshi - Hawaii
Giff & Chris Gates, CEO Gates Furniture - Oregon
Gil Gilbertson, Josephine County Sheriff - Oregon
Dwight Grover, Shihan - Virginia
Pat Haley, Kyoshi - California
Dr. Brian Hancock, M.D. - Oregon
Charles Harrington, Publisher of Hawaii Parent and Military Guide - Hawaii
Hajime Ide, President of Uniao Brasil Karate-do - Brasil
John Isabelo, sensei - Hawaii
Kazumasa Itaki, Hanshi - Japan
Rony Kluger, Hanshi - Israel
Ubiratan de Souza Lima, Shihan - Brasil
Joel Lovingfoss, President of International Color Imaging - Hawaii
Tony Mendonca, Shihan - Oregon
Chuck Merriman, Hanshi - Connecticut
Takayuki Mikami, Shihan - Louisiana
Joe Mirza, Hanshi - Illinois
James Miyaji, Hanshi - Hawaii
Kiyoshi Nishime, Shihan - Ohio
Walter Nishioka, Shihan - Hawaii
Joni Sharrah, Shihan - Washington
Danilo Torri, Shihan - Connecticut
Kevin Quinn, DEA - Virginia
Clinton Williams, Shihan - Virginia

APPENDIX 2
KEIZU (GENEALOGICAL TABLE)

TKFI Shihan Kai members and senior instructors at the honbu dojo.

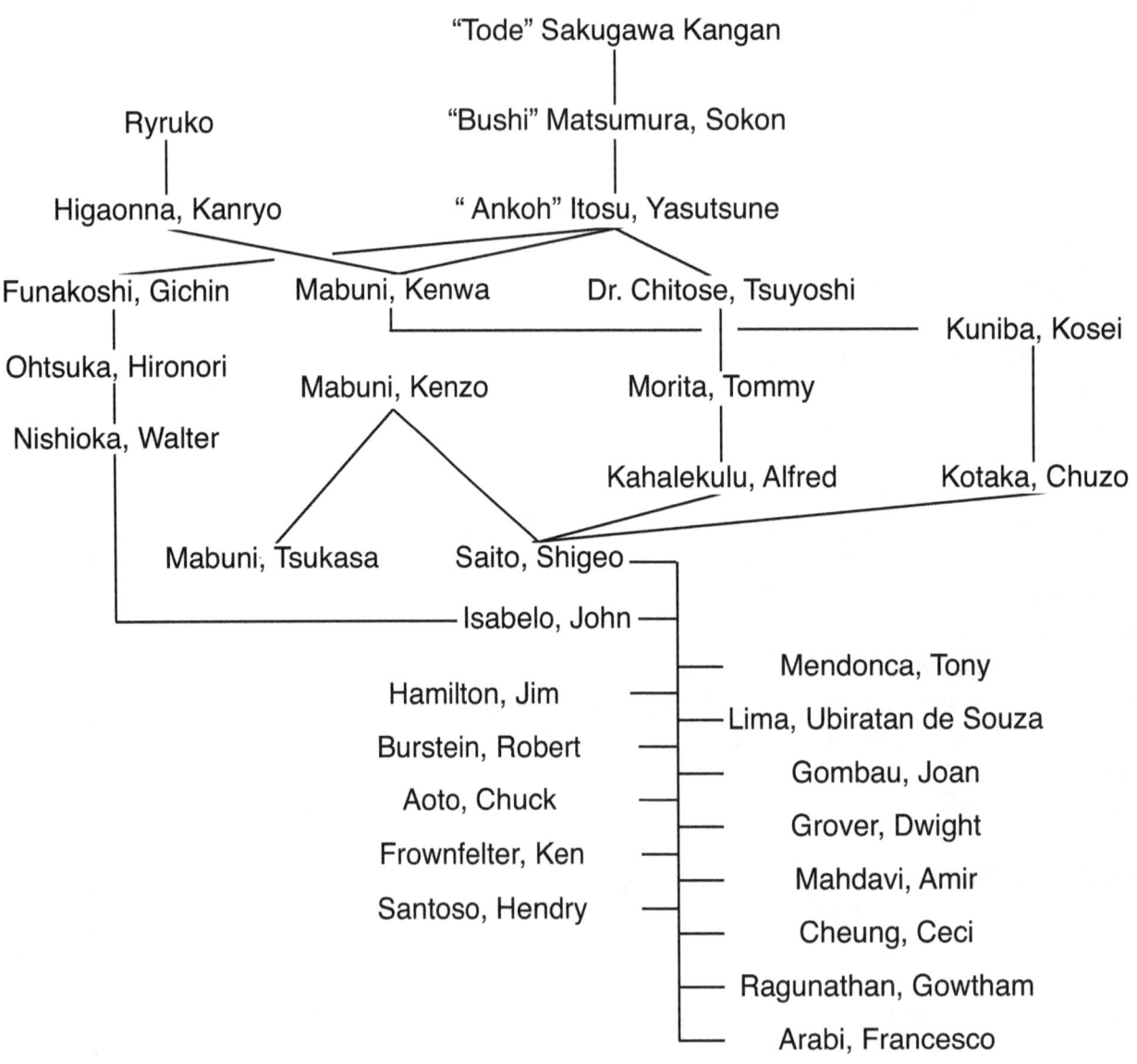

APPENDIX 3
COMBINATIONS

Stay relaxed and be sure to complete each technique correctly before executing the next move. Shift, feint, and use correct footwork. Pause after each series of movements. Perform the combination on both sides. Elise Gattey's combination incorporates a jab, reverse thrust, kick, backfist, hook kick and another reverse thrust.

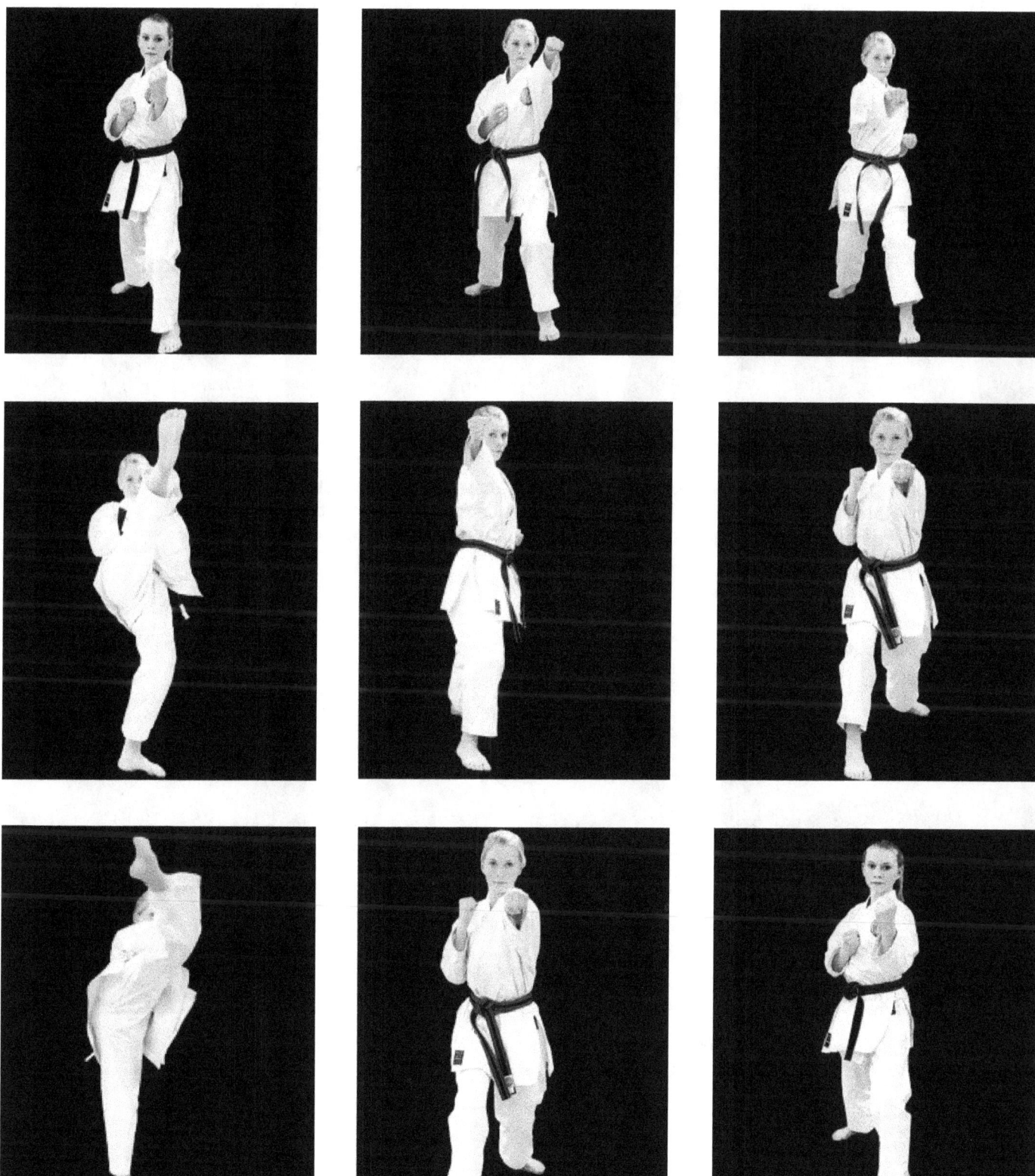

APPENDIX 4
FUN DRILLS

Karate training should also be fun. Our instructing duty and obligation is to make sure that every student we teach has the opportunity to enjoy the martial arts. Here are few examples of enjoyable drills to incorporate in your training.

Immovable stance drills
A

Both students begin with a strong stance as Jennifer and Matthias demonstrates. They each hold one end of the belt with their left hand. The objective is to break the balance of their partner by using their hips while pulling or slacking the belt and without letting go of the belt. Whoever moves their foot first loses the match.

B

Both students begin with a shiko stance. The objective is to break the balance of their partner by pushing or pulling on the hands. Whoever moves their foot first loses the match.

APPENDIX 5
CATALOG OF KATA

KIHON KATA	- Basic Formal exercise.
Hachiji Dachi Kihon	- Kata performed in natural shoulder stance.
Kihon Nijugo	- Basic 25.
ZENKUTSU DACHI KIHON KATA	- Kihon kata performed in front stance.
Zenkutsu Dachi Dai Ichi	- Down block, step forward and lunge thrust.
Zenkutsu Dachi Dai Ni	- Down block, outward block, rising block, front kick with rear leg, step forward and lunge thrust.
NEKOASHI DACHI KIHON KATA	- Kihon kata performed in cat stance.
Nekoashi Dachi Dai Ichi	- Down block in cat stance, step forward and lunge thrust.
Nekoashi Dachi Dai Ni	- Down block, outward block, rising block in cat stance, front kick with front leg and step forward and lunge thrust.
Kihon Zuki	- Basic thrusting kata. (Reverse thrust, vertical thrust, horizontal uppercut, vertical uppercut, hook thrust, roundhouse thrust, lunge thrust, double thrust).
Kihon Uke	- Basic blocking kata. Rising block, outward block, downward block, inward block, knife hand block, hooking hand block, inward open-hand block, two-handed circular block.
Kihon Nijuho	- Basic 20 ways/method. Rising block & reverse thrust, outward block & reverse thrust, inward bock & reverse thrust, downward block & reverse thrust, knife-hand block & reverse thrust (4 sets).
SHITO-RYU HONGATA	- Shito-ryu True Kata Methods.
Itosu-Ke (Itosu lineage)	
Bassai Sho	- To Breach a Fortress, minor version.
Bassai Dai	- To Breach a Fortress, major version.
Chinte	- Winning hands or Calmness.
Chinto	- Fighting to the East.
Gojushiho	- 54 Steps.
Jiin	- Temple Ground.
Jion	- Temple Sound.
Jitte	- Temple Hand or Ten Hand.
Juroku	- 16.
Kosokun Dai	- Chinese Military official, major version.
Kosokun Sho	- Chinese Military official, minor version.
Matsukaze	- Pine Tree Wind.
Naihanchi	- Sideway Fighting.

Pinan Shodan	- Peaceful Way 1.
Pinan Nidan	- Peaceful Way 2.
Pinan Sandan	- Peaceful Way 3.
Pinan Yondan	- Peaceful Way 4.
Pinan Godan	- Peaceful Way 5.
Rohai	- Vision of a Crane.
Wanshu	- Name of a Chinese official.

SHITO-RYU HONGATA — Shito-ryu True Kata Methods.

Higaonna-Ke (Higaonna lineage).

Kururunfa	- Come, Stop, Tear/Break.
Nipaipo	- 28 Steps.
Niseishi	- 24.
Saifa	- Final Break or Tear.
Sanchin	- Three Battles or Conflicts.
Seienchin	- Calm Within a Storm.
Seipai	- 18.
Seisan	- 13.
Shisochin	- Four Calm Monks.
Sochin	- Men "Monks" of Peace.
Suparinpei	- 108.
Tensho	- Rolling Palms.
Unshu	- Cloud Hand.

KENWA MABUNI SHITO-RYU KATA

Aoyagi (Aoyanagi in Okinawan)	- Green Willow.
Happo Sho	- 8 Ways.
Juroku	- 16.
Kensho	- Innocent Light.
Kenshu	- Excellent Fist.
Miyojo	- Pure Brightness.
Shiho Kosokun	- Name of a Chinese official, 4 direction version.
Shinpa	- New Break.
Shinsei	- Pure heart.

SUPPLEMENTAL KATA A

Ananku/Annanko	- Southern Light.
Chatanyara Kusanku	- Name of a Chinese Official, Chantan Yara's version.
Tomari Bassai	- Breach a Fortress, Tomari version.
Matsumura Bassai	- Breach a Fortress, Matsumura version.

SUPPLEMENTAL KATA B
(Ryuei-ryu Influence)

Anan	- Possibly a place in the Republic of Vietnam.
Heiku	- Black Tiger.
Pachu	- To Twirl a Ball.
Paiku	- White Tiger.

SAITO KE

Futen No Kata	- Kai bo Kata, Whirlwind.
Makoto	- To assert one's true identity.
Saitoshi Shodan	- Kumite combination in kata format 1.
Saitoshi Nidan	- Kumite combination in kata format 2.
Saitoshi Sandan	- Kumite combination in kata format 3.
Saitoshi Yodan	- Kumite combination in kata format 4.
Saitoshi Godan	- Kumite combination in kata format 5.

 Saito-Ha Shito-Ryu Karate-Do

APPENDIX 6
TERMINOLOGY

PRONUNCIATION GUIDE
a = ah, as in father
i = ee, as in meet
u = oo, as in threw
e = eh, as in feather
o = oh, as in dough

GENERAL TERMS
ABUNAI - dangerous. Any technique that poses a threat or is potentially dangerous to the person performing the technique.
DESHI - student disciple.
DO - the way.
DOGI - the formal name for training uniform worn during lessons of the way.
DOJO - a training center where "The Way" is practiced.
HANSHI - refers to a senior expert considered a "teacher of teachers." This title is used by many different arts for the top few instructors of that style, and is sometimes translated "master" or "exemplary warrior".
HIDARI - left.
KARA - empty or void of something.
KARATE-DO - Okinawan and Japanese martial art. The way of karate.
KARATEKA - student of karate.
KATA - prearranged formal exercise drills.
KIAI - spirit shout.
KOHAI - Junior Class Member.
KYOSHI - refers to an advanced teacher. Can be a more modest synonym for sensei.
MAE - front.
MIGI - right.
MEIJIN - Grandmaster, title awarded by a special board of examiners.
MOKUSO - command to "quiet the mind and body." To bring your mind to the present.
NANAME - generally 45° - (yonjugodo)
OSHIERU - to teach by example. To show. To walk the talk.
OTAGAI NI - to face your fellow student.
TE - hand.
REI - bow of respect.
RENSHI - instructor.
RYU - a traditional style or school.
RYUHA - multiple or separate schools or styles of any art.
SEIZA - kneeling down in formal seated posture.
SEMPAI - Senior Class Member. One looked up to for leadership.

SENSEI (gata) - Teacher(s).
SHIDOIN - Assistant Instructor.
SHIHAN - Master Teacher, exemplary teacher or Chief Instructor.
SHOGO - "title," "name," "degree," are martial arts titles developed by the Dai Nippon Butoku Kai.
SHOMEN - front of the class area in the Dojo.
SOKE - current Headmaster of a style or school.
USHIRO - back.

COUNTING:
ICHI - one
NI - two
SAN - three
SHI - four
GO - five
ROKU - six
SHICHI - seven
HACHI - eight
KU OR KYU - nine
JU - ten
NIJU - twenty
SANJU - thirty
YONJU - forty
GOJU - fifty
ROKUJU - sixty
SHICHIJU - seventy
HACHIJU - eighty
KUJU - ninety
HYAKU - one hundred
SEN - one thousand

EVERYDAY CONVERSATIONAL JAPANESE PHRASES
"OHAYO GOZAIMASU" - "Good Morning."
"KONNICHI WA" - "Good Day or Good Afternoon."
"KOM-BAN WA" - "Good Evening."
"OGENKI DESUKA?" - "How are you?"
"SAYONARA" - "Good-Bye."
"DO ITASHIMASHITE" - "You're welcome" or "Don't mention it."
"DOKO" - "Where?"
"(DOMO) ARIGATO GOZAIMASHITA" - "Thank You (very much) for what you have done for me."
"DOZO" - "Please."
"HAI" - "Yes".
"HAJIMEMASHITE. DOZO YOROSHIKU." - "I am pleased to meet you."
"IIE." - "No."

"KOKO" - "Here."
"ONEGAI SHIMASU" - (requesting something) "Please Train Me."
"OSU" - Greeting or can be used to mean "Keep trying" and "Perseverance."
"SHITSUREI SHIMASU" - "Excuse me" or "Pardon me."
"SOKO" - "There."
"WATAKUSHI WA JIM DESU" - "I am Jim."

KIHON WAZA (BASIC TECHNIQUE)

DACHI - Stance
KATA - Form, shape or pattern
KERI - Kicks
TSUKI - Thrusts
UCHI - Strikes
UKE - Blocks

UNDO (EXERCISES)

DACHI (STANCE)

HAN ZENKUTSU DACHI	- Half front stance
HEIKO DACHI	- Forward parallel stance (natural walking length)
HEISOKU DACHI	- Feet together, closed toed
KOKUTSU DACHI	- Back stance
KOSA DACHI	- Crossed leg stance
MOTO DACHI	- Short stance. In kumite, rear heel is up
MUSUBI DACHI	- Heels together, feet pointed out
NAMI HEIKO DACHI	- Parallel, shoulder width, feet straight
NEKO ASHI DACHI	- Cat foot stance
SAGIASHI DACHI	- One-legged stance
SANCHIN DACHI	- Hour-glass stance
SHIKKO DACHI	- A horse riding stance (feet pointed out)
SOTO HACHI DACHI	- Shoulder width (feet pointed out)
UCHI HACHIJI DACHI	- Modified hour-glass sanchin stance
ZENKUTSU DACHI	- Forward stance

JODAN UKE (HEAD AREA BLOCKS)

AGE UKE	- Rising block
KO UKE	- Wrist block
KOSA UKE	- Crossed arm block
KOTE UKE	- Back of hand block
KURI UKE	- Inside out, circle block with knife edge of hand
NAKA UKE	- Forearm inward block
SASHITE	- Inward sweeping block
TSUKI UKE	- Thrust block
UCHI OTOSHI	- Inside out circle forearm drop block

WA UKE	- Two arm circle block
YOKO BARAI	- Forearm outward parry

CHUDAN UKE (MIDDLE BODY BLOCKS)

GASSHO UKE	- Praying hands block
HARAI UKE	- Middle area downward block (from higher stances)
HIJI UKE	- Elbow block
HIJISASAE UKE	- Two hand outer block, closed fist at elbow
HIRAYUKI	- Two hand knife edge pushing block
KAKIWAKE	- Wedge block
KAKETE	- Hooking hand block
KENSASAE UKE	- Two hand outward block, open hand supports fist
KO UKE	- Wrist block
KOSA UKE	- Crossed arm block
KOTE UKE	- Back of hand block
NAKA UKE	- Inward block
NINOUDE UKE	- Forearm inward block
OURA UKE	- Large circle inverted forearm block
SEIRYUTO UKE	- Ox hand block
SHOTEI UKE	- Palm Heel Block
SOTO (YOKO) UKE	- Forearm outward side block
SUKUI UKE	- Scooping block
SHUTO UKE	- Knife hand block
TSUKIDOME	- Withdrawing forearm block (after thrust) - also called hikite
UKENAGASHI	- Inward flowing block
URA UKE	- Inverted block (small circle with back of hand or wrist)
WA UKE	- Two arm circular block
YOKO KENTSUI UKE	- Side hammer-fist block
YOKO (SOTO) UKE	- Forearm outward side block

GEDAN UKE (LOWER BODY BLOCKS)

FURISUTE	- Scoop and throw block
GEDAN BARAI	- Downward sweeping block protecting lower area (from lower stances)
HIZAGAESHI UKE	- Knee sweeping across block
KATATE SUKUI UKE	- One hand scooping block
KOSA UKE	- Crossed arms block
SHUTO BARAI	- Knife hand parry
RYOTE SUKUI UKE	- Two hand scooping block
SUKUIDOME	- Scoop and catch block
UDE UKE	- Forearm block
WA UKE	- Two arm circular block

TSUKI (PUNCHES)

In karate and its variants, tsuki is used generally as a part of a compound word for any one of various punches, and virtually never stands alone to describe a discrete technique. (Note that in a compound word, where tsuki does not come first, its pronunciation and writing changes slightly; this is translated as zuki).

AGE ZUKI	- Rising punch.
AWASE-ZUKI	- U-punch.
FURI-ZUKI	- Circular punch, knuckles facing inward.
GYAKU-ZUKI	- Reverse punch.
HIRAKEN-ZUKI	- Fore-knuckle punch (leopard punch).
IPPONKEN-ZUKI	- One-knuckle punch.
KAGI-ZUKI	- Hook punch.
MOROTE-ZUKI	- Double-fist punch.
SEIKEN-ZUKI	- Standard fore-fist punch.
TATEKEN-ZUKI	- Vertical fore-fist punch.
URA-ZUKI	- Uppercut, close punch.
WA-ZUKI	- Two arm circular punch.

UCHI (STRIKES)

HAITO UCHI	- Ridge hand strike.
HIJIATE	- Elbow smash strike.
HIRA BASAMI UCHI	- Full hand scissors strike.
KENTSUI UCHI	- Hammer fist strike.
NUKITE UCHI	- Spear hand strike.
SHUHO UCHI	- Mountain hand (back knuckles of a peaked hand) strike.
SHUTO UCHI	- Knife hand strike.
URAKEN UCHI	- Back knuckle strike.
YUBI HASAMI UCHI	- Thumb and forefinger scissors strike

KERI (KICKS)

CHUDAN GERI	- Ball of foot middle level kick.
FUMIKOMI GERI	- Heel stomping kick.
HIZAGAESHI GERI	- Knee sweeping across kick.
HIZA GERI	- Knee kick.
JODAN GERI	- Ball of foot upper level kick.
KAKATO GERI	- Heel of the foot kick.
KOSHU GERI	- Heel back rising kick.
MAE JOSOKUTEI GERI	- Ball of the foot front kick.
MAWASHI GERI	- Roundhouse with instep or ball of foot kick.
MIKAZUKI GERI	- Crescent kick.
SOKO GERI	- Instep kick.
SOKUTO GERI	- Knife edge of foot to knee level kick.
TOBI GERI	- Jump kick.

YOKO GERI KEAGE   - Side snap kick.
YOKO GERI KEKOMI   - Side thrust kick.

OTHER USEFUL TERMS

A

Abunai - dangerous.

Aka - red.

Antei - balance or stability.

Aoi - blue.

Arigato gozaimashita - the phrase, "Thank you for what you've already done."

Ashi - foot, feet, leg or legs.

Ashi barai - foot or leg sweep.

Ashi guruma - leg wheel. Attacker is thrown or pulled over your reaping leg.

A so desu ka - the phrase, "Oh, is that so?"

Atama - one's head.

Ate - smash.

Atoshibaraku - a few seconds left.

Atsui - hot. As in temperature or as in spicy food.

Azato, Ankoh - Okinawan teacher who taught Funakoshi Gichin (Tominakoshi in Okinawan).

B

Bachi - retribution, bad karma.

Banzai - ten thousand years, meaning long life.

Barai - a wide swing or arc.

Bo - a wooden staff or stick.

Bodiharma - Daruma in Japanese. Founder of Zen Buddhism.

Bokken - wooden sword.

Bubishi - part of an ancient Chinese manuscript on combative techniques.

Budo - way to stop war or aggression.

Bugei - formal name for ancient martial arts.

Bunkai - having to be cut into many parts. Intellectual analysis of the parts of kata.

Bushi - warrior.

Bushido - "Way of the Warrior."

Butokuden - the hall of martial virtues.

C

Chakugan - the spot on which you place your sight.

Chan - Chinese pronunciation of Zen.

Chantan Yara - martial arts teacher, said to have taught in the Tomari district of Okinawa.

Cha obi - brown belt. There are three levels of brown belt.

Chiisai - small, as in size or stature.

Chikara - physical strength.

Chinte - kata based on the movements of the White Heron.

Chinto - fighting to the East.
Chito-ryu - a Japanese style of karate-do founded by Dr. Tsuyoshi Chitose (1898 -1984).
Choku zuki - straight punch.
Chotto matte ittei kudasai - the phrase, "Just a moment please."
Chuan Fa - a generic term for styles of Chinese fighting.
Chudan - middle area.

D
Dachi - stance.
Dai - large, great or major.
Daijobu - all right, ok, safe.
Dame - incorrect, not like that.
Dan - literally means step, as in stages. These are generally the stages of the black belt.
Dan zuki - consecutive punches with the same hand.
De ai - to counterattack when an opponent loses focus.
De ashi - stepping forward with the rear foot.
De ashi barai - a sweeping attack to an opponent's forward or advancing leg or foot.
Densho - a written record of a Ryuha's most important techniques and philosophies.
Deshi - disciple or follower of the way.
Do - the way.
Dogi - the formal name for the prescribed uniform worn during lessons.
Dojo - a place to learn "The way."
Dojo Kun - dojo oath.
Dojo yaburi - a challenge visit to a dojo.
Domo - adverb meaning very much or indeed. Often times incorrectly used for thanks.
Domo arigato gozaimasu - the phrase, "Thank you very much."
Dozo - "please."

E
Edo - an older name for what is now Tokyo.
Ei - one of the traditional kiai sounds. Included are ya, toh and ai.
Eiku - Okinawan boat oar.
Eishin ryu - the deep river valley excellent fist system of iaido.
Enbu - A demonstration or presentation.
Enbusen - Both the lines or direction of movement in the performance of a kata.
Enchosen - to prolong a matter of combat.
Enpi - monkey's elbow, also hiji.
Enryo - the warrior who embraces death and welcomes it is unbeatable for you can take nothing away from him.
Ensho - heel of the foot, also kagato.

F

Fudoshin - immovable spirit.
Fukushin - title of a judge or lower level referee.
Fumikiri geri - cutting kick.
Fumikomi - thrusting in, or to forcefully enter.
Funakoshi, Gichen - (1868 - 1957), Father of Shotokan Karate-do.
Furi tsuki - a circular roundhouse punch.

G

Ganbatte - the verbal command of encouragement or to try hard!
Ganmen - face.
Gata - the suffix gata makes the word plural.
Gasshuku - a training camp or training seminar.
Natsu gasshuku - summer training camp.
Fuyu gasshuku - winter training camp.
Gedan - lower area.
Gedan barai - a large lower or descending sweeping movement.
Genki - Lit: - good ki. Being well or healthy in body and spirit.
Geri - to kick.
Giri - a debt of loyalty or of moral obligation.
Godan - the fifth level of Black Belt.
Goju - hard and soft.
Goju Ryu - a karate-do style founded by Okinawan Chojun Miyagi.
Gojushiho - fifty-four steps of the Shamtung black tiger.
Gomen nasai - the phrase, "I'm sorry."
Go no sen - to seize the initiative later.
Go shaku bo - a five foot long wooden staff.
Goten - the hand that is not attacking, but defending at the same time the other hand goes out.
Gyaku - reverse.
Gyaku mawashi geri - a reverse roundhouse kick.
Gyaku tsuki - reverse thrust.

H

Hachi dan - the eighth level of Black Belt.
Hachiji dachi - the natural open toed stance.
Hachi kyu - the eight beginner's rank.
Hachimaki - a white cotton sweat head band.
Hai - "Yes."
Hai dozo - "Yes, please."
Haiku - a form of Japanese poetry.
Haishu uchi - striking with the back of the hand.
Haisoku - the instep of the foot.
Haito uchi - striking with the ridge of the hand.

Hajime - the command to begin!

Hajime mashite - the phrase, "How do you do?" (to be followed by "watashi wa Saito desu, dozo yoroshiku." "I am Saito, please favor me.") Generally used only when meeting someone for the first time.

Hakama - traditional divided skirt like trousers.

Hakutsuru - White Crane.

Hana - nose.

Hangeki - a counterattack.

Hanko - half hard. A name that Kenwa Mabuni sensei used for his style prior to the adoption of the name Shito-ryu.

Hanmi dachi - a half facing stance.

Hanshi - a honorary title given to a Master Instructor.

Hansoku - a foul in a martial art sporting contest.

Hantei - a decision, as in a match.

Han zenkutsu dachi - a half length forward stance.

Happo - eight directions.

Hara - belly and the seat of all physical consciousness.

Harai uke - a sweeping deflection or block.

Hayaku - speed or acceleration. Used as a training command to encourage a student to move quicker.

Heian - the Heian period of Japanese history was roughly from 794 - 1185. The capital was moved to Kyoto.

Heian kata - The basic kata series taught by Gichen Funakoshi. Funakoshi altered the Pinan and changed their names to Heian. He also switched the order of the kata believing that the second kata, Pinan Nidan was easier to learn first, with Pinan Shodan taught second. Funakoshi sensei learned the Pinan series from Kenwa Mabuni.

Heiho - referring to combative strategy.

Heiko - parallel.

Heisoku - instep.

Henka - variations.

Henshu - switching hands.

Hidari - left.

Hidari mawari - left or counter-clock-wise turning.

Hiji - elbow.

Hiki - withdraw. To pull back.

Hiki ashi - stepping (pulling) straight back.

Hiki te - pulling hand.

Hirabasami - full hand scissors.

Hiraken uchi - a hand strike or punch using the second knuckles.

Hito - a human. People.

Hitsui - one's knees.

Hiza - knee.

Hizagaeshi - knee sweeping across.

Hiza geri - knee kick.

Honbu - headquarters dojo (spelled with an "n" but pronounced as an "m").
Hone - bones.

I
Iaido - the way of drawing a weapon.
Iaito - a practice katana.
Ibuki - breath control techniques.
ichi - the number one.
Ichiban - number one, as in "the best."
Iie - "No."
Ikimasu - to go.
Ikkyu - the final grade of the mudansha (colored belt) ranks.
Ippon - one point associated with combative fighting matches.
Ippon ken - one knuckle fist.
Ippon shobu - one point match.
Irrashai mase - the verbal greeting, "Welcome, come in."

J
Ja mata - the phrase, "See you later."
Jiin - kata meaning "temple ground."
Jikan - time out.
Jion - kata meaning "temple sound."
Jiite - kata meaning "temple hand."
Jiyu - free or unrehearsed.
Jiyu kumite - free sparring.
Jodan - upper level.
Jogai - out of bounds.
Ju - the number 10.
Judan - the tenth level of Yudansha, or black belt ranks.
Juji - crossed or to cross.
Juji uke - cross hands block.
Ju kumite - a soft flowing style of sparring training. This type of training eliminates speed, thus developing rhythm and timing.
Juroku - an intermediate level kata formulated by Kenwa Mabuni, meaning 16.
Jushin no antei - correct stability of the center of gravity.
Jutsu - a suffix that denotes an art or science, one that deals with actual combative application as its forte, verses the "do" methods which are not meant for combat, but as a vehicle for personal, moral and spiritual development.

K
Kachi - victory. To win.
Kagato - one's heel. (also kakato).
Kagato geri - a kick with the heel of the foot.

Kage - shadow.
Kagi - hook.
Kagi tsuki - hook punch.
Kai - the Japanese name for a boat oar.
Kaicho - the leader or founder of a group or style. A headmaster of a style.
Kaiden - referring to deep initiation to a schools principles and techniques.
Kake - hook.
Kakiwake uke - wedge block.
Kakushite - hidden hands.
Kakuto uchi - striking with the bent wrist.
Kama - a classical weapon made up of a wooden handle with a sharpened curved blade protruding at a right angle on one end.
Kamae - a term used to refer to a posture.
Kamae te - the verbal command to assume a direct posture.
Kan - a building or school.
Kancho - a casual title sometimes given to the founder of a ryu.
Kan geiko - morning or winter training. This exhaustive annual training generally taking place outside, on the coldest day of winter.
Kanji - Chinese written characters, used by Japanese along with Hiragana and Katakana.
Kankyu - speed.
Kansa - arbitrator.
Kansetsu - joint.
Kansetsu geri - joint kick.
Kao - face.
Kara - empty or void of something.
Karada - body.
Karate - an Okinawan and subsequently Japanese Gendai Budo (martial way).
Karate-do - simplistically put, the way of karate.
Karate-do gaku - the evolution and improvement of karate through practice, research, experimentation, and personal adaptation of one's understanding of the art.
Karateka - A casual term used to refer to a student of karate. The more polite way to refer to a serious student would be a "deshi" or student disciple.
Karate ni sente nashi - there is no first attack in karate, or no initial aggressiveness.
Kata - form, shape or pattern.
Kata - one's shoulder.
Katakana - the ideographs used to translate foreign language sounds in Japanese.
Katchi - victory, or to win.
Kaze - wind.
Ke age geri - rising kick.
Keiko - training or practice class, not limited to just physical training.
Keito - chicken beak.
Keizu - geological table. The family tree of founders, headmasters, instructors and, at times, students.
Kekomi - to thrust in.

Kempo - the pronunciation of what should be spelled kenpo. Kenpo is what the Japanese and Okinawans called the Chinese external pugilistic fighting arts.

Ken - fist or sword.

Kendo - martial sport, roughly based on the actions of the classical Japanese sword styles of ken jutsu.

Kenjutsu - the art of the sword.

Kenpo - fist way.

Kenshu - rigorous daily classes or training.

Kentsui - hammer fist.

Keri - combining form of the word keru (to kick).

Keru - to kick.

Ki - commonly referred to as the universal energy, life energy, life force or internal energy.

Kiai - spirit convergence. The dynamic expression of the meeting of the spirit. Harmonized energy.

kihon - generally used to mean the basics, but more accurately the practice of the minute portions of a movement that are repeated until some semblance of perfection has been achieved.

Kihon kata - the basic training forms of a school.

Kihon kumite - the basic prearranged sparring, or attack and defensive training scenarios.

Kihon waza - basic techniques.

Kiken - when one person wishes to surrender during a submission technique. The nonverbal signal of kiken is to tap the opponent or the floor multiple times.

Kime - simplistically put, one must focus all of their mental and spiritual energy onto a single moment or action.

Ki o tsukete - term used for be careful. Also used in the dojo for a command meaning "attention!"

Kishin no yoi - prepare-spirit-mind.

Kizame tsuki - a short jabbing, closed fisted strike with the front hand.

Kobudo - a common name used to refer to all modern adaptations of ancient classical Okinawan and Japanese weapons arts.

Kodansha - the higher ranking Yudansha, or Black Belt holders, generally holders of the rank of Rokudan through Judan.

Kohai - the Junior Student.

Kokutsu dachi - back stance.

Kokyu - breathing, respiration. Breath or breath control.

Kon - the Okinawan name for the wooden staff.

Konban wa - the phrase, "Good Evening."

Koryu - ancient or older martial arts.

Kosa dachi - crossed legged stance.

Koshi - ball of foot.

Kote - the wrist.

Ko uke - receiving, intercepting or blocking with the bent wrist.

Ku - the number nine.

Kuchi - mouth.

Kumade - a bear hand.

Kumibo - partner practice (or training), with the bo.

Kumite - crossing or exchanging hands. Kumite is also referred to as the attacking hand, or to attack. Modern usage refers to the sporting style of sparring with an opponent.
Kun - Okinawan name for the wooden staff that is referred to as a bo in Japan.
Kurobi - a black belt.
Kururunfa - a revised goju kata referred to as holding your ground.
Kusshin - To expand or contract one's body or posture to avoid or keep one from receiving the full force of an attack.
Kuzushi no heiho - the combative strategy of unbalancing your opponent.
Kyoshi - teaching expert rank. Generally Rokudan or Nanadan in the Kyu/Dan ranking system.
Kyu - the number nine.
Kyu - a name for each of the lower levels or rank below that of Shodan or Black Belt.
Kyudan - the second highest rank in the Kyu/Dan ranking system.
Kyushaku bo - a nine foot wooden staff.

M
Maai - spatial distance.
Mabuni Kenwa - the founder of Shito-ryu karate-do.
Mae - front.
Mae geri - front kick.
Make - defeat.
Makiwara - to wrap with straw. Also referred to a striking post.
Man'naka - the center.
Matsukaze - "pine tree wind." Also a name of a kata with variations from the kata Wankan.
Matte - the verbal command, or request to "Wait!"
Mawari ashi - a rotating step.
Mawashi geri - a rotating kick, most commonly called a roundhouse kick.
Mawashi tsuki - a roundhouse punch.
Mawatte - the verbal command to rotate.
Me - eyes.
Meijin - one who is considered a martial arts genius.
Menkyo kaiden - the levels off rank, or understanding in a classical ryu. Differing from the modern practice of awarding rank based upon skills in the modern martial arts ways, Menkyo Kaiden ranks are most often awarded on the level of understanding more so than the physical prowess.
Metsuke - eye contact, focal point, eye control.
Michi - path, or way.
Migi - right. the right side, or to the right.
Mikazuki - crescent moon.
Mikzuki geri - crescent kick.
Misete kudasai - the verbal request please show me.
Mite - a verbal command to look!
Miyagi, Chojun - Miyagi is the Japanese pronunciation of the Okinawan name Miyagusuku. He is best known for being the founder of what is called Goju-ryu karate-do.
Mizu - water.

Mizu no kokoro - "Mind like water."
Mokuso - to bring your mind to the present.
Morote tsuki - a two-handed thrust.
Moto dachi - a short fighting stance. At times the rear foot heel is raised.
Mu - simplistically this refers to the state of nothingness; the empty mind, void of all conscious thoughts.
Mudansha - those without rank.
Mune - one's chest.
Musubi dachi - an informal attention stance where the heels are together and the toes pointed outward.

N

Nafuda - name tag. In traditional dojo, these are made out of small strips of wood.
Nagashi - flowing.
Nage - the contraction of the word nagemasu (throw).
Naha - the major seaport town on the island of Okinawa.
Nahate - martial arts ways that came from instructors in and around the area of Naha.
Naihanchi - the Okinawan karate-do name for the classical kata performed in the horse riding stance.
Naka - middle.
Nakadaka ken - fist with the 2nd knuckle of the middle finger protruding.
Naka uke - middle level reception, or deflection from outside to inside.
Nami ashi - the wave foot. Referring to a foot movement wherein one lifts one's leg to avoid, or flow with, a strike or sweeping technique.
Nanadan - the name of the seventh black belt.
Naname - diagonal.
Neiseishi - A kata said to refer to the movements and techniques of the Chinese style, referred to as "monk fist boxing."
Neko - cat.
Neko ashi dachi - cat foot stance.
Ni - the number two.
Nidan - the second level of black belt.
Nihon - Japan or Japanese.
Nihon-go - the Japanese language.
Nihon nukite - a two finger, thrusting strike.
Ninoude uke - forearm inward block.
Nipaipo - a classical Okinawan kata meaning "28 steps."
Nippon - the same as Nihon, but used when referring to Japan.
Nodo - throat.
Nukite - spear hand strike.
Nunchaku - a classical Okinawan weapon. A horse bridle that had a similar construction to weapons found in China.

O

O - a prefix to denote great or large.

Obi - classically, a wide cloth sash wrapped numerous times around the waist to warm the tanden and to support the lower back.

O genki desu ka - the phrase, "How are you?"

Okinawa - the largest island in the Ryukyu Archipelago.

Okinawa te - Okinawan hand. Often said to have been one of the original indigenous fighting arts of Okinawa.

Omedeto gozaimasu - "Congratulations." As spoken to a classmate that has been awarded a new rank.

Onegai shimasu - the phrase "I make a request." Commonly used in the dojo to mean please do this with (for) me.

Oroshi - to strike downward.

Osae - press down.

O sensei - great teacher.

Oshi shinobu osu - to be patient with yourselves and with others.

Oshieru - to teach.

Osoi - slow, without speed.

Osu - a contracted form of "Oshi Shinobu Osu." Commonly used to mean keep trying, try hard, and have patience. Also commonly heard as a greeting, or acknowledgment in a Japanese Dojo.

O tagai ni rei - the phrase "Face your fellow students and pay your respects."

Otearai - bathroom.

Otoshi - drop.

Otsuka, Hironori - the founder of Wado-ryu Karate-do.

Oyasumi nasai - the phrase, "good night."

Oyo - application. The physical reenactment of the self-defense or combative scenarios within a kata.

P

Pachu - an Okinawan Ryuei ryu kata, meaning "to twirl a ball."

Paiku - an Okinawan Ryuei ryu kata, meaning "white tiger."

Passai - classical Okinawan kata, called "Bassai" by the Japanese, meaning "to breach a fortress."

Pinan - (Pingan) mening "peaceful mind" or "stay safe or safe from harm."

R

Rakka - to receive an attack with much force.

Reigi - etiquette, protocol, or courtesy.

Rengo - a federation or alliance.

Renoji dachi - an upright stance with the feet placed in a position that resembles the Roman letter r.

Renshi - classical teaching title, generally around the Yondan rank in the Kyu/Dan ranking system. Not automatically awarded.

Renshu - training, wherein one is learning. The repetitious execution of techniques to imbed them into the muscle memory.

Rohai - a classical Okinawan kata. Said to be based on the movements of the White Heron. Also called

Meikyo.
Rokkyu - the sixth Mudansha rank in the Kyu/Dan ranking system.
Roku - the number six.
Rokudan - the sixth level of Yudansha (black belt) ranking in the Kyu/Dan ranking system.
Rokushakubo - a six foot hard wood staff.
Romanji - the Roman alphabet.
Ryu - dragon.
Ryu - a traditional style, or school of thought or actions.
Ryuha - multiple or separate schools or styles of any particular art.
Ryusui - to receive an attack with circular redirection.

S

Sabaki - motion. When you move your legs and feet it is called ashi sabaki. Body movement is called tai sabaki.
Sagi ashi dachi - the body and foot posture commonly called The Crane, or one legged stance.
Sai - a forked trudgeon.
Saifa - final breaking point. A classical kata based on the movements of the monkey.
Sakugawa, Kanga - often referred to as Tode Sakugawa, a student of Kushanku. He is know to be the most influential teacher of Sokon (Bushi) Matsumura.
Sakugawa no kon - a basic kata of the bo, developed by Tode Sakugawa.
Sakura - the Cherry Blossom flower.
Samui - cold.
Samurai - one who serves.
San - the number three.
San - the honorific suffix to a formal name, whether they be male or female.
Sanbon kumite - prearranged three attack training scenarios.
Sanbon tsuki - triple alternating punches.
Sanchin - breathing method to harden ones body to withstand attacks.
Sanchin - a classical Okinawan kata meaning man's three internal battles.
Sanchin Dachi - a pigeon-toed, or three-point stance.
Sandan - the third level of Yudansha in the Kyu/Dan ranking system.
San kyu - the third level of Mudansha in the Kyu/Dan ranking system.
Sanseiryu - thirty-six hands or thirty-six schools (ways). Kata deals with close-in fighting.
Sasae - to prop, or to support.
Sashite - the verbal command to "Stab!"
Sashi-te - to extend one's hand. To intercept an attack and strike the enemy at the same time.
Sayonara - informal way of saying, "Goodbye." More politely, or on formal occasions, the correct phrase would be shitsurei shimasu.
Sebone - one's spine.
Seiken - a squared fist for punching.
Seipai - an Okinawan kata meaning "eighteen hands."
Sei retsu - the verbal command to line up in an orderly fashion.
Seiryuto uchi - striking with the bottom edge of a shuto hand position (ox hand).

Seisan - an Okinawan kata meaning "thirteen." Thirteen techniques against thirteen different attacks.
Seiyunchin - the modern spelling or Seienchin. A classical kata meaning "lull in the storm."
Seiza - to sit correctly. Kneeling down in a formal seated position.
Sempai - the one who came before, in a senior/junior relationship.
Sen - initiating or initiative.
Sen no sen - to seize the initiative at the same time or simultaneously with the physical attack.
Sensei - one who was born before. The honorific title for a teacher. Someone who has previously walked the path that a student wishes to travel and as such, is able to guide the student on their journey.
Sensei ni rei - face the teacher and pay respects.
Sen sen no sen - the highest level of defense initiatives in the Japanese combative mindset. To seize the initiative at the moment of the opponent's intention, but before a perceivable physical action.
Shaku - a linear unit of measure, approximately one foot. Exact measurement is 11.930542 inches.
Shiai - a word to refer to a match or contest.
Shichi - the number seven.
Shichidan - the seventh level of Yudansha in the Kyu/Dan ranking system.
Shidoin - Assistant Teachers.
Shihan - a honorific title for a teacher who is not only a guide but a role model for those he teaches. This term comes from Shihansha, or the Chinese compass. Like a compass, a Shihan must always point the right way (despite exterior circumstances).
Shiho - transmission. Four methods, or four corners.
Shikaku - disqualification during a sporting match.
Shikko - a horse riding stance, wider and lower than the Okinawan naihanchi dachi, with the feet pointed out at thirty degrees.
Shimpa - a Shito-Ryu specific kata formulated by Kenwa Mabuni, meaning "New break" or "Mind Wave."
Shin - truth, true heart, or sincerity.
Shinai - a practice sword made up of bamboo.
Shinken - a live or real sword.
Shinpan - a referee, or judge.
Shiro - the color white.
Shisei - one's form, posture, or moral character.
Shisochin - a classical kata from China, meaning "Fighting Four Monks."
Shita - underneath, from below.
Shitachi - in a two person training drill, Shiitachi is the attacker. Uke is the receiver.
Shito-ryu - a style formulated by Kenwa Mabuni in 1928.
Shitsurei shimasu - the verbal apology, "I'm sorry, excuse me."
Sho - small, lesser, minor. Opposite of Dai.
Shobu - a match, engagement, or fight.
Shodan - first step, or first man. The first black belt awarded in the Kyu/Dan ranking system.
Shodan-ho - a probationary shodan black belt ranking.
Shomen - the front.

Shomen ni rei - the verbal command to "face the front and respectfully bow."

Shotei otoshi uke - a downward palm heel deflection.

Shotei - the heel of one's palm.

Shotokan - the name that was given for the style Gichen Funakoshi formulated. Shoto was Funakoshi's pen name.

Shugyo - rigorous daily training.

Shuhari - the three stages of learning and mastery. Shu (Mamoru), the student emulates his master without question. Ha (Yabureru), the student begins to formulate his own interpretations to fit his own body and soul. All techniques are mastered. Ri (Hanareru), the student embodies the core principles of movement and psychological state. This state takes multiple decades of training and study as well as years of teaching and introspection. At this stage a student needs no other instructor than the art itself.

Shurite - the martial arts practiced in and around the area of Shuri, Okinawa.

Shushin - the referee in a sporting event.

Shushi no kon - a bo kata from Okinawa. Said to have been devised in the early 20th century by an Okinawan kobujutsu teacher by the name of Chinen.

Shuto - sword hand.

Sochin - an Okinawan kata, meaning "Men" or "Monks of Peace."

So desu ka - the phrase, "Is that so?"

Soke - term originally used in feudal Japan to signify a family that had exclusive commercial rights to something. Today it is used to refer to a current headmaster of a style or school.

Sokutei - the sole of the foot.

Sokuto - the outside, or blade edge, of the foot.

Sore made - the phrase, "End of Contest." The verbal statement that the match is over.

Soto - exterior or outside.

Sugoi - amazing.

Sukui - scoop.

Sumimasen - excuse me, to get someone's attention.

Suna kake - to flick sand at your opponent.

Sun dome - stopping your attack one inch from the target.

Suparinpe - a classical Okinawan kata sometimes called Peichurin. This kata may contain 108 separate attack and defense scenarios. It is also said that this kata represents the battle of man's 108 evil passions.

Suri ashi - the sliding or gliding step in which the front foot slides forward, and the rear foot slides up to regain the original posture.

Sutemi ni heiho - the combative strategy of sacrificing. To sacrifice, or accept a small injury to oneself in order to inflict a greater injury to one's opponent.

Suwatte - the casual command to sit down.

T

Tabi - the common name for the traditional Japanese split toed cotton socks. Modern ones are rubberized.

Tachi - referring to standing.

Tai - body.
Taikai - grand or large, meeting or gathering.
Tai otoshi - body dropping. To throw an opponent's body to the ground.
Tai sabaki - body movement.
Tanden - also known as hara. One's physical center of gravity.
Tanto - a short blade or knife.
Tatami - floor covering traditionally made of straw.
Tate - to stand erect.
Tate tsuki - vertical punch.
Tegua - an often heard term in older Okinawan dojo for the weapons arts practiced there.
Teisho - palm heel.
Te kubi wrist.
Ten - heaven.
Teni - to move one's body from the line of attack.
Tettsui uchi - iron fist strike.
Te waza - hand techniques.
Ti - an Okinawan term for hand.
Tobi - common term for jump, or jumping.
Tobi ashi - jumping or springing.
Tobi geri - any jumping kick.
Tode - "China Hand."
Tokui - one's favorite.
Tomari te - martial arts practiced in and around the area known as Tomari, Okinawa.
Tomeru - to stop.
Tonfa - an Okinawan hand held weapon that was a mill grinding handle, or a crutch.
Tsubo - pressure point.
Tsukami - grasping.
Tsuki - to thrust.
Tsuki uke - thrust block.
Tsuki waza - thrusting techniques.

U
Uchi - the contraction of the verb utsu (to strike).
Uchi - inner or inside.
Uchi hachiji dachi - a ready stance with feet turned in. They are positioned as the number eight written in kanji.
Ude - arm, forearm.
Uke - one who initiates the attack and receives the defensive technique.
Uke - the slang translation to block. More correctly from the root word ukeru, to receive.
Undo - any exercise.
Unshu - a karate-do kata meaning "Cloud hands." Originally taught to Kenwa Mabuni by Aragaki Seisho.
Ura - back, the back of, or to the rear.

Uraken uchi - to strike with the back of the fist.
Ushiro - to the rear.

W
Wa uke - two arm circular block.
Wado ryu - a style of karate formulated by Hironori Otsuka.
Wakari mashita ka - the phrase, "Did you understand?"
Wakari masu - the phrase, "I understand."
Wakari masuka - the phrase, "Do you understand?"
Waki - the side. Side of the chest.
Wansu - also referred to as "Wanshu." A classical Okinawan kata also called "Empi."
Washide - eagle hand
Watashi - I, oneself.
Waza - technique.
Waza no kankyu - speed control.

Y
Yakusoku - prearranged.
Yame - the verbal command to "Stop!"
Yasumi - to break, or to rest.
Yoi - preparation. To prepare your mind for combat. A preparatory instruction to get ready.
Yoko - the side.
Yoko geri - side kick.
Yon - the number four. Also spelled shi.
Yondan - the fourth level of Yudansha in the Kyu/Dan ranking system.
Yonhon nukite - four finger spear hand.
Yonkyu - the fourth Mudansha level in the Kyu/Dan ranking system.
Yori ashi - a forward yori ashi movement consists of stepping forward with the front foot then dragging the rear foot up.
Yowai - weak.
Yubi - finger.
Yubi hasami - thumb and forefinger scissors.
Yudansha - those with rank. Black belt holders.
Yudansha kai - an association of black belt holders, or a governing board of an organization.

Z
Zanshin - remaining mind.
Zenkutsu dachi - a forward-leaning training stance.

APPENDIX 7
THE AUTHOR'S JOURNEY

As a child growing up in Hawaii, outdoor activities were all I ever enjoyed. Without the distractions of the TV, internet, cell phones and modern technology, it wasn't often that you would catch me indoors. I would meet my friends to play marble games, fish, sand surf, body surf, board surf, slide on algae-covered reefs and catch Moi (Pacific threadfin, also called "the fish of kings") under my feet on the beach.

Growing up in Sunset Beach, a small community on the North Shore of Oahu, most of my friend's mothers were also stay-at-home moms, and were always present to watch over their children, and the neighborhood children as well. They all were from the same "school" on how they viewed respect, obedience, responsibility and accountability. If I was at my friend's home and demonstrated negative behavior, his mother would immediately set me straight and then call my mother to give her a detailed report!

In the summer we all had seemingly endless chores to do, but my friends and I learned that if we all chipped in and helped each other we could play sooner. My parents also enrolled me and my brothers in the local Christian School where we enjoyed learning our core subjects, along with the "spiritual food" for everyday living. This schooling reinforced our shared values, and was provided to us on a reduced tuition, thanks to Glen and Ruth Powel, our minister and his wife, who made it possible for my brothers and I to attend. This childhood training prepared me to easily accept the martial arts.

At age 11 I was drawn to judo, primarily because a few of my buddies talked me into taking lessons because, they said, it was "so much fun." The practice was in Kahuku, a small sugar plantation town, just a few miles away from home. After a serious discussion with my dad about commitment, I entered a dojo for the first time. I learned that the martial art I was about to learn was indeed was called Judo (Gentle Way) and was created by Professor Jigoro Kano. He developed the techniques from the Samurai's Jiu Jutsu, and made his art form less dangerous so more people could enjoy doing it.

The first smell of my brand new muslin dogi (training uniform) made me feel confident immediately. I was exposed to ukemi (breakfalls) and balancing drills, then various throws and takedowns, pins, chokes and joint locks. Although I enjoyed the lessons of sensei Palimo and Matsuda senpai, I became a bit frustrated by having to yield to numerous falls from all the more advanced students. I wanted something more suitable for me but never discussed this with my dad since I had promised him that I would not complain or quit.

About a year later, on a typical warm Hawaiian summer day, several of my friends and I were sitting around deciding what clean mischief we were going to get into when a car pulled up towards us. The door opened and a big Hawaiian man wearing construction clothes got out and approached us. He introduced himself as Mr. Kahalekulu, and invited us to learn karate with some of his other students. He said he was the head instructor and that the cost would be $5.00 per month. Classes would be held in Sunset Beach, twice a week, at small house on the mauka (mountain) side near Banzai Pipeline, a famous surfing spot. "If you're interested, ask your parents if you can participate," Mr. Kahalekulu said with a smile.

I hadn't the slightest idea what karate was, but I thought that this was a good way to get out of judo practice and learn something new without serious consequences from my dad. I asked my mom if I could join, and she asked me to talk to my dad. It was easier to approach my mom at that time, but she almost always instructed me to talk to my dad. I already knew that but I had to try anyway. So I talked with my dad, and to my surprise he agreed. I could walk to and from practice, and I suspect that was the key point which led to his approval. Of course, being a classical Japanese dad, he had to again remind me about commitment and responsibility. "If you work around the house, do your homework, no fight with your brothers, no get lazy, and no answer back mommy, you can do karate," he pointed out in his broken English. And he added, "Saito name very important so you cannot do anything to dishonor name. Ada wise (otherwise) poho (waste time), daddy work hard to make name good, so no forget." I knew at that time, from that beginning, that karate was to become a lifelong journey for me. And it is now my way of life.

The small house was off a dirt road, nestled in the foothills of evergreen Ironwood trees. Two single-bulbed lights illuminated the training area and shown out onto the mountainside of the screenless windows. The training was strict, but the newness of doing something entirely different than judo kept me training hard. The loud shouts (kiais) echoed in the darkness, and probably scared off the Pupukea Man, our version of Big Foot. Kahalekulu sensei would often use the "Shinai" (bamboo sword) to "assist" us in our learning process. Scratching an itch wasn't allowed, even if the pesky mosquitoes landed on my face. To do so was quickly resolved by a whack of the shinai. If my stance was off or my wrist bent, the shinai would always be a quick reminder to fix my faults. Although it didn't hurt much, the loud noise it created was just enough of a reminder to keep me, as well as my fellow students, focused.

At first we were not allowed to spar until our kihon (basics) were perfected, but we were awed by the more advanced and older student's display of kumite. Our patience wore thin for not being able to spar, so after class a few of us who walked home stopped at Ehukai Park, (home of the famous Banzai Pipeline) and there we would engage in sparring, imitating our senior students and throwing in a few forms we picked up watching Chambara (sword fighting) movies at the theater. One of the forms we all used was named the "Shooting Star" where we would stand on one leg and place one arm above our head and the other arm in a down block position. We were all serious, shouted a lot, and kicked and punched at each other. I'm sure that if we had taken some film clips of our stunts it would have won a prize for "Best Comedy" at the film awards.

Eventually the house where we practiced fell to the termites who had also been busy practicing beneath us. Kahalekulu sensei was able to secure a beach house owned by a physician overlooking Sunset Beach to be our temporary dojo. The dojo floor was bare concrete, and being an intermediate student, Kahalekulu sensei would call upon me to demonstrate his sweeping and throwing techniques. The wooden floor at the other dojo was hard enough, taking a fall on concrete was quite painful.

After graduating from Sunset Beach Christian Elementary School, I attended Kahuku High School. "Ka huku" meaning "the projection," is located at the northernmost point of land on Oahu and was about 5 miles from our home. I was a bit nervous to attend high school, and my shyness didn't help either. But my karate training gave me enough courage to catch the bus each day, approach my classmates, and be able to have conversations with them.

Back in those days little martial arts history was taught. Instructors were more concerned about keeping us on a positive path with their strict rules of the dojo and harsh training routines. This was necessary because in those days "Dojo Yaburi," also known as known as the "dojo challenge," was still being practiced. This practice was inappropriate, however there were some instructors that felt that the only way to demonstrate their superiority was to challenge and attempt to defeat the head instructor and top student from another school in order to humiliate them in front of their students. We did have one instructor and his top students visit our dojo in Sunset Beach, however after watching all of us practice he decided to leave peacefully. Dojo yaburi is almost unheard of in these modern times.

Eventually I found out that sensei Kahalekulu learned his karate from Tommy Morita, who at that time was the representative of Dr. Tsuyoshi Chitose (aka Chinen Gua in Okinawa), who was the founder of the Chito-ryu karate-do, in Kumamoto City, Japan. Since Morita sensei also studied kung fu and kenpo, he incorporated some of these techniques with his Chito-ryu style, which were passed on to his instructors, and then these were eventually taught to me.

Very impressionable at that time, we were awestruck when the men demonstrated breaking techniques. Sonny Morales, who worked for the Honolulu City & County Sanitation Department, could "Nukite" (spear-hand) three 1" pine boards pressed together, a feat I have never seen anyone else do. He said that while he was on his daily garbage runs he heaved the heavy garbage cans with his finger tips to strengthen them. Others would break boards held by two assistants, and I might add, without any spacers! The crisp sound of the boards breaking sounded sweet to my ears, and now I had another goal to focus on. My friends and I would constantly strike the makiwara (padded striking post) in preparation for our breaking opportunities.

Occasionally, when the 25th division of Schofield Barracks would have their maneuvers, soldiers would march some 20 miles to their "war zone" above our house. Tanks, jeeps and trucks also traveled on the Kamehameha Highway which was just in front of our house. At times, tanks would spit black rubber pieces from their tracks that would land to the side of the highway. We gathered these rubber blocks and would use them as a target, hitting against them with our knuckles and the side edges of our hands. The callouses and black residue left on our knuckles was our trademark, and many who saw those marks knew instantly that we were martial artists and that it would not be wise to mess with us. We would meet nearly every Saturday to break rocks, boards, bricks and whatever we could get our hands on. Sometimes we found success in breaking these items, but there was one challenging red brick that only bruised our bones, as it was stubborn as we were. After striking it with a hammer fist several times in a row, we would grasp our fist, placed it close to our body and display our agony and defeat with a distorted face and painful sounds. I should have kept that brick just to remind me of the great times we shared.

Kahalekulu sensei was assisted by Versola senpai, and twice a week they also taught karate at a Catholic School in Wahiawa, a town in Central Oahu near Schofield Barracks and Wheeler Air Base. I was asked to accompany them to the school but little did I know, at that time, that they were grooming me to be an instructor as well.

Although a starting quarterback for 4 years at Kahuku High School, I was very shy. Karate certainly helped me overcome my insecurities, and I became more assertive and confident. I became more involved with community activities and organized community dances, and even a luau. I was active with ANSO, the Alliance of North Shore Organization, and was honored with the North Shore's "Man of the Year" award for my services.

I received my black belt some four years after my first introduction to karate, and by this time the Vietnam War was in full swing. Some of us decided to enlist in the Air Force rather than wait to be drafted into the army. Basic training was held at Lackland AFB in Texas, Dental Specialist training at

Gunter AFB in Alabama, and Medical Specialist schooling at Sheppard AFB in Wichita Falls, Texas. I was selected to be a "rope" (a student leadership position that promotes and develops leadership skills}. Airmen chosen for this honor must meet high standards of military bearing, perform well academically and have no behavioral issues. With this special leadership responsibility, it was my duty to assign duties, assist airmen with their problems, and march the airmen to and from school, to the chow hall, and anywhere else our drill sergeants commanded us to go. During our marches, I enjoyed leading them with "cadence call" which is the traditional military "call-and-response" work and march song. I was also able to teach a few airmen some karate during our breaks, which didn't come too often.

My first duty assignment was at the dental clinic at Norton AFB in California. As soon as I was acclimated to the base I was able to secure an on-base building to begin a karate training program. Assisted by Donald Kluge, who was a Master of Ophthalmic Prosthetics and Crown and Bridge Specialist, our dojo was well-received by fellow airmen, their dependents, and the public from the surrounding areas.

Around 1967, Kahalekulu sensei decided to retire from teaching due to health reasons. He asked me to take over the teaching duties, and informed me that Tommy Morita had decided to represent Nagamine Sensei, the founder of Matsubayashi-ryu Shorin-ryu, and had resigned from the Chitose Sensei's organization. Kahalekulu sensei promoted me to Godan and I began teaching under the Go Shin Jutsu name. Although Kahalekulu sensei no longer taught karate, I still considered him to be our Chief Instructor and therefore invited him to attend our tournaments and special functions.

I eventually ended up in Hawaii, serving out the remainder of my tour at Wheeler AFB. Since karate was still very close to my heart, I quickly made arrangements to teach at the Pupukea Recreation Center, just north of Waimea Bay. Teaching was always rewarding for me, not only because it kept me practicing karate fundamentals and kata, but also because it allowed me to see the growth in my students. I knew there was something special about offering this type of training; it provided students with physical exercise, mental stimulation, and care for their emotions, and it secured them in a strong social network. My karate knowledge was still limited in all areas, but this added to my hunger to learn more for a higher level of understanding.

Eventually I had several advanced students that assisted me, and we enjoyed great training together. John Isabelo, Ben Ballesteros and John Widmer were faithful to our training and were the backbone of our dojo. Quite often after class we would enjoy playing table tennis or singing Hawaiian songs accompanied by Mark Proprios and his superb ukulele strumming. Ballesteros, Isabelo and Widmer eventually found themselves serving with the Honolulu Police Department. John Isabelo worked as a homicide detective, and later as an investigator for the Attorney General's office in Hawaii. He continues to teach for our organization today.

In the early 1970s, restlessness stirred me into finding a sensei in order to broaden my horizons. After speaking to several sensei, including James Miyaji, Fumio Demura and Chuzo Kotaka, I decided to join with Kotaka's International Karate Federation based out of Hawaii. I was particularly drawn to the precision and beauty of Shito-ryu, a stye formulated by Master Kenwa Mabuni.

I relocated to Southern California once again, in hopes of furthering my education and possibly attending dental school at Loma Linda University. John Isabelo remained dedicated to the karate-do and kept the Sunset Beach dojo active. Several months later I had opened several dojos in San Bernardino, Fontana, Banning, Loma Linda and Redlands, and taught the Kotaka method of Shito-ryu, also serving the International Karate Federation as National Director for over 25 years. During those years I taught John Sells and Ray Castilonia, who also later decided to make karate their life-long journey. Sells is a current member of the Seito Shito-ryu organization, and the historian who authored Unante. Castilonia founded the Aoinagi-ha Shito-ryu group in California. Meanwhile, in Hawaii John Isabelo trained with Walter Nishioka, the founder of the International Karate League (previously known as Statewide Karate League) and he continues to teach a modified version of Shorin-ryu and Wado-ryu. Other black belts, such as Manuel Corona, continued teaching karate in Rialto, California. Rollin Ramsaran earned his Ph.D. degree in theology and is presently the Dean and Professor of New Testament at the Emmanuel School of Religion.

A highlight of my years teaching in California was organizing the annual Inland Empire Karate Championships in Rialto, CA. Mike Visser, who received his black belt from Nakano from the Big Island (and who was a member of the Nishioka Shihan's Statewide Karate League) co-directed these championships with me. We invited Fumio Demura and his Japanese Deer Park Demonstration Team, emceed by Dan Ivan. Included on his team were Sho Kosugi, Kiyoshi Yamazaki, Tadashi Hiraoka and Doug Ivan. Ray Dalke also honored us with his attendance, demonstrating Shotokan Karate for the many in attendance. We also enjoyed some great training at my San Bernardino dojo with Ray Dalke and the instructors from his UC Riverside Karate Club, Mike Visser, Joe Pagliuso and Doug Kretch from the United States Karate Organization, along with some of my senior instructors.

I was always told, as were many other karate enthusiasts, that soon karate was going to be an Olympic Sport. So, just to keep in tune for this possibility, I participated in a few tournaments. I had my share of first place acknowledgments for both kata and kumite, and especially enjoyed the tournaments held by Fumio Demura at the Japanese Deer Park in Buena Park, Tak Kubota's tournament in Southern California, and James Miyaji and Chuzo Kotaka's tournaments in Hawaii. These stood out mainly because of the caliber of athletes from Hawaii, the mainland, and Japan that participated.

Since the IOC kept rejecting karate as an Olympic Sport, I made the decision to focus more on organizing tournaments and training officials.

At the end of 1978 I decided to leave California to re-evaluate my goals. I turned over my dojo to Yukinori Kugimiya, a long-time friend who was a representative of Dr. Chitose's Chito-ryu group

I returned to Hawaii and began teaching at the Pupukea Recreation Center. During the day I ran an art gallery in Haleiwa, a charming town on the North Shore of Oahu, the home of Matsumoto Shave Ice and the Haleiwa Boat Harbor.

I had a thirst for more in-depth knowledge, so I arranged a few one-on-one training sessions from Kotaka Sensei. Although he had much technical knowledge, his views and philosophy leaned more to winning and competition. His brand of karate and his drive to be a successful businessman did not satisfy my needs. I was looking for something with more of substance, yet I remained faithful and loyal, thinking that it was not yet my time to fully understand my place in karate.

In June of 1980 I made the decision to return to the mainland, and then decided to head up the I-5 from Northern California to find my new home. I stopped at each potential city, and the more north I traveled, the more beautiful the landscape became. As I entered Oregon, the mountains, valleys and rivers stirred my inner spirit. When I reached Grants Pass, Oregon, a city in Josephine County located off Interstate 5 northwest of Medford, I immediately fell in love with the beauty of the Rogue River, the laid-back attitude and the friendliness of the folks I met. In August of that year I decided to make Grants Pass my permanent new home.

In 1981, my dad and I converted the garage of my house into a dojo, and soon I had a handful of students eager to learn from the newcomer in the area. A couple of years later we outgrew the space at the house, so I leased a commercial space in town. To ease my lease obligation, I incorporated tanning, toning and massage services with the martial art activities.

In 1986 I took a few students to Ray Dalke's UCR Karate Championship. It was at this event I was introduced to Joe Mirza, the Chairman for AAU (Amateur Athletic Union) Karate. He expressed a need for volunteers to assist him in strengthening AAU Karate and invited me to join in his mission. I accepted his invitation and the following year was appointed the Regional AAU Director for the Pacific Northwest. In 1989 I became the AAU National Karate Treasurer and in 2000 I was named the National Executive Director for AAU Karate.

Now fully immersed in the AAU Karate program and beginning to see the potential in organizing a healthy environment for competition for athletes throughout the country, I encouraged Chuzo Kotaka to become involved in the AAU to expose the IKF students to a national arena of competition. After thoughtful consideration, he finally agreed to join. Since then, IKF athletes have enjoyed earning numerous awards in the competitions and have become National and International AAU Champions.

Encouraged to become involved with the Oregon AAU to establish a strategic position, especially on voting issues at the national level involving all sports, I accepted opportunities to serve in other AAU capacities. In 1992 I was elected as Oregon AAU Vice President and Commissioner for Oregon AAU Martial Arts. The following year I was elected President (later called Governor) of the Oregon AAU, and served there until 2010. In 2008, I was appointed to the Board of Directors of the Amateur Athletic Union. In 2010, I resigned from the AAU in order to spend more time working with my own karate plans.

In 1996, Lana Lavenberg, a student of mine, encouraged me to meet with David Basset, (an engineer, builder, and former test pilot), to begin plans for building my own dojo. David felt he had a parcel of land, which was adjacent to some of his other commercial properties, that would be an ideal location for our new karate home. The property was easily accessible, in a safe place and very visible. With God's grace, everything went smoothly with the planning, financing and finally the construction of the new well-designed dojo. There are so many plusses to owning your own dojo that I now sometimes wonder why it took me so long to do so. Nevertheless, the timing was perfect and I am still eternally grateful to Lana and David.

In 2000, I became a member of the Nihon Karate-do Kai under the leadership of Kenzo Mabuni Soke. During those memorable times spent with Mabuni Soke at our home and at the dojo in Grants Pass, at several National Championships, at his home in Japan, and even at our wedding in Hawaii, I shared my plans and my vision to carry on his legacy. I also discussed the politics that I felt were eroding the principles and expectations karate was built upon. I revealed to him that I was on "the road less traveled" and that I always spoke my mind when others would remain silent. I fought for those who were always humble, loyal and passionate in doing the right thing, but were too timid or afraid to speak their mind. Many probably thought I was being disrespectful, especially to the higher-ranking black belts, when I would oppose their self-serving motives. I observed instructors actions and the way they treated their students and colleagues, and challenged them with views that didn't quite fit the karate spirit. Mabuni Soke agreed that more senior instructors should conduct themselves as leaders with a better purpose, rather than lean on their rank for respect and power. I asked Soke what he thought was the best way for me to continue the Shito-ryu legacy and his teachings. To my surprise, after many hours of discussions with Rumi Kosugi (my "daughter") interpreting, Soke Mabuni gave his blessing to pursue my vision of Shito-ryu independently, without the constraint of any of his personal organization's policies or rules. As many in the karate circles throughout the world know, this gesture of trust and goodwill is almost unheard of. In fact I am the only instructor that Soke has ever given his blessing to remain independent. Kazuo Sakai Shihan, the Secretary of Nihon Karate-do Kai wrote, "I know this case with you is an exception, as you are the only person Soke Kenzo Mabuni has permitted to belong to our organization who does not need to obey the rules and regulations of Shito-Ryu Karate Do Kai and USA Shihan Kai." I remain deeply honored.

In 2008, when I had reached my 46th year in the martial arts, I felt it was time to initiate Saito-ha Shito-ryu karate-do. If it wasn't for the latitude, trust, confidence and friendship given to me by Soke Mabuni, I would not have arrived at this decision. I once again alerted the Japan Seito Shito-ryu organization of my decision, and the following message was sent to me from Tsukasa Mabuni Soke, the third Soke of the Shito-ryu International Karate Do Kai, and her Saiko Shihan Kai (Head Council of Teachers), "We feel so sad to hear of your decision, but we respect and support your decision. As you know, the spirit of the human beings of Shito-ryu karate is fully the same, even though you have your own ha. It means we are the same field of karate forever, and would like to keep good relations. So when you need our support or help, please contact us anytime."

This special opportunity of founding Saito-ha Shito-ryu required teamwork, dedication and wisdom. We needed to remain committed to our mission of preserving the Shito-ryu legacy. No doubt, the path ahead would be challenging. We would be constantly examined and even criticized, however the endorsements, encouragements and support reassured me that this decision to move ahead was prudent. So a Shihan Kai was formed, a group of my senior instructors, and I appointed Tony Mendonca as the director of this elite leadership group.

Our first launching of Saito-ha Shito-ryu took place in Albany, New York, on July 2, 2008. The TKFI Shihan Kai invited several instructors, their families, and friends from across the country to witness this historic event. The packed room provided encouragement, hope and support. Endorsements came from many respected martial arts masters and professional friends throughout the world. To provide opportunities for others to participate in this newly formed system and method of Shito-ryu, the Shihan Kai decided to hold launching ceremonies in Brasil, Oregon, Hawaii and Italy.

The second ceremony was held during the Instructor's Gasshuku in Grants Pass, Oregon in August of 2008 at the All Sports Park Pavilion. Organized by the TKFI Shihan Kai, the humble ceremony touched everyone's heart and rekindled a flame of eternal brotherhood.

A third glamorous ceremony was held during our international training in Brasil, July 19, 2009. Several Mayors, government officials, military representatives and business leaders participated in wishing our organization a successful future. This ceremony was organized by Ubiratan Souza de Lima, and one of the highlights was a grand festival with fireworks, dancing, and tasty foods, including corn-on-the-cob.

The fourth ceremony took place in October, 2009, in Hawaii at the beautiful and historic Wai'oli Tea Room, Oahu's hidden treasure and Honolulu's pride and joy since 1922. Several shihan, and sensei, with their lovely brides, graciously attended the ceremony conducted by Tony Mendonca and Ceci Cheung. Among the well-respected instructors and their wives were Walter Nishioka, James Miyaji, Lee Donohue, John Isabelo and Charles Goodin.

Our final formal ceremony was held the following year in the beautiful country of Italy. After a fantastic Italian meal, the TKFI Shihan Kai joined together in promising to stay committed, united and fulfilling the mission of our organization.

The planning and incorporation of the values of Saito-ha Shito-ryu Karate-do requires leadership and teamwork. It is easy to stand alone and teach "safely," however for us to hold each other accountable in training, knowledge and growth I thought it best to officially organize the Traditional Karate-do Federation International. This "family" of instructors and students throughout the world work in unison to strengthen each other in mind, body and spirit. It provides an opportunity for those without a home to join us, and be accepted as our brothers and sisters. It is not my objective to have a large organization with thousands of members to boost my living standards. Instead, I would rather have dedicated members who truly understand the meaning of good character, loyalty, faithfulness, commitment, high moral principles and leadership, and who truly embrace our purpose.
Our mission statement reads:

"The Saito-ha Shito-ryu Karate-do of the Traditional Karate-do Federation International aspires to bring together members to prosper Saito-ha Shito-ryu Karate-do with high standards. The organization is dedicated to the promotion, preservation and education of the martial arts and its traditions, with service to the community in the spirit of karate-do. The TKF International Saito-ha Shito-ryu Karate-do strives to be the most reputable and respectable organization worldwide, and pledges to uphold the classical styles of Shito-ryu as founded by Kenwa Mabuni, promoted by Kenzo Mabuni, and advanced by Del Saito Soke through the incorporation of his modifications of the style."

We take pride in our members accountability, integrity, and honor. Each member is asked to sincerely commit to achieving the goals of the TKF International Saito-ha Karate-do with veracity, engaging in community outreach activities, and striving for self-improvement of the mind, body and spirit. Furthermore, the TKFI principle of karate teaching is to allow individual members to passionately train to better define themselves as individuals, while learning the importance of trustworthiness, perseverance, courtesy, humility, courage and wisdom.

The TKFI Karate-do competition programs offer quality competition and training as a supplement to the general program of the TKFI organization. The program is intended to enhance the physical, mental and moral development of all athletes; to provide an avenue for competition on a local, national and international level; to integrate into a curriculum that will encourage our athletes to choose a drug-free lifestyle; to showcase TKFI Karate champions, instructors, coaches, and officials as role models; and to promote good sportsmanship and exemplary citizenship, as well as safety, in competition.

Success is based on teamwork, not on one's ego and selfish motives. Although there will be differences of opinions, it will be much easier to find resolve with issues as long as our goals and our mission is a common one. It is through this strength of unity that we can overcome any personal disturbances, knowing that we have friends that will always provide encouragement and support. Unity will keep us healthy in every sphere of life.

Having my own organization makes it so much easier to assist students who need a structured environment in order to become upright citizens with a purpose. I am not obligated to pay outrageous promotion fees and other dues to an organization, which in the past I had to pass on to my students. Instead, I can work with each student, or with families, to make it affordable for them to train regularly. If my bills are paid each month and I am fortunate to have a few dollars left to fish, golf or to treat my wife to a movie or dinner, I am grateful.

Moving on to our present-day organization, it would be remiss of me not to mention my senior instructors and advisors who have remained loyal and stood by their oath of commitment. Many instructors have come and gone, for whatever reason, which is often how life unfolds. My hope is that we were able to teach them something of value and substance that they can manifest in what they are trying to pursue in life. Those that continue with outstanding leadership, commitment, and dedication are Tony Mendonca, Rumi Kosugi Tajalle, Ubiratan de Souza Lima, Ceci Cheung, Dwight Grover, Joan Gombau, Jim Hamilton, Robert Burstein, Chuck Aoto, John Isabelo, Amir Mahdavi, Gowtham Ragunathan, Francesco Arabi, Alessandra Arabi, Ken Frownfelter, Hendry Santoso and Basilio Bara. Others who believe in what we are accomplishing continue to volunteer in their special ways at all of our dojos worldwide. Those teaching, assisting, organizing and supporting at the honbu dojo include Sebastian Gattey, Matthias Gattey, Kelsey Kitts, Michele Barnes, Misty Hamilton, Jerred Shoemaker, Sherry Archambault and Lisa Pickart.

I continue to teach in hopes that my students will learn and understand the "warrior spirit," and use it in order to prevail in their lives. I feel too many folks become too complacent by not paying attention to their civic duties and by taking freedom for granted. Through the study of karate-do, I hope to aid in restoring and perpetuating the character necessary for human decency, and to continue fighting to keep our Constitution and God-given rights alive. Learning fighting skills gives one the techniques needed to defend oneself against their own ego, stresses, dissatisfactions and temptations of daily life. Too often our fellow men render themselves helpless and give in when things appear too difficult to tackle.

As I am writing this book, the COVID-19 pandemic has caught everyone by surprise. As I hear and see the reactions throughout the world, I am, on one hand, uplifted in seeing so many families actually spending more quality time with each other. They are sprucing up their yards, going over school work with their children, playing more board games and even are preparing meals together. Neighbors seem to slow down and take more time to get to know each other. On the other hand, I am deeply concerned by the power exercised by some of our politicians who use fear as a common denominator, leaving many feeling helpless and powerless. Crises such as this should serve as a wake-up call for us to stand together. Beware of the few power-mongers out there who are using the reactions of the general public to satisfy their future ambitions, as the consequences will not be not beneficial to those they should be serving.

Scaring away the COVID virus.

KARATE IS ALSO ABOUT HAVING FUN

Mark and Sebastian Gattey must practice zanshin.

Jade Elardi passes her final kyu test.

Monthly pot luck dinners with changing food themes are always well attended.

Faithful golfing buddies Mick Jennings, Dave Presely, Chuck Briere and Tom Trader.

Hanging out with Jake Shimabukuro, internationally renowned ukulele virtuoso from Hawaii.

Polar plunging for a good cause.

APPENDIX 8
MEMORABLE PHOTOS PAST & PRESENT

WITH KENZO MABUNI SOKE

Mabuni Soke and Toshio Saito, author's dad.

A special dinner with Mabuni Soke, his wife Hiroko and his Shihan Kai members in Osaka, Japan.

Enjoying a delicious meal with Mabuni Soke.

Soke Kenzo Mabuni, a humble and wise master of Seito Shito-ryu Karate-do.

Mabuni Soke at his home in Osaka, Japan.

Sharing some great memories with the author's teacher at Osaka Castle.

Over a hundred participants at Kenzo Mabuni Soke's clinic held at the Grants Pass dojo.

Officials with Kenzo Soke and Hiorko Mabuni at the International Karate-do Taikai, held in Grants Pass, Oregon.

Mabuni Soke demonstrating kakiwake uke.

James Miyaji, Lim Sison, Kenzo Mabuni, Minobu Miki and Masayuki Shimabukuro.

Kenzo Soke teaching in Grants Pass, Oregon.

Students are in complete awe when Soke is teaching.

Mabuni Soke with Mr. Yamaoka and Hirokazu Kanazawa.

Mabuni Soke with students at the Grants Pass dojo.

Instructors flank Kenzo Mabuni Soke in a historic taikai and seminar held in his honor, in Grants Pass, Oregon.

Tsukasa Mabuni Soke with her husband and mother Hiroko.

"Mama" Hiroko Mabuni in Osaka, Japan.

CONTRIBUTORS TO MARTIAL ARTS

Sharing great stories with Osamu Ozawa and Dan Ivan.

Chuck Merriman, an outstanding Goju-ryu sensei, who always adds humor in his conversations.

Tomohiro Arashiro and Kazumasa Itaki in Grants Pass, Oregon.

With Hirokazu Kanazawa in Las Vegas.

Preparing for a meeting with Hidetaka Nishiyama and Mike Harrigan in Chicago.

Ray Dalke, a Riverside Hall of Fame recipient, and the highest ranking American in Shotokan Karate.

Takayuki Mikami, one of JKA's top instructor who currently teaches in New Orleans.

Fumio Demura and Dallas Grady Watanabe at the Oregon State Championship, in Grants Pass.

Sadaharu Fujimoto, a talented sensei known for his breaking skills.

Instructors representing various styles always willing to share their expertise with others.

Ubiratan de Souza Lima, TKFI Director of South America and President Hajime Ide in Mirassol, Brazil.

Rony Kluger from Israel, a loyal friend and one of the great Goju-ryu masters of today.

With my karate brother, Bobby Chinen.

Alex Miladi and Pat Haley in Chico, California.

World champions, Takashi Katada and Yukimitsu Hasegawa.

Launching in Hawaii was attended by John Isabelo, Walter Nishioka, Lee Donohue, James Miyaji and Charles Goodin.

Honoring Al Kahalekulu sensei at the Invitational tournament in Waialua, Hawaii.

Maile and Robert Koncal, directors of Kachi Karate Hawaii, with "Papa 3" on their wedding day.

Leone Bara & Toni Romano, the backbone of the World Traditional Okinawa Karate Federation.

Special times with David Krieger, President Emeritus of the Nuclear Age Peace Foundation, Grace Sherwin, Rollin Ramsaran and Peggy Grimm.

John and Lisa Limcaco with Sho Kosugi at the Oregon State Karate Championship in Grants Pass.

Alisa Au, U.S. WKF World Champions with Christophe Pinna, French WKF World Champion.

Takeshi and Kenzo Nakasone, owners of the world famous Shureido gi.

George Kotaka, U.S. WKF World Champion and a positive role model for athletes throughout the world.

PERMANENTLY ETCHED

Pat Haley having fun with some of the Shihan Kai members in Osaka, Japan.

Happy times with instructors at Kazumasa Itaki's Charity Tournament celebration party, in Tachikawa City.

The author teaching in Virginia at Dwight Grover's dojo.

Tony Mendonca and Rumi Kosugi Tajalle Matsuyama have endured many years of hard training.

Children in Tanzania love karate and especially Francesco Arabi.

Annual higher kyu and dan testing at the honbu dojo.

A royal welcome in India by Kaysavan Ragunathan and his instructors.

Enthusiastic students learning kumite techniques in Iran.

Sunset Beach dojo fortunate to train near the beach all year long with assistant instructor Ben Ballesteros.

Ray Dalke showing Robert Burstein and Matt Collins the proper way to hit the makiwara.

The author teaching in Deva, Romania.

Joan Gombau keeping a watchful eye on his students in Catalonia.

The author conducting a Eiku workshop in Sao Jose Rio Preto, Brazil.

TKFI Summer Camp at Camp Erdman, in Mokuleia on the North Shore of Oahu.

Students enjoying the warm Pacific waters while enduring intense training.

Summer camp participants enjoying a tour at Waimea Falls in Hawaii.

Gerard Gombau trains for hours to be a victorious competitor.

Vallori Abbey and sister Vanessa perfecting their countering techniques.

The formidable team from Israel led by Rony Kluger at the Olympic Training Center in Colorado Springs.

Back in the days in Hawaii where training was so hard that students have difficulties smiling.

Sharing some time with "the champ" Evander Holyfield.

Students at the San Bernardino dojo in the early 1970s.

After a good workout in Catalonia organized by Joan Gombau.

Dick Thompson with Clara and Toshio Saito, the author's parents.

The Katada family in Yamanashi, Japan.

TKFI students doing very well with Hamed Zafaranlou under the directorship of Dr. Amir Mahdavi Shihan in Iran.

The author, with Robert Burstein, trains female Iranian students who wear the traditional hijab head covering.

Masumi Timpson, a well known koto master, with some of her assistants at the Asian Cultural Festival.

Proud students receiving their hard earned Dan and Kyu certificates at the Mirassol dojo in Brazil.

Luisa, Ubiratan de Souza Lima's daughter, giving "Grandpa Soke" a tour of our Karate Camp in Brazil.

Joana Gombau spends many hours keeping her students active at our TKFI dojo in Catalonia.

Jim Hamilton takes to the air in preparation for the Police Olympics.

John Isabelo, Joel & Venus Lovingfoss, TKFI leadership team in Hawaii.

John and Carmen Isabelo, devoted friends forever.

Kirby, our chimpanzee black belt, auditions to be our dojo mascot.

Kari, Tysen, Kasen, and Bev enjoying the day with Grandma Saito.

Enthusiastic karatekas after a strenuous workout.

Junki Yoshida and his wife Linda, also known for his *Mr. Yoshida's Gourmet Sauce,* at his beautiful home in Troutdale, Oregon.

Relaxing with Brendal, a 420 lb. bengal tiger, after a gruelling photo shoot.

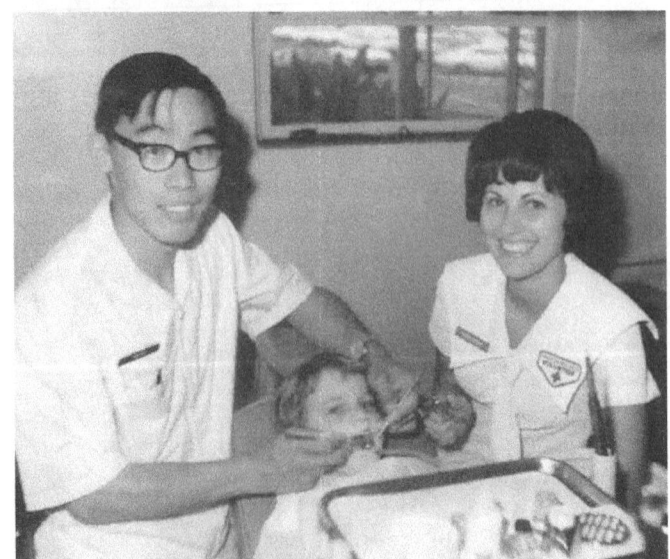
Enjoying dentistry while serving in the Air Force.

Author teaching with baby Evelyn so her mother Morgan may train.

Jerry Chew officiating Dallas Grady's match in Oregon.

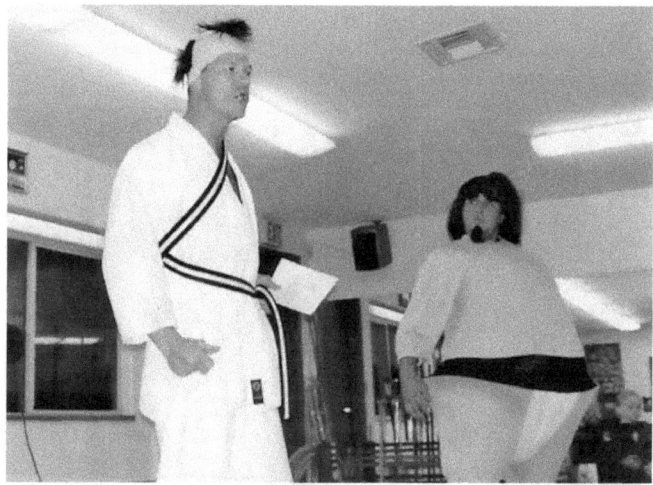
Jim Hamilton and Tony Mendonca keep students roring in laughter with their skits.

Tony Mendonca awarded the Joel Ferrell Award for his athletic ability at the AAU Junior Olympic Games.

Granddaughters Kaila and Elise with their dad Robert and the author's wife Ida in Kauai.

Ted Nakamura, childhood friend, also known for his famous Ted's Bakery in Sunset Beach, Hawaii.

FUN WITH TALENTED FRIENDS

Noble Willingham an accomplished television and film actor.

E.T. the Extra-Terrestrial's Henry Thomas.

Having fun in Paramount's production, "Fire in the Sky."

Dick Fosbury, Gold medalist in the 1968 Summer Olympics in the high jump event and creater of the Fosbury Flop.

Robert Clouse, film director, who directed "Enter the Dragon," starring Bruce Lee.

Stunt coordinator for Robert Clouse in Jacksonville, Oregon.

Professional make-up artist making a punched face look very real.

Referees' clinic in Anchorage, Alaska.

Florence Griffith Joyner, "Flo Jo," won 3 gold medals and a silver at the 1988 Summer Olympic Games.

Jim Ryun, first high school athlete to run a mile in under four minutes, and Silver Medalist running the 1500 m at the 1968 Sumer Olympics.

Steven Lopez, Gold medalist as an American Taekwondo competitor in the 2000 and 2004 Olympics.

A great round of golf with Issac Curtis, wide receiver for the Cincinnati Bengals.

Olga Korbut, "Sparrow from Minsk," won four gold medals and two silver medals at the Summer Olympic Games. Had a nice time together in Florida.

Jacqueline Bisset, film actress known for her roles in *Detective*, *Bullitt*, *The Sweet Ride* and *The Deep*.

Reggie Williams, previous linebacker for the Bengals and Vice President of Disney's Wide World of Sports, a driving force in hosting NBA "bubble" at the sports complex in Orlando.

Hiroshi Wajima, retired Yokozuna in sumo wrestling.

Buick LaSabre commercial.

HONBU DOJO - OUR HOME

Hoe hana...

to framing...

to drywall...

to a brand new dojo.

Ribbon cutting ceremony at our Grand Opening.

Ceremony organized by Dwight Ellis, Chamber Director and the Grants Pass Ambassadors.

A home where many are welcome to learn and share the lessons that karate has to offer.

A serene Japanese garden.

Koi pond for all to enjoy.

Teamwork made this all possible.

Honbu dojo open all year long to serve the community and international dojo members.

Saito-Ha Shito-Ryu Karate-Do
For The Modern Warrior

COLLAGE OF TREASURED MOMENTS

APPENDIX 9
THROUGH THE LOOKING GLASS

MARTIAL ARTS DEGREES - MOST RECENT
2009 - Master Teacher degree of Budo - Karate-do International, by the State of Israel, Ministry of Education, Culture and Sports.
2009 - 10th degree Black Belt, Dento Karate-do Rengo Kai - International.
2005 - Third Degree Black Belt, Iaijutsu, Nippon Kobubo Jikinshin-Kai USA.
1998 - Eight Degree Black Belt, Shito-Ryu Nippon Karate-Do Kai.
1998 - Hanshi (highest teaching title - shogo), Shito-Ryu Nippon Karate-Do Kai.
1990 - Shihan Menkyo Sho, Shito-Ryu Nippon Karate-Do Kai.

TRAINING EXPERIENCE
- Saito-ha Shito-ryu, 2008 to present.
- Seito Shito-ryu, 1998 to 2008.
- Eishin-Ryu Iaijutsu, 1996 to present.
- Kotaka-Ha Shito-ryu, 1974 - 1999.
- Chitose-ryu Karate-Do, Hawaii, 1962 - 1974.
- Kodokan judo in Hawaii, 1961 - 1962.

ORGANIZATION AFFILIATIONS
- Member of the Committee for Awarding Degrees and Titles of the World Traditional Okinawa Karate-do Federation, 2014 to present.
- Technical Advisor and Vice-President of the World Traditional Okinawa Karate-do Federation, 2014 to present.
- Founder and President of the Traditional Karate-do Federation International, 2008 to present.
- Governor's representative for Zones C & D and member of the National AAU Board of Directors, 2006 to 2010.
- Director, Del Saito's Martial Arts Training Center, 2000 to present.
- National AAU Karate Executive Director, 2000 to 2010.
- Oregon District Governor, September, 2004 to 2010.
- Member of Nippon Kobudo Jikishin Kai-USA, 2000 to present.
- Member of the Nihon Karate-Do Kai, 2000 to 2008.
- Oregon AAU President, July 1993 to 2004.
- Oregon AAU Martial Arts Chairman. 1992 - 1993.
- Oregon AAU Karate Chairman, 1989 to 2004.
- AAU Secretary Treasurer, August, 1998 to 2000.
- AAU Region 12 Director, 1987 to 2004.

OFFICIATING EXPERIENCE
- Refereed and judged at numerous tournaments throughout the United States, 1966 to present.
- Certified AAU Class A Official, 1988 to 2010.
- Refereed at AAU National Championships and at the AAU Junior Olympic Games, 1988 to 2010.
- Member of the National Council of Referees, 1989 to 2010.
- Conducted Officials' clinic throughout the United States to certify referees, judges and other officials.
- Refereed at the International Goodwill Games, 1990.
- Selected as one of 15 officials in the US to officiate at the US team trials held at the US Olympic Training Center in Colorado Springs, on February 17 & 18, 1995.
- Selected to Council of Referees at the Pan American Union Karate Organization U.S. Team Trials in

Chicago, April 22, 23, 1995
- Obtained PUKO International Judging license in Medellin, Columbia, on May 28, 1995.
- Refereed at the PUKO Games in Medellin, Columbia in May, 1995.
- Selected as one of five Referees to represent U.S. at the WKC World Karate Championships in Hamilton Ontario, Canada, May 24-26, 1996.
- Appointed to the WKC Referee's Council, May 26, 1996.
- Organized the TKO/AAU team to Osaka, Japan for 5th Taikai. Team won 9 gold, 6 silver and 3 bronze medals.

TEACHING EXPERIENCE
- Teaching for the World Traditional Okinawa Karate-do Federation, 2014 to present.
- Teaching internationally for the Traditional Karate-do Federation International, 2008 to present.
- Conducted clinics, lectures, workshops, and training in self defense tactics for Law Enforcement, SWAT teams, Air Force bases, schools, universities, hospitals, Veterinarian clinics, YMCA, YWCA, and community organizations, 1967 to present.

AWARDS
- Diplomatic Passport, Knights of Malta, 2016
- 8 September Award for Service in Education by the City Council of Mirassol, Brazil, 2012
- Kansha Sai Award in Mirassol, Brazil, by Ubiratan Shihan, 2012.
- Commendation by the people of Hawaii for teaching, promoting and preserving traditional karate-do, presented by Neil Abercrombie, Governor, State of Hawaii.
- 25 Year AAU Service Award, 2010.
- Oregon AAU Appreciation Award, 2010.
- Presented Soke degree by International Budo Academy, Israel, 2009
- President's Leadership Award, 2004.
- AAU Karate Hall of Fame, Man of the Year, 1997.
- AAU President's Leadership Award, 1997.
- AAU Communication Award, 1995.
- International Karate Hall of Fame, 1994.
- AAU Rookie Newsletter Editor of the Year, 1994.
- Oregon AAU Leadership Award, 1990.
- National AAU Outstanding Service Award, 1990.
- National IKF Outstanding Instructor Award, 1986.
- North Shore's Man of the Year Award (Hawaii), 1969.

OTHER ACCOMPLISHMENTS
2015 - Reporter in Paramount Studio's **Fire in the Sky** with James Garner.
1994 - 1995, owner of Graphics and Imaging Unlimited.
1991 - Authored "Karate-do, The Way Of Shito-ryu" (Library of Congress number 91-67331, ISBN 0-9631274-0-3).
1984 - 2010, Director of the Annual Oregon Karate Championships.
1990 - 1997, President of the Board, Pine Valley School.
1990 - 1991, Executive Vice President of Mountain Alloys. (Foundry, machining and manufacturing plant).
1990 - Stunt Coordinator for motion picture producer and director Robert Clouse (Director of **Enter the Dragon**).
1989 - 1990, Publisher/Editor of the Grants Pass Chamber of Commerce Profile & Directory.
1989 - 1990, Co-owned Osprey Publications.
1978 - 1979, General Building Contractor.

1970 - 1973, Dental & Maxillo-Facial Lab technician with Donald Kluge.
1966 - 1970, Served four years in the U.S. Air Force, in the dental profession.

COMMUNITY AFFILIATIONS
- 2009 to present - Member, Grants Pass Elk's Lodge.
- 2001 - 2006, President, Grants Pass Asian Cultural Society.
- 1993 to present - Member, The American Legion.
- Past Board Member, Grants Pass Family YMCA.
- Organizer of WAG (Wipe Away Graffiti).
- Past Vice-President, Crime Stoppers of Josephine County.
- 1989 - 1991, Member of the Grants Pass/Josephine County Chamber of Commerce.

MAGAZINES AND BOOK FEATURED IN
- Karate Illustrated
- Furyu, The Budo Journal
- Martial Arts Masters Magazine
- The Complete Idiot's Guide® To Karate (provided all the kobudo photos)

SUGGESTED READING
- <u>Bubishi</u>, by George Alexander and Ken Penland
- <u>The 7 Habits of Highly Effective People</u>, by Stephen R. Covey
- <u>A Book of Five Rings</u>, The Classical Guide to Strategy, by Miyamoto Musashi
- <u>Karate-do, History and Philosophy</u>, by Takao Nakaya
- <u>The Dojo Desk Reference</u>, A Translation of Hyaku Jiten no Bugei, by Akatsuki Sakiyama
- <u>Unante, The Secrets of Karate</u>, by John Sells
- <u>Living Karate, The Way of Self-Mastery</u>, by Masayuki Shimabukuro
- <u>The Art of War</u>, by Sun Tzu
- <u>As a Man Thinketh</u>, by James Allen

Please visit our website at tkfikarate.com

"Karate assists you in formulating a purpose in life. Make it a good one and you'll live healthier and happier."
D. Saito

NOTES

www.ingramcontent.com/pod-product-compliance
Lightning Source LLC
Chambersburg PA
CBHW081936170426
43202CB00018B/2935